THEMES IN SOCIAL THEORY

Series Editor: Rob Stones

The series explores how cutting-edge research within the social sciences relies on combinations of social theory and empirical evidence. Different books examine how this relationship works in particular subject areas, from technology and health to politics and human rights. Giving the reader a brief overview of the major theoretical approaches used in an area, the books then describe their application in a range of empirical research projects. Each text looks at contemporary and classical theories, provides a map of primary research carried out in the subject area and highlights recent advances in the field. The series is a companion to the *Traditions in Social Theory* series, founded by Ian Craib and edited by Rob Stones.

Published:

HEALTH AND SOCIAL THEORY
Fernando De Maio

Coming Soon:

TECHNOLOGY AND SOCIAL THEORY
Steve Matthewman

ENVIRONMENT, NATURE AND SOCIAL THEORY
Damian White, Alan Rudy and Brian Gareau

POLITICS AND SOCIAL THEORY
Will Leggett

HUMAN RIGHTS AND SOCIAL THEORY
Lydia Morris

INTERNATIONAL MIGRATION AND SOCIAL THEORY
Karen O'Reilly

TRADITIONS IN SOCIAL THEORY

Founding Editor: Ian Craib
Series Editor: Rob Stones

This series offers a selection of concise introductions to particular traditions in sociological thought. The books deepen the reader's knowledge of particular theoretical approaches and enhance their wider understanding of sociological theorizing. Each book will offer: a history of the chosen approach and the debates that have driven it forward; a discussion of current debates within the approach (or related debates that take different approaches); and an argument for the distinctive contribution of each approach and its likely future value. The series is a companion to the *Themes in Social Theory* series, edited by Rob Stones.

Published:

PHILOSOPHY OF SOCIAL SCIENCE
Ted Benton and Ian Craib

CRITICAL THEORY
Alan How

STRUCTURATION THEORY
Rob Stones

MARXISM AND SOCIAL THEORY
Jonathon Joseph

MICRO SOCIAL THEORY
Brian Roberts

Coming Soon:

POST-STRUCTURALISM AND AFTER
David Howarth

THE DURKHEIMIAN QUEST: IN SEARCH OF SOLIDARITY
AND THE SACRED
Willie Watts Miller

Further titles are in preparation across both series

Health and Social Theory

Fernando De Maio

Department of Sociology and Anthropology,
Simon Fraser University, Canada

First published 2010 by
PALGRAVE MACMILLAN

Palgrave Macmillan in the UK is an imprint of Macmillan Publishers Limited, registered in England, company number 785998, of Houndmills, Basingstoke, Hampshire RG21 6XS.

Palgrave Macmillan in the US is a division of St Martin's Press LLC, 175 Fifth Avenue, New York, NY 10010.

Palgrave Macmillan is the global academic imprint of the above companies and has companies and representatives throughout the world.

Palgrave® and Macmillan® are registered trademarks in the United States, the United Kingdom, Europe and other countries.

ISBN-13: 978–0–230–51741–7 hardback
ISBN-13: 978–0–230–51742–4 paperback

This book is printed on paper suitable for recycling and made from fully managed and sustained forest sources. Logging, pulping and manufacturing processes are expected to conform to the environmental regulations of the country of origin.

A catalogue record for this book is available from the British Library.

A catalog record for this book is available from the Library of Congress.

10   9   8   7   6   5   4   3   2   1
19   18   17   16   15   14   13   12   11   10

Transferred to Digital Printing 2013

To *CEA*

Contents

List of Tables and Figures

Tables

Figures

Foreword

A simple aim lies at the heart of this series. This is to deepen understanding of the role of social theory in the creation and validation of the most valuable empirical research in the social sciences. The series rests upon a commitment to explore the vast terrain upon which theory and the empirical meet, and extends an invitation to readers to share in this exploration. Each book takes on a specialized substantive area of research such as health, international migration, crime, politics, technology, human rights and the environment, and excavates the character of the theory-empirical interplay in relation to key themes within the specialized area.

The authors of the volumes all write clearly and accessibly even when the material they are dealing with is intrinsically difficult. They have a close knowledge of the relevant field, an enthusiasm for the kind of theoretically informed empirical research that has been produced within it and have themselves a flair for theoretical analysis. Within the general rubric of the series each author (or team of authors) has her or his own style and approach and a distinctive authorial voice. This should translate into a sense of pluralism within the series as a whole, meaning that the investigation of the theory-empirical terrain will take on the broad and varied character required to push forward our understanding in the most open and constructive manner possible.

Each book in the series aims to bring together in one volume some of the most significant theoretically informed empirical work in that subfield. The opening chapters of each book will outline the main theoretical approaches associated with substantive research in the area, and subsequent chapters will bring out how these approaches have been important in facilitating a range of key empirical studies. It will become apparent that a researcher's focus on a particular empirical case has often led her/him to draw on more than one theoretical approach, and then to creatively combine them in a form appropriate to the empirical case. The value of the substantive findings and arguments produced by each highlighted study is paramount, and will be clearly indicated.

It is hoped that the books from the series will play their part in helping to bridge the harmful gap between theory and the empirical that is still too often present within the social sciences, and that they will not only be used on second and third year undergraduate courses, to train and sensitize the next generation of social analysts, but will also be helpful to researchers at all levels. The books will demonstrate that there is already a large existing literature in each sub-field that has indeed combined theory and the empirical, and they will clarify the descriptive, explanatory and critical power produced by such combinations.

The notion of 'themes' referred to in the series title in fact signals two kinds of themes. The *first* kind is *substantive* and refers to the overall theme of the respective volume – health, environment, human rights and so on – and, more subtly, to the sub-types of thematic content to be found within each of the different clusters of studies highlighted in each volume and indicated through the titles of the more substantive chapters. The *second* type of theme is *methodological*, and refers to the ways in which theory and the empirical are brought together within each of the studies highlighted. I prefer to refer to this set of themes under the label of 'conceptual methodology', rather than just 'methodology', in order to emphasize the ways in which particular theoretical ideas or concepts (and combinations of these) guide more formal methods such as observation, documentary analysis, surveys, interviews and so on, towards certain types of empirical data. Concepts and theories, here, are seen to have identifiable methodological and empirical consequences.

It is relatively self-evident that the *key substantive themes* that emerge in, for example, Fernando De Maio's volume on health – such as those around health inequalities and demographics, the functioning of the sick role or the practices of pharmaceutical companies – will be distinct from those in other volumes such as Karen O'Reilly's on international migration or Steve Matthewman's on technology. This is not to say that there couldn't be fruitful overlap; it is very easy to envisage research projects looking at the health implications of international migration or at the use of technology in health care. However, it is to say that one might expect a series of distinctive thematic concerns to emerge from a focus on studies that have health as their primary concern. It is probable that the lessons to be learnt from the *conceptual methodological themes* will be more general. Here, more commonality is likely to emerge across sub-fields in the ways that theory and the empirical are combined together, notwithstanding their different subject matters.

All the authors in the series take it for granted that particular ways of seeing, hearing, interpreting and understanding – to name just some of the ways we apprehend the world – are involved every time a so-called empirical fact is given that status by somebody. That somebody, in turn, may be any kind of everyday participant within society, deploying their own cultural and social standpoint on the world, whether they are a political power broker, a homeless migrant, an environmental activist or an academic researcher. Whoever it is who does the apprehending, all empirical facts – and the stories and arguments through which they are joined together into an account of the social world – are already infused with their ideas and ways of seeing associated, in turn, with the particular cultures and sub-cultures they belong to. Embedded within these cultures are concepts, presuppositions, categorizations, that can range from a mixture of the simply inherited and/or confused at one end of the spectrum to a mixture of the systematically reflected upon and/or analytically lucid at the other end of the spectrum. Social theory contributes profoundly to our ability to apprehend the social world in ways that are nearer to the latter end of the spectrum than the former.

The degree of rigour and intellectual seriousness implied by these standards, brought into close liaison with the imaginative ways of seeing that good social science seeks constantly to renew, are what should make the activities and claims of social science stand out. Our claim should be that the accounts we produce add something further to public and civic culture, and to political life, than say news journalism or the everyday understandings of ordinary people. Social science has its own generic standards, standards that we constantly need to explore, reflect upon and improve, not least with respect to the relationship between social theory and substantive studies. It is only by doing this that we can genuinely carry forward the ambitious aspirations of a public social science that can play its rightful and much needed part in a thorough and continuing interrogation of the social.

Rob Stones

Acknowledgements

I am grateful to Rob Stones for developing this series and for encouraging me to write this book. His support and incisive feedback on the manuscript were invaluable, and his own publications are a solid foundation for any exploration of social theory.

Some of the material on health inequities presented in this book stems from my graduate work at the University of Essex. While at Essex, I benefited from supervision from Joan Busfield, Tim Liao, and David Pevalin, as well as support from other members of the Department of Sociology and the Department of Health and Human Sciences. Along with supporting my graduate work, Joan Busfield provided very helpful comments on a draft of this manuscript. Ewen Speed contributed insightful comments on the proposal for the book, and brought my attention to exciting parts of the literature with which I was unfamiliar. At Essex I had the privilege of working with Dan O'Neill; he was a wonderful colleague and friend and will be missed.

An early plan for this book was presented at a seminar at the Department of Sociology, University of Illinois at Urbana-Champaign; I am grateful for the suggestions raised during my visit. At Simon Fraser University, I benefited from the support and encouragement from colleagues in the Department of Sociology and Anthropology, the Latin American Studies Program, and the Faculty of Health Sciences. Funding from the SFU President's Research Grant supported this project in important ways. Ryan Klausing, Pepita Elena and Eagan Kemp were superb research assistants and rewarding students. I would like to especially thank the students who participated in my Contemporary Issues in Medical Sociology course. Much of the material in this book has been refined as a result of our discussions and their questions. Funding from the Social Sciences and Humanities Research Council of Canada has supported my work on the social determinants of health and the health transitions of immigrants.

Emily Salz, Beverley Tarquini, Anna Marie Reeve, Sheree Keep and the staff at Palgrave Macmillan were central to the project. I am also grateful to Sunita Jayachandran and her colleagues at Integra for the services rendered on this book.

Most importantly, I would like to thank my family for their support during this project. My parents, Susana and Domingo De Maio, have been steadfast in their encouragement from the very beginning, as has been my brother Paul. Sharyn and Phil Allen have kindly forgiven their son-in-law for bringing his computer along during holidays. My partner, Christy

Allen, inspired me with her own work and pushed me in discussion on all aspects of this book. She has done more than anyone else to teach me about the craft of writing.

Writing a book about health and illness while loved friends and family members dealt with life-threatening conditions was difficult. For me personally, it underscored a tension that runs throughout this book: that we can be awed by the power of modern medicine, that at times access to advanced medical technologies is the most important thing in the world. Yet at the same time, we need to worry about medicine's reductionist tendencies, its neglect of underlying social determinants, and its ability to depoliticize human suffering, and our inability to distribute its benefits equitably. I hope that this book may help readers to see health and health care as fundamentally social, and that it contributes to an understanding of health as an outcome of social justice – a lesson that Virchow and Engels tried to teach us more than 150 years ago. And although this is an old lesson, it is often absent from many discussions of health and health care in the world today.

1

Introduction

Health is traditionally understood as a personal trouble, and rightfully so, since it is individuals who experience illness. It is individuals who suffer asthma attacks, or undergo kidney dialysis, and it is individuals who die prematurely from coronary heart disease. Sociological research seeks to describe, analyze, and ultimately understand the lived experience of these situations. It also aims to examine what it means to be ill, and how illness affects the lives of individuals and their families. Such research may be applied in nature and seek to develop ways of improving social policies or medical interventions – by documenting how user fees may deter a person living in poverty from using hospital services, for example, or by closely examining the "illness narrative" of a person undergoing treatment with the goal of developing more effective treatment regimes. Alternatively, medical sociological research may hold a more abstract focus; in such cases, illness experiences are analyzed in order to develop our understanding of core sociological concepts, such as gender, normative roles, identity, and power. And the social patterning of diseases may be examined to better understand class divisions or socio-economic inequalities.

An important overarching theme of this book is the notion that whilst we need to appreciate the personal troubles associated with any illness, we also need to acknowledge that illness and disease – be it asthma, diabetes, heart disease, tuberculosis, HIV/AIDS, or any other condition – is socially patterned. This implies an underlying public issue, or the effects of structural forces, rather than a focus on biography alone. Indeed, to the extent that social conditions influence patterns of morbidity (illness) and mortality throughout the lifecourse, and that because the organization of health care systems reflect decisions about the way to provide support for those in need of medical treatment, health ought to be considered a public issue. Seen in this light, a population's health is a reflection of complex and interactive social, political, historical, cultural, and economic forces. In other words, there is a political economy to disease; the structure of health care systems reflects political struggles, and social conditions are inextricably intertwined with biomedical outcomes (Farmer, 1999; Wilkinson, 2000). Even the way we think about disease reflects complex social and political forces.

In many ways, understanding health and illness requires what the American sociologist C. Wright Mills (1959) called the "sociological imagination", a kind of thinking that involves understanding and drawing connections between personal troubles and public issues. Mills conceptualized sociology as a discipline interested in the inter-connections in our biographies, history, and society. For Mills,

> the individual can understand his own experience and gauge his own fate only by locating himself within his period...he can know his own chances in life only by becoming aware of those of all individuals in his circumstances. In many ways it is a terrible lesson; in many ways a magnificent one.
>
> (1959: 5)

Mills' sociological imagination requires us to link personal circumstances with structural economics and politics; it requires us "to be aware of the idea of social structure and to use it with sensibility" (1959: 10–11). This influential approach to social research enables us to see ill health – surely one of the most personal of all personal troubles – as explicitly social. Applied in medical sociology, the distinction between personal troubles and public issues leads us to a diverse array of empirical and theoretical possibilities. The works examined in this book utilize a wide range of methodological approaches covering the entire quantitative–qualitative spectrum, reflect myriad ontological and epistemological positions, and engage with sometimes contradictory theoretical traditions. On some levels these works will seem to have little in common with each other, as they reflect drastically different approaches to research. Yet they are all part of the grand tradition of health-related social research; their differences and, at times, commonalities will offer important lessons on the nature of social research in general, and enhance our understanding of health issues in particular.

Also central to this book is the notion that health is inherently a sociological concept. This is because at the most basic of levels, determining if we are healthy or not involves social comparisons. We judge our health in comparison to the standard of living of our peers (Kaplan and Baron-Epel, 2003; Sen, 2002). The very definition of what is "health" and what is "illness" is socially constructed, and varies by culture in time and place (Samson, 1999). For example, recent empirical work in Canada highlights significant cultural variation in the reporting of pain and mental health problems (Kopec et al., 2001). And my own research on health inequities in Argentina shows that people who live in some of the least healthy parts of the country (as evidenced by rates of life expectancy and infant mortality significantly worse than the national average and by the presence of infectious diseases not found elsewhere in the country) may nevertheless report being in good health (De Maio, 2007a). Amartya Sen (2002) has documented similarly incongruent findings from studies of life expectancy and self-reported health in India. All this reflects the notion that health is socially constructed; social forces, including culture, shape how we respond to pain and suffering, how we conceptualize our bodies, and how we define health and illness. Examples in this book will use a wide range of conceptualizations of health, including epidemiological indicators of life expectancy (with low life expectancy being an indicator of an increased likelihood of premature death), as well as individual-driven accounts of pain and suffering as markers of illness.

The sociological foundation of health as a concept can also be seen at the societal level, considering that "health" involves decisions regarding how to structure health care systems: is health a private good, to be purchased under market mechanisms? Or is it a public good, guaranteed by human rights or citizenship? Health also reflects societal power relations: what conditions are considered illnesses? What conditions are considered to be outside of the medical sphere?

And lastly, health is a sociological concept in the sense that social conditions ultimately determine levels of population health (Marmot and Wilkinson, 2006). As sociologists and epidemiologists have firmly documented, social position – our place in society's hierarchy – is strongly related to our risk of developing illness and partly determines how long we may expect to live. This notion has been a central theme in sociological research on health, from the origins of our discipline in Engels' *The Condition of the Working Class in England* (1987 [1845]) to more contemporary medical sociological and social epidemiological research on health inequities.

Sociology offers a unique perspective on the study of heath and illness, for it allows us to understand the nature of health "problems" in a more holistic way than is usually afforded by the more clinical, biomedical perspective that usually dominates discussion of these issues. In other words, it changes the "frame" within which we seek to understand health and illness. Consider Peter Berger's definition of a sociological problem, as developed in his classic book *Invitation to Sociology*:

> ...not so much why some things "go wrong" from the viewpoint of the authorities and the management of the social scene, but how the whole system works in the first place, what are its presuppositions and by what means it is held together. The fundamental sociological problem is not crime but the law, not divorce but marriage, not racial discrimination but racially defined stratification, not revolution but government.
>
> (1963: 37)

This influential definition of a "problem" encourages us to see health research as something that should not only focus on wait times for specific surgeries, or on the relative efficacy of a particular pharmacological treatment over another (the kind of health "problems" that typically make the daily newspapers), but also on wider issues such as the social determinants of health, health inequities, the structure of health care systems, the medicalization of everyday life, and the social interaction embedded in the medical encounter itself.

This perspective encourages a comprehensive frame of analysis; of course we remain interested in when things go wrong, like an outbreak of a new infectious disease, such as SARS in 2002/2003 and swine flu in 2009, or the increasing burden of mental health problems in industrialized countries. The key is to go beyond that to also incorporate a systemic and structural focus. This encourages an historical and truly contextual analysis, one that integrates analysis of personal agency and social structure and can acknowledge their complex interconnections. Social theory plays a central role in this endeavour.

Empirical and Theoretical Levels of Research

A key feature of this book, and the series of books to which it belongs, is its emphasis on the dynamic connection that exists between empirical and theoretical levels of research. The relationship between these at-times disparate strands of scholarship has been perhaps best discussed by Robert K. Merton, who argued that empirical research does not merely play the passive role of testing hypotheses and concluded that it was not "enough to say that research and theory must be married if sociology is to bear legitimate fruit. They must not only exchange solemn vows – they must know how to carry on from there" (1968: 117). Arguably, sociological research has not been able to accomplish such a union, leading to a situation where empirical and theoretical research often seem to have little to do with one another, or are at best superficially connected.

Medical sociology offers a particularly interesting example of how this "marriage" unfolds in practice. To examine the connection between empirical and theoretical strands of research in medical sociology, I want to raise three inter-related questions: To what extent has empirical research in medical sociology been informed or inspired by theoretical ideas? To what extent has empirical research been constrained by theoretical or epistemological assumptions? And has empirical research in medical sociology fed back to the larger discipline and led to the development or refinement of theoretical concepts? These questions enable a critical analysis of the interplay between empirical and theoretical research, including the ways theory shapes the kind of empirical evidence that is valued, and how that empirical evidence is interpreted. At the crux of these questions is a basic but important point: theory both drives and constrains empirical research. Theory implicitly and explicitly shapes what we consider to be "knowledge".

Appreciating the complex relationship between the empirical and theoretical is fundamental to understanding the development of medical sociology. This requires us to revisit Mills' warnings against both grand theory and abstracted empiricism – the former is characterized by highly abstract theorizing that cannot readily be connected to historical and structural contexts, and the latter describes research that, through its intense focus on method, loses touch with underlying problems of structure and politics. Mills saw both tendencies as "withdrawals from the tasks of the social sciences" (1959: 50) and warned against "the blindness of empirical data without theory and the emptiness of theory without data" (1959: 66). Recognizing the prevalence of these characteristics in sociology, Mills urged us to instead centre our research gaze on the intersection of biography, history, and society. He described this as the "promise" of social science and argued that "any systematic attempt to understand involves some kind of alternation between (empirical) intake and (theoretical) assimilation ... concepts and ideas ought to guide factual investigation, and ... detailed investigations ought to be used to check up on and re-shape ideas" (1959: 74). Appreciating these complex connections in medical sociology will enable us to develop a more holistic understanding of some of the most pressing health issues of our time:

- The global HIV/AIDS pandemic.
- The seemingly ever increasing rates of mental health problems, including depression and anxiety, throughout the world.
- The rapidly increasing rates of obesity in both developed and developing countries.
- The fact that social inequities in health exist in all countries in the world, regardless of the quality and nature of their health care systems.
- Life expectancy data that indicate that whilst people in the richest nations may expect to live about 80 years, people born in the poorest nations in the world can expect half that amount – about 40–45 years, with life expectancies in some sub-Saharan countries now dipping below 40.
- The emergence (and sometimes re-emergence) of preventable infectious diseases and the development of new, drug-resistant strains of diseases such as tuberculosis that severely threaten the lives of billions of people (particularly poor people) around the globe.
- The pressures to reform health care systems throughout the world in order to achieve adequate levels of care and access and balance the goals of equity and efficiency, whilst at the same time, enable access to expensive new treatments.

Indeed, whether or not we perceive these issues as "problems" partly depends on both data and theory. Importantly, all of these issues can be examined using myriad sociological perspectives. For example, what might conflict theory contribute to an analysis of the global HIV/AIDS epidemic? Does it help us to better interpret the prevalence of HIV/AIDS, which by the best current estimates afflicts over 33 million people worldwide (UNAIDS, 2007)? Does theory help us to understand why only 30 per cent of people estimated to be in need of anti-retroviral treatment in low- and middle-income countries actually receive it (WHO, 2008b)? Social research examines the structural factors shaping infection and treatment and brings attention to the political economy of the disease in all areas of the globe. Or, does it help us to conceptualize more adequately the root causes of infection? More generally, can empirical data or theoretical frameworks help us to decide how, as a society, we address this growing problem and provide timely treatment for those infected with the AIDS virus? As we will see in this book, medical sociology and related disciplines such as medical anthropology, particularly through the work of Paul Farmer (2003), have made substantial contributions on these issues.

Looking even further, other questions arise: what might a Foucauldian analysis of mental health pharmacological treatments look like? Can social theory be used to examine the very meaning of mental illness and how psychiatric categories of disease are constructed and change over time (Busfield, 1996; Horowitz, 2002)? Do Durkheimian notions of social integration and social cohesion contribute to analyses seeking to explain patterns of health inequities? Do feminist conceptions of patriarchy help to frame the "problem" of depression in a particularly useful way? Do conceptualizations of profit and competition – with connections to conflict theory and the tradition of political economy – help us to better understand the power of the pharmaceutical industry? Can the sociological traditions of symbolic interactionism and structural functionalism help us to understand issues related to medical care? All of these theoretical traditions indeed have much to offer empirical researchers, and in turn, empirical research of these health issues can enable us to refine theoretical constructs.

But whilst we might assert that theory can play an important part in understanding contemporary health problems, the explicit role of sociological theory in medical sociology is and has been quite controversial. Currently, widely different assessments can be found in the literature. For example, William Cockerham, in the *Blackwell Companion to Medical Sociology*, asserts that: "the link between medical sociology and sociological theory is crucial to the subdiscipline. Theory binds medical sociology to the larger discipline of sociology more extensively than any other aspect of the sociological enterprise" (2001: 3). In contrast, Graham Scambler's influential book *Sociological Theory and Medical Sociology* begins by positing: "when sociologists have been invited or felt the need to comment on the current state of medical sociology...they have almost invariably included a lament on its theoretical impoverishment. This has generally been attributed to its detachment from mainstream social theory" (1987: 1). Scambler's assessment echoes a 1975 review published in *Social Science & Medicine*, where Malcolm Johnson argued that medical sociology was "theoretically impoverished, not only through its failure to contribute significantly to sociology's conceptual stock, but also through its shyness in utilizing theoretical constructs in its research" (1975: 227). What is at the root of these contradictory assessments? What is the basis of Scambler's and Johnson's concerns that medical sociology has been theoretically impoverished? Has so much changed in medical sociology in the past three decades that these assessments may all be accurate?[1]

Scambler's concern stems from the (largely unacknowledged) limitations that exist in much of medical sociology due to the enduring dominance of positivist approaches to research. The notion of epistemology (the branch of philosophy concerned with the nature of knowledge and truth) is central to this book and will be examined in the subsequent chapters.[2] Epistemology is key to coming to an understanding of the dynamic connections between empirical and theoretical work. As Trigg thoughtfully points out: "The philosophy of the social sciences cannot be an optional activity for those reluctant to get on with the 'real' empirical work. It is the indispensable starting-point for all social science" (1985: 205). Epistemological positions underlie many of the debates explored in this book.

Outline of Chapters

The present chapter introduces the main themes of the book and, in the following pages, lays out its structure. Chapter 2 examines the earliest manifestations of what we now define to be medical sociology in the works of Friedrich Engels and Rudolph Virchow. It also identifies the intellectual space of medical sociology in comparison to the discipline of epidemiology. This comparison helps us to understand the problems medical sociologists have traditionally been concerned with and also helps us to develop a richer understanding of the evolution of the field.

Chapter 3 traces medical sociology's theoretical contours and explores landmark conceptual advances – among them, Talcott Parsons' development of the *sick role*, Erving Goffman's work on *stigma*, Irving Zola's writing on *medicalization*, Eliot Freidson's work on the *profession of medicine*, and contemporary research by Richard Wilkinson on the *social determinants of health*. Tracing these developments illuminates the main theoretical approaches associated with medical sociology, and enables an assessment of their contributions to the field over the past 60 years.

In many ways, the theoretical approaches dominant at any given point in time in medical sociology reflect their overall popularity within the field of sociology. Whilst structural functionalism was very important in the early development of medical sociology as a subdiscipline in the 1950s (primarily because of Parsons), it gave way to the symbolic interactionist-inspired medical sociology of Howard Becker and Anselm Strauss in the 1960s. The 1970s and 1980s witnessed a growing engagement with symbolic interactionism, political economy and conflict theory, and the work of Michel Foucault. The 1990s saw post-modernism quickly rise in prominence in both medical sociology and the general discipline – only to experience a recent downturn in popularity (Cockerham, 2007).

Interestingly, all of these theoretical perspectives can be seen at play in contemporary medical sociology. It is perhaps this richness of theoretically informed work that led to the establishment of the journal *Social Theory & Health* in 2003. Theoretically centred or theoretically informed articles can also be regularly found in the main scholarly journals publishing medical sociological research, including the *Journal of Health & Social Behavior, Social Science & Medicine, Sociology of Health & Illness*, as well as the *American Journal of Public Health*. It is also not uncommon to see theoretically informed work published in the major biomedical journals, including the *British Medical Journal*, the *Journal of the American Medical Association*, and the *Lancet*. In tracing the history of medical sociology and the debates which have received particular attention, we will not only analyze the changing theoretical contours of the discipline but also gain insight into the future directions of health research.

Chapters 4–7 examine the interplay between empirical and theoretical work in different areas of current debate in medical sociology. Health inequities are the primary focus of Chapter 4. In many ways, they are the fundamental medical sociological issue, linking health and illness to society like no other. More specifically, Chapter 4 examines how health issues reflect larger patterns of social divisions, arguing that population health levels are sensitive indicators of the quality of a country's social fabric (Kawachi and Kennedy, 2002; Sen, 1999). We will examine the large (and rapidly growing) literature on *within-* and *between-*country inequities. These studies – mostly quantitative, but epistemologically connected to both positivism and to critical realism – will provide us with important lessons on the connections between empirical data, theory, and epistemology in medical sociology.

Many of these studies are centred on the notion that *social forces* are ultimately the most important determinants of health, arguing that our health depends more on social conditions like housing and income than on magnetic resonance imaging (MRI) machines or hospital-based technologies. From this perspective, health is a product of the society in which we live. Indeed, a tradition in this branch of medical sociology engages with the philosophy of John Rawls (1972) and argues that health is a product of social justice (Daniels et al., 2000).

An important recent development in this literature has been Wilkinson's income inequality hypothesis, a conceptual model proclaimed to be one of the "big ideas" of our time in a 1996 editorial in the *British Medical Journal*. Chapter 4 closely examines the income inequality hypothesis, its empirical underpinnings, and theoretical relevance. It has been the subject of a great deal of debate; a rare situation which has brought into the open important epistemological issues and unresolved theoretical debates building from the works of Durkheim, Marx, Veblen, Bourdieu, and others. Much of the debate has integrated advanced empirical analysis and nuanced theorizing, a discussion that has traversed the distance between the *Journal of Critical Realism* and the *Journal of the Royal Statistical Society*. This body of research has also attempted to integrate biomedical research on stress mechanisms and neurohormonal connections to macro-level analysis of social structure and meso-level work on social interaction – an issue discussed in Chapter 4 under the Foucauldian concept of *embodiment* (Freund, 2006; Krieger, 2005; Krieger and Davey Smith, 2004).

In addition, Chapter 4 touches upon ethnographic research revealing the lived experiences of health inequalities, such as Laurie Abraham's (1993) *Mama Might Be Better Off Dead* as well as the medical anthropology of Paul Farmer in *Aids & Accusation* (1992), *Infections and Inequalities: The Modern Plagues* (1999), and *Pathologies of Power: Health, Human Rights, and the New War on the Poor* (2003). The work of these authors – characterized by interpretivist and critical realist epistemologies – enable us to more fully grasp the suffering that lies behind quantitative analyses of health inequities. At the same time, these ethnographies are informed by concepts such as *structural violence* and *institutionalized racism* and reveal the wide-ranging theoretical foundations of empirical research on health inequities.

Chapter 5 closely examines health care systems, an area of study with contemporary political relevance. It is not an overstatement to suggest that health care reform is one of the most ubiquitous political issues in both developed and developing countries, with both experiencing rapidly rising costs of health care. Costs associated with health care are widely seen as one of the most substantial pressures on state and household budgets; in the United States, for example, medical expenses are the leading cause of personal bankruptcy (Angel et al., 2006).

Within Chapter 5, I examine the literature on the comparative study of health care systems and how theoretically informed empirical research has approached the study of a health care system's myriad goals, including effectiveness, efficiency, and equity (Blendon et al., 2002; Caplan et al., 1999). Drawing from a Marxist political economy, work in this area has examined how global capitalism has shaped the structure of health care systems (Navarro, 2002b). For example, researchers have critiqued the exportation of private US-style managed care systems to developing countries in Latin America (Iriart et al., 2001; Waitzkin and Iriart, 2001). These studies are intertwined with debates on capitalism, globalization, the retrenchment of the welfare state, and political economy (Navarro, 1999) – issues of particular relevance to sociology.

The discussion of health care systems in Chapter 5 also engages with medical sociological research on the power of health professionals, and the ways in which different health care systems deal with that power. Freidson's landmark *The Profession of Medicine* (1970a) – one of medical sociology's canonical books – is explored in depth; it is an excellent example of how theoretical positions develop through debate and further research. In particular, Freidson's critique of the Parsonian model of the professions leads us to a new understanding of the role of medical doctors. As we will see, the symbolic interactionism of Freidson refined Parson's original work, and brought our attention not only to the traits and characteristics of the medical profession, but also its ideology – the very ideas that underlie its claims to autonomy. Examples from Canada and Venezuela are then presented to examine the controversial roles that the profession of medicine can play in struggles for health care reform.

Chapter 6 investigates the medicalization of everyday life, one of the most important concepts in the canon of medical sociology. It was initially developed by Irving Zola (1972), who argued that medicine itself was becoming an institution of social control, a "new repository of truth" as more and more of social life began to be seen through the lens of medicine. As we will see in Chapter 6, Zola's analysis is built upon the 1950s and 1960s structural functionalism of Parsons, as well as Eliot Freidson's social constructionist refinements of Parsons' work.

The concept of medicalization was also central to the radical critique of medicine offered by Ivan Illich, who famously noted that "medicine is but a device to convince those who are sick and tired of society that it is they who are ill, impotent, and in need of technical repair" (1976: 9). The discussion of medicalization offered in Chapter 6 will examine how disease constructs are created, following the example of alcoholism's shift from *sin* to *crime* to *illness*, before examining the tremendous power held by the pharmaceutical industry in defining what is health and what is sickness. The pharmaceutical industry – whilst a relatively new area of interest for sociologists (Busfield, 2003, 2006b; Hollander, 2006) – today holds unprecedented power in shaping discourse surrounding health and illness. Recognition of the economic issues underlying the power of the pharmaceutical industry brings to light significant conflict, which Conrad has recently summarized: "[i]t may well be to the shareholders' advantage for pharmaceutical companies to promote medications for an ever-increasing array of human problems, but this in no way insures that these constitute improvements in health and medical care" (2005: 11). Chapter 6 investigates the ways in which current debates regarding the power of the pharmaceutical industry reflect the warnings developed by Illich (1976) in *Limits to Medicine*, and at the same time, the chapter examines how our understanding of medicalization has changed as a result of social research published in the last few decades. Due to both empirical and theoretical advances, the concept of medicalization is now understood to be a complex and multi-faceted term (Ballard and Elston, 2005).

Chapter 7 examines research on the *medical encounter*, an area of significant research productivity in medical sociology. Like other topics in the book, the literature on the medical encounter has incorporated a wide range of empirical approaches, including in-depth interviewing (Lupton, 1997a; Werner and Malterud, 2003), questionnaires (Waitzkin, 1991), conversation analysis (Campion and Langdon, 2004), and even secondary analysis (May et al., 2004). Work in this area has included positivist (Waitzkin, 1991), interpretivist (Werner and Malterud, 2003), and critical realist (Porter, 1993) epistemologies. The integration of these different methodological and epistemological approaches offers many lessons; above all, a comparison of these works reminds us of the different ways in which researchers have approached the generation of knowledge and will encourage us to develop a reflexive attitude towards our own positions on research strategies.

Research on the medical encounter has primarily focused on its structure, how doctors and patients negotiate power in the consultation, the type of "turn-taking" incorporated into their conversations, and how knowledge and preferences are transferred from one to the other. Work in this area has contrasted different "ideal types" of physicians and patients, including physicians as "perfect agents" and patients as "informed patients" (Gafni et al., 1998). The former describes a knowledgeable physician who assumes authority over the patient to make decisions, and justifies this imbalance by the asymmetry of information, experienced by the two parties (physicians in this case holding professional expertise on which they can base treatment decisions). Gafni et al. describe this ideal type: "the doctor possesses the knowledge needed for making a treatment decision regarding the patient's illness and for assessing the expected effectiveness of health care interventions in improving the patient's health status" (1998: 347). The position is described as that of a perfect agent because it assumes that the doctor's decision-making process is informed by knowledge of the patient's preferences. The latter ideal type, that of the "informed patient", describes a situation where authority to make treatment decisions rests with the patient; the physician in this case is responsible for transferring knowledge needed to make the decision to the patient.

These Weberian "ideal types," whilst not reflective of all empirical circumstances, offer us models on the spectrum of the different kinds of interaction and communication that are possible in the medical setting. Work in this area has also closely investigated breakdowns in the medical encounter: what happens when a patient presents symptoms that are not recognized by the medical authority? What happens when a patient seeks treatment that a doctor cannot or will not provide?

Cases where the experience of the patient clashes with the medical training of the physician offer important clues to the underlying structure of the medical encounter. Studies in this area have explored the notion of "medically unexplained symptoms" from the perspective of both physicians (Reid et al., 2001; Wileman et al., 2002) and patients (Johansson et al., 1996; Ware, 1992; Werner and Malterud, 2003), offering unique viewpoints on what can be frustrating, tension-filled encounters characterized by credibility claims (patients wanting to be "believed") and knowledge claims (physicians seeking to maintain authority in situations where they may not be able to alleviate painful symptoms or provide effective curative treatment). Ultimately, research on "contested" medical encounters reveals the negotiation that ultimately leads to the creation of new disease constructs. It also has the potential to feedback to the substantial sociological literature on small groups and interaction which has emerged from the ground-breaking work of Erving Goffman.

Research on the medical encounter displays a sophisticated use of social theory. For example, Lupton (1997a) uses the medical encounter as a means to explore notions of consumerism, risk, and Anthony Giddens' *reflexive project of the self*. Werner and Malterud (2003) use the medical encounter as a means to examine the notion of "doing gender". And much of this research builds from Goffman's work on *interaction order*, a foundational concept of micro-sociology. Perhaps the most important contribution of this work to sociology, however, lies in the linkages between the micro-politics of the medical encounter and the macro-politics of health inequities. Analysis of these links raises the question of how interactions between doctors and patients reproduce what Waitzkin calls "macro-level structural patterns of domination and oppression" (1983: 119). Research on the medical encounter is therefore particularly well-suited to integrating much of what concerns medical sociologists, and clearly benefits from concepts we can trace to a range of theorists, from Marx to Parsons to Foucault.

Chapter 8 offers a re-evaluation of the role of social theory in medical sociology. Drawing from the work of Merton, the chapter assesses sociology's contribution to our understanding of health, and highlights the interplay between theoretical and empirical work in medical sociology. The chapter also discusses some ideas regarding the future direction of health-related social research.

Whilst this book is primarily concerned with social theory, methodology is also central to all of the chapters. As we will see, medical sociology has a rich tradition of both qualitative and quantitative research. And like sociology in general, it has experienced problems in integrating findings from these seemingly disparate approaches to empirical data. At times it seems like sociology is firmly shaped around the so-called quantitative–qualitative divide, with each tradition advancing more or less on its own. David Mechanic's insight on this issue, published almost 20 years ago, is still useful today:

> As quantitative multivariate methodologies have come to dominate research work in medical sociology, investigators have split into two cultures separating quantitative and qualitative studies. These cultures share little communication, publish in different journals, and, for the most part, ignore and sometimes belittle each other's research contributions.
>
> (1989: 187)

This is a most unfortunate situation, and one that hardly lives up to the promise of social science as envisioned by Mills. Instead of a sociology that seeks to understand the connections between biography, history, and society, we currently have a sociology deeply divided along methodological grounds.[3]

This book, focused as it is on the interplay between theoretical and empirical realms of research, draws from both quantitative and qualitative aspects of empirical medical sociology. In this way, *theory* may bridge the quantitative–qualitative divide by reminding us of the overarching questions that have interested medical sociologists for decades. Theory brings our attention back to what is at stake: unnecessary sickness and preventable death, inequalities that are avoidable, unnecessary, and unfair, and unequal access to health care – essentially, suffering that people endure and the social forces that underlie it.

2
Foundations of Medical Sociology

This chapter examines the intellectual roots of medical sociology, compares its perspective to the modern-day discipline of epidemiology, and identifies an important distinction between sociology *in* medicine and sociology *of* medicine. Analysis of these issues enables a critical assessment of the field, including its inherent tensions and possible future directions.

Health and Revolution

We can trace the roots of contemporary research on health inequities to Friedrich Engels' classic treatise *The Condition of the Working Class in England* (1987 [1845]). In that work, Engels – most famous for his many years of friendship and collaboration with Karl Marx – developed the notion of the social production of disease.[1] This perspective posits that ill health is produced by the very way in which society is organized, and that class exploitation results in premature mortality and unnecessary morbidity for workers and their families. Capitalist exploitation of the working class, from this perspective, is embodied in poor health outcomes.

Engels' analysis used both descriptive prose and basic statistics to document the miserable living conditions faced by the working class and how these affected their health. He examined the aetiology and epidemiology of a number of diseases afflicting the working class, including the major killers, typhoid and tuberculosis. He compared death rates in the major cities and the countryside, concluding that

> ...in general, epidemics in Manchester and Liverpool are three times more fatal than in country districts...affections of the nervous system are quintupled, and stomach troubles trebled, while deaths from affections of the lungs in

14

cities are to those in the country as 2 1/2 to 1. Fatal cases of smallpox, measles, scarlet fever, and whooping cough, among small children, are four times more frequent....

(1987 [1845]: 137)

Engels interpreted these differences as symptoms of the underlying social hierarchy that distinguished between a labouring class that lived in the major cities and a bourgeois class that resided in the countryside:

The manner in which the great multitude of the poor is treated by society is revolting. They are drawn into the large cities where they breathe a poorer atmosphere than in the country; they are relegated to districts which, by reason of the method of construction, are worse ventilated than any others; they are deprived of all means of cleanliness, of water itself, since pipes are laid only when paid for, and the rivers so polluted that they are useless for such purposes; they are obliged to throw all offal and garbage, all dirty water, often all disgusting drainage and excrement into the streets, being without other means of disposing them; they are thus compelled to infect the region of their own dwellings. Nor is this enough...

(1987 [1845]: 129)

Ultimately, he concluded that society itself plays a role in determining who is healthy and who is not, who lives and who dies. Engels famously wrote that

When one individual inflicts bodily injury upon another, such injury that death results, we call the deed manslaughter; when the assailant knew in advance that the injury would be fatal, we call his deed murder. But when society places hundreds of proletarians in such a position that they inevitably meet a too early and an unnatural death, one which is quite as much a death by violence as that by the sword or bullet; when it deprives thousands of the necessaries of life, places them under conditions in which they *cannot live* – forces them ... to remain in such conditions until that death ensues which is the inevitable consequence – knows that these thousands of victims must perish, and yet permits these conditions to remain, its deed is murder...

(1987 [1845]: 127, emphasis in original)

His analysis remains remarkably relevant to our twenty-first century world; with but a few changes, his description of the health effects experienced by the English working class in 1845 applies to the majority of the world's population today. For example, Engels writes – with a quality of prose now largely extinct in contemporary social research – of the pathogenic effects of poor working conditions, unsafe and unsanitary housing, unequal access to the services of trained physicians, and the predatory practices of companies seeking to profit from ineffective and often-times harmful "treatments" and "cures". In many ways, these are the same issues that people, particularly the poor, contend with today (Kim et al., 2000).

Engels argued for social change, but explicitly warned that a mere expansion of medical services would not be sufficient. Instead, he called for a socialist revolution, and argued that nothing short of worker control of the means of production would be needed if the health of the working class was to be improved. Building his charge that society murders the poor, Engels describes the accidental death of six children in London during one week in late 1844. His text is worth quoting at length:

> Nowhere are so many children run over, nowhere are so many killed by falling, drowning, or burning, as in the great cities and towns of England. Deaths from burns and scalds are especially frequent, such a case occurring nearly every week during the winter months in Manchester, and very frequently in London, though little mention is made of them in the papers. I have at hand a copy of the *Weekly Dispatch* of 15 December 1844, according to which, in the week from 1 December to 7 December inclusive, *six* such cases occurred. These unhappy children, perishing in this terrible way, are victims of our social chaos, and of the property-holding classes interested in maintaining and prolonging this chaos. Yet one is left in doubt whether this terribly torturing death is not a blessing for the children by rescuing them from a long life of toil and wretchedness, rich in suffering and poor in enjoyment. So far has it gone in England; and the bourgeoisie reads these things every day in the newspapers and takes no further notice of the matter. But it cannot complain if after the official and non-official testimony here cited which must be known to it, I broadly accuse it of social murder. Let the ruling class see to it that these frightful conditions are ameliorated...The English bourgeoisie has but one choice, either to continue its rule under the unanswerable charge of murder and in spite of this charge, or to abdicate in favour of the labouring class. Hitherto it has chosen the former course.
>
> (1987 [1845]: 137–138, emphasis in original)

Engels' analysis of the deaths of these six children is based on the notion that their deaths were a sign of inequity – a central concept in medical sociology that is usually defined as an inequality that is avoidable, unnecessary, and unfair (Whitehead, 1992). Engels links their preventable deaths to the "social chaos" of the time; in other words, their deaths were not merely attributable to the physical effects of their burns but to the contextual effects that shaped their living conditions (note that Engels' analysis displays characteristics congruent with Berger's definition of a sociological problem and Mills' sociological imagination). Health, for Engels, and much of the contemporary medical sociological community, is socially produced; as such, understanding patterns of disease requires us to go beyond a narrow focus on an individual's physical state. A close reading of the medical sociological literature reveals that the deaths described by Engels in 1844 are not dissimilar to the preventable deaths currently recorded every day around the world as a result of unsafe and unhealthy working and living conditions.

Engels' description of health inequities and his analysis of its root causes in society are similar to the assessment put forth recently by Richard Wilkinson, a widely cited professor of epidemiology at the University of Nottingham: "...perhaps we should liken the injustice of health inequalities to that of a government that executed a significant portion of its population each year without cause" (2005: 18). Wilkinson's work on income distribution as a social determinant of health has been immensely important in the past 15 years, and has influenced high-level government reports in the UK (Acheson, 1998), Canada (Romanow, 2002), as well as the World Health Organization (WHO) Commission on the Social Determinants of Health (2008a). Thus, whilst the discipline has changed substantially from the days of Engels (as we will see in further detail in the coming chapters), it remains grounded in the belief that inequalities in health are unnecessary and unjust, and that solutions to the problem of health inequalities require social and political action. Of course, there is heated disagreement amongst researchers when they discuss what actions would be helpful and how they should be brought about.

The concern over unjust living conditions and health inequities was not only displayed in Engels' writings, it is also clearly seen in the writings of Rudolph Virchow (1821–1902), a celebrated Prussian physician, pathologist, politician, and anthropologist (Brown and Fee, 2006; Rather, 1985; Virchow, 1958). He is not widely known among general sociologists, but his contributions to medicine and public health were profound. Amongst his many achievements: the introduction of the terms "leukemia" (a type of cancer found in bone marrow which prevents the normal manufacture of red and white blood cells), "thrombosis" (coagulation, or clotting of the blood in any part of the cardiovascular system), and "embolism" (when a blood clot or other object circulates and causes a blockage of a blood vessel in another part of the body) (Eisenberg, 1986; Hajdu, 2005). These terms are still very much in use today in clinical medicine. However, as impressive as these medical achievements may be, Virchow's legacy owes even more to his contributions to public health and social medicine.

An overview of Virchow's life history offers a window into the development of medical sociology. He studied medicine at the Army Medical School in Berlin, graduating in 1843. After graduation, he took a position at the Charité Hospital in Berlin, one of the most famous teaching hospitals in the city, and continued his research in physiology, anatomy, and embryology, making significant advances in all of those fields (Reese, 1988).

It is an understatement to merely note that Virchow lived in a time of tremendous social change. In 1848 (the year Marx and Engels published *The Manifesto of the Communist Party* and the year of revolutions in Italy, France, Germany, and Hungary), Virchow – then a young 26 year old recent graduate from medical school – took up arms and joined a revolutionary movement, finding "his place on the barricades in Berlin" (Hajdu, 2005: 203) with "a rusty sword and an antiquated rifle" (Reese, 1988: 107). During this time, Virchow was elected vice-president of the Berlin Revolutionary Committee, and called for the establishment of a constitutional government, protection of freedom of the press, and notably, universal health care for workers (Hajdu, 2005).

History tells that the European revolutions of 1848 were quickly defeated. Virchow found his position at the Charité Hospital suspended, but he refused to repent for his political actions and had no choice but to leave Berlin (Taylor and Rieger, 1984). He moved to Bavaria, where he accepted a professorship and completed major works on cellular pathology, considered by most medical historians to be his most important works (Eisenberg, 1986; Reese, 1988). Virchow brought cells to the centre of medical thinking – they became not only the basic biological unit of organisms, but also the locus of pathology (Waitzkin, 2006). His research represents a true paradigm shift in medicine. Reese notes that

> the concept of cells as the building blocks of the organism and the locus of disease may seem self-evident to modern physicians and scientists, but it was revolutionary in mid-19th century Europe. When cells are recognized as the essential components of life, no place remains for theories of disease relying on notions of evil humors, strange fluxes, disturbed animisms, or other supernatural explanations of illness.
>
> (1988: 106)

Reese goes on to compare the publication of Virchow's *Cellular Pathology* to Darwin's *Origin of Species*: "Virchow's notions of cells as the locus of disease is clearly as important an organizing principle in medicine as evolution is in biology" (1988: 107). Similar praise is given by Eisenberg: "It is no exaggeration to herald Virchow as the principal architect of scientific medicine" (1986: 245). The way we theorize about health and illness today, then, owes much to Virchow's research.

By 1856, the political climate in Berlin had changed and Virchow was allowed to return to the city. Before his death in 1902, Virchow went on to found and lead the German Progressive Party and served for 13 years in the Reichstag. His concern for public health was reflected in his politics: he improved Berlin's water supply and sewage system, established hospitals and clinics to serve the poor, introduced legislation for food inspection, improved the working conditions of nurses and other health personnel, and called for medical examinations for school-age children (Reese, 1988; Taylor and Rieger, 1984).

Virchow's legacy to medical sociology is unquestionably most significantly shaped by his investigation of a typhus outbreak in Upper Silesia (today a part of Poland), which he carried out in early 1848. By most accounts this was the galvanizing life event that found him joining the revolutionary movement in Berlin upon his return. In the winter of 1847–1848, Upper Silesia, an economically depressed Prussian province, experienced a famine that affected tens of thousands of people. Typhus (a potentially fatal infectious disease that is spread amongst humans by lice and fleas) reached epidemic levels. In response to public outcry, the government appointed Virchow to a commission to study the situation, write a report, and develop recommendations for how to deal with the situation. Virchow spent three weeks in the field, observing the epidemic first hand. Taylor and Rieger note that his ensuing report "was revolutionary for its time and even now it continues to set a standard for any attempt to understand and change the social conditions that produce illness. It is unquestionably a classic" (1984: 202). Although we may consider it a classic now – at the time, the Prussian authorities who had commissioned Virchow to write the report found it scandalous.

Virchow's report is rich in sociological insight (and notably, cites with approval Engels' *The Condition of the Working Class in England*, sharing with it features of historical materialism). He never deviates from the view that the typhus epidemic and the famine were inter-related and that to understand one or the other, you had to understand Upper Silesia's social–political history and structure. Virchow's report describes a materially deprived and politically apathetic population, noting that

> they were poorer and more ignorant, more servile and submissive than almost any other people in the world; they had lost all their energy and self-confidence...In Ireland the people fought back, armed and unarmed, when their conditions became unbearable. They appeared on the battlefield, rebellious against law and property. In Upper Silesia they starved to death in silence.
>
> (Virchow, in Taylor and Rieger, 1984: 205–206)

Whilst acknowledging the medical features of typhus, Virchow emphasized that social context ultimately shaped its contagion and effect on the population. His report explicitly focused on material conditions such as poverty, housing, diet, and sanitation. For Virchow, these were the keys to understanding the nature of the famine *and* the typhus epidemic. In doing so, his analysis foreshadows Mills' sociological imagination:

> ...we have moved from medicine into the social field, and in so doing we have had to consider some of the fundamental issues of our times. Thus, for us, it is no longer a question of the medical treatment and care of this or that person taken ill with typhoid, but of the well-being of one and half million fellow citizens who find themselves at the lowest level of moral and physical decline. With one and a half million people you cannot begin with palliatives, if you want

to achieve anything you have to be radical...That is why I insist that free and unlimited democracy is the single most important principle. If we get free and well-educated people then we shall undoubtedly have healthy ones as well.

(Virchow, quoted in Taylor and Rieger, 1984: 205–208)

Like Engels before him, Virchow clearly recognized the primacy of the social determinants of health.

Both Virchow and Engels understood the public issues underlying the personal troubles individuals experience as poor health. Virchow notes

There cannot be any doubt that such a typhoid epidemic was only possible under these conditions and that ultimately they were the result of the poverty and underdevelopment of Upper Silesia. I am convinced that if you changed these conditions, the epidemic would not occur. In theory, the answer to the question as to how to prevent future outbreaks in Upper Silesia is quite simple: education, together with its daughters, freedom and welfare.

(in Taylor and Rieger, 1984: 206)

Among Virchow's long-term recommendations were unlimited democracy, devolution of decision making, taxation reform, universal education, and the disestablishment of the Catholic church, whose response to the epidemic received his scathing criticism (Eisenberg, 1986; Reese, 1988; Taylor and Rieger, 1984). His report was not well received by the authorities.

Virchow's experience in Upper Silesia galvanized his radical views on the role of medicine in society. He famously concluded that "disease is not something personal and special, but only a manifestation of life under (pathological) conditions...Medicine is a social science and politics is nothing else but medicine on a large scale..." (1985 [1848]). Virchow teaches us that the role of the physician is social and political, not merely scientific (Mackenbach, 2009). In this light, the practice of medicine ought not to be separate from social activism and should work towards social justice.

Virchow returned from Upper Silesia in March 1848 – just in time to join the revolutionary movement in Berlin. His report was ignored by the Prussian government. He contributed to and co-edited *Medical Reform* from July 1848 to June 1849, arguing that "Medical statistics will be our standard of measurement: we will weigh life for life and see where the dead lie thicker among the workers or among the privileged" (quoted in Taylor and Rieger, 1984: 203). His writing in *Medical Reform* called for a revolutionary change in the practice of medicine. At the same time, he emphasized the notion that social and economic conditions have important health effects and that these relationships could be investigated using scientific methods.

The spirit of Virchow is very much alive in contemporary medical sociology, particularly strands of research engaged with political economy and conflict theory. However, his influence has been sporadic. According to Waitzkin, since "Virchow's classical work in social medicine appeared during the mid-nineteenth century, succeeding generations have largely forgotten its message and only later have rediscovered the conditions of society that generate illness and mortality" (2006: 5). This cycle of forgetting and re-discovering reflects the changing theoretical and methodological contours of health-related social research.

Medical Atomism and Sociological Collectivism

Analysis of Virchow's contribution to our understanding of health and illness raises a fundamental tension that continues to exist in contemporary medical sociology. On the one hand, Virchow's research on cellular pathology was a key step towards the biomedical model of disease that we are familiar with today. Reese calls this Virchow's most important contribution: "the idea that cells are fundamental units constituting all tissues and organs, and that disease in the organism results when cells fail to perform their normal, specialized functions" (1988: 106). Cellular pathology remains central to biomedical research, some of it published in *Virchow's Archive*, a respected academic journal. Contemporary pharmacological research is a notable legacy of this model, as is cutting-edge research on genomics.

On the other hand, Virchow's report on typhus in Upper Silesia and his politically charged writings on the social determinants of health lie at the heart of contemporary work on health inequities and the tradition of social medicine (Saracci, 2009; Tajer, 2003; Waitzkin et al., 2001). For example, Virchow's work and political activism were a noted inspiration to Salvador Allende, the late President of Chile and medical doctor deposed in the September 1973 *coup d'état* lead by Augusto Pinochet. Allende's influential book *The Chilean Medico-Social Reality* (1939) presents an analysis heavily influenced by Virchow's ideas; the book conceptualizes a clear relationship between disease and social structure. Acknowledging the importance of Virchow's analysis and foreshadowing later developments in world systems theory, Allende emphasized the effects of economic underdevelopment and international dependency, as well as the effects of the country's foreign debt on the health of Chileans. He advocated social, rather than purely medical, solutions to Chile's population health challenges:

> Allende proposed income redistribution, state regulation of food and clothing supplies, a national housing program, and industrial reforms to address occupational health problems. Rather than seeing improved health care services as

a means toward a more productive labor force, Allende valued the population's health as an end in itself and advocated social changes that went far beyond the medical realm.

(Waitzkin et al., 2001: 1593)

As an elected Senator in the early 1950s, Allende introduced legislation that established the Chilean National Health Service – the first program in the Americas built upon the notion of universal access to health services (Waitzkin, 2006).

Virchow's (and later, Allende's) conceptualization of public health and the role of medicine are fundamentally *social* in nature. However, this notion at times may clash with the medical atomism that is also a legacy of Virchow's ideas. The tensions between the medical individualism/atomism exhibited in Virchow's work on cells and sociological collectivism, at the core of his view of public health and the role of medicine in society, remain central to debates on health and illness in contemporary research.

Both Engels and Virchow saw disease as something produced by underlying structures and forces in society – poverty, class oppression, and working conditions. And both their analyzes conceptualize disease simultaneously as personal troubles and public issues, giving readers an in-depth description of health conditions and the lived experience of the working poor. At the same time, they frame these conditions in terms of societal organization, power, and inequality.

Tracing the links between these nineteenth century writings and research today brings to light the degree to which social scientific approaches to health issues have changed over time. This is particularly the case with respect to research on health inequalities. For Himmelstein

...much recent empirical work on inequalities in health is, in essence, a statistical restatement and verification of this tradition [early socialist scholarship on poverty and health]; Virchow and Engels' prose descriptions have been translated into the modern scientific language of epidemiology. But in the translation from socialism to epidemiology, something has been lost. In analysing typhus, Virchow found the social seeds of disease and prescribed the overthrow of a social system...Too often, today's researchers describe the phenomenology of inequality and injustice, but leave its origins and perpetrators obscured...They would redistribute wealth, but not renounce the market relations and property rights that engender inequality.

(2002: 1279–1280)

This comment brings attention to important differences that exist between the work of Engels and Virchow and contemporary medical sociological research in general and work on health inequalities in particular. Not only have methodology and writing styles changed, but the overall frame of recent work has taken on a different perspective. Most importantly, the implications that researchers look to draw from empirical work have changed as well. Himmelstein laments this change, noting that above all, it has a political effect that encourages reformist rather than revolutionary thinking. I explore these differences in greater detail in the chapters that follow. First, it is important to understand in greater depth the intellectual space of medical sociology.

Medical Sociology and Epidemiology

To better understand the development of medical sociology as a distinct field of research, a useful comparison can be made with other approaches to the study of health. Bezruchka (2006) argues that health can be considered from three fundamentally distinct levels: that of the cell, of individuals, or of a population. Based on a clinical biomedical model, we can conceptualize the body as made up of a great number of different cells, from those in the brain to those in the blood and to those that compose the lining of organs (indeed, advances in genomic research brings us to levels even smaller than that of the cell). At the cellular perspective, health is achieved when cells have their required needs, primarily nutrients like glucose and oxygen. Bezruchka points out that what "maximizes" health at the level of the cell is quite distinct from what "maximizes" health at the level of the individual: "The argument could be made that since human beings are but an assembly of cells that need oxygen and glucose plus some trace elements, then humans need just what their cells need to be healthy. If cells benefit from oxygen and glucose, the more we get, the better" (2006: 15). Of course, we can easily see the fallacy in this argument – what is best for any given individual cell is not necessarily best for the human being. Bezruchka rightfully points out that "the logic of doing what is best for our component parts – our cells – and generalizing this prescription to the community of cells that comprise a human being may not be the best advice for us humans to be healthy" (2006: 15).

At the individual level, health is "maximized" through a common set of health tips: do not smoke, eat a balanced diet, exercise, get enough sleep, and so on. This kind of advice may maximize the health of any one individual – but there are no cellular-level versions of these recommendations: "you cannot ask cells to exercise or to not smoke or to wear a seat belt..." (Bezruchka, 2006: 15). However, the logic is that if you do follow the advice on what makes an individual healthy, your cells will be healthy as a result. The same may be true with population factors – if we follow "good health practice" at the level of the population, then individuals and their cells will be healthy as a by-product.

Table 2.1 Life expectancy and prevalence of smoking (Japan and selected countries)

	Japan	United Kingdom	Germany	Italy	United States	Canada
Life expectancy at birth, males (years)	78.7	76.7	76.2	77.2	75.2	77.9
Prevalence of smoking, adult males (per cent)	47	27	37	31	24	22
Life expectancy at birth, females (years)	85.7	81.2	81.8	81.8	80.4	82.6
Prevalence of smoking, adult females (per cent)	15	25	28	28	19	17

Source: UNDP (2007).

Research points to Japan as an example of this (Marmot, 2004; Takahashi et al., 2008). Japan has the highest life expectancy at birth in the world, with women expected to live 85.7 years and men 78.7 years (UNDP, 2007). However, among rich countries, Japan also has by far the highest rates of smoking for adult men, which we know has pathogenic effects (see Table 2.1).

This is a paradox: a society that does not follow a key piece of individual-level health advice has the best population health profile in the world. Perhaps it is because something is happening at the population level (in contrast to the individual or cellular levels). As shown in Chapter 4, there is some empirical evidence and theoretical reasoning to suggest that Japan's level of income distribution – one of the most equitable anywhere in the world – may be a key driver of its health status (Marmot, 2004).

These varying approaches and different levels of study enable us to develop distinct narratives about health and illness. Importantly, they point us towards very different theoretical explanations for what ultimately *causes* disease. For Bezruchka,

> there are factors that exist at a population level that produce health that have no individual counterparts, just as individual health advice had no cellular counterparts. If the population factors are gotten right, then what individuals in that population do or don't do for their own health may not matter as much. They are healthy as a by-product.
>
> (2006: 16)

This may explain, at least in part, the apparent paradox of Japan.

Different levels of analysis highlight substantially different causal explanations, from those based on biological agents, such as bacteria or viruses, to nutritional agents, such as fats and carbohydrates; from chemical agents, such as toxic pollution, to physical agents, such as climate, and finally to social agents, such as occupation, social class, and income inequality. These levels of analysis encourage different kinds of theoretical reasoning.

Epidemiology is the academic discipline most closely aligned to the population health perspective. In the strictest sense, epidemiology is the study of epidemics, outbreaks in disease that spread out over a population. However, a broader definition is generally accepted today – epidemiology is the branch of medicine that specializes in studying the causes of disease, its distribution, and ways of controlling its spread in populations (De Maio, 2008b; Kawachi, 2002). This definition suggests that considerable overlap exists between epidemiology and medical sociology, which is also interested in the causes of disease, its distribution, and ways of controlling its spread in populations. However, much of modern epidemiology is concerned with identifying the prevalence of individual-level *risk factors* for disease. This approach to epidemiology highlights the importance of *compositional* factors (characteristics of individuals), such as whether or not one smokes, or the type of diet one consumes, or whether or not one uses a seat belt when driving a car. As discussed above, although these recommendations help to maximize the health of any given *individual*, it is a fallacy to assume that at a population level, they are the things that must be done to promote health.

So how does one decide whether to approach health and illness from a biomedical or social perspective, that is, at the level of individuals or groups/populations? *Theory* plays a crucial role in helping to determine the level of analysis of a research project. For example, a feminist-informed empirical study would not be satisfied with investigating only individual-level risk factors for health; instead, concepts such as patriarchy would have to be included in the analysis. This requires a different research "frame"; one that is relational and social, rather than atomistic and individualistic. Similarly, a Marxist-informed analysis would not be complete if only socio-economic status, measured by income and educational attainment, were considered (Muntaner, 2003). Historical and political context would need to be incorporated, and measures of class position, not just social stratification, would need to be included.

The epidemiological approach has been criticized for focusing too much on individual-level risk factors and ignoring the social and political processes that lead to disease. For some critics, the way in which epidemiology is practiced limits its true potential as a source of knowledge for improving the health of populations (Bezruchka, 2006). For Raphael et al., "epidemiology has been the primary tool wielded by the medical profession in quest of the causes of disease and illness. Its application, however, has been narrow, with little appreciation of the complex of political, economic, and social factors that set the stage for the onset of disease and illness"

(2006: 5). This is a far cry from the work of Engels and Virchow, who identified the social, political, and economic foundation of epidemics.

Sociologically, a traditional epidemiological approach is not very satisfying – it rests upon an individualistic conceptualization of disease and, in many ways, ignores social context and structure (De Maio et al., 2008). In response to this criticism, recent years have seen the growth of *social* epidemiology (see Berkman and Kawachi, 2000; Cwikel, 2006), a branch of the discipline that increasingly recognizes context and focuses on the social causes of disease.

Medical sociology overlaps with social epidemiology on a variety of dimensions. Both approaches are interested in the causes of disease, its distribution, and ways of controlling its spread in population. However, not being as closely associated with medical research, medical sociology does not enjoy the status usually afforded to epidemiology. In contrast, medical sociology is perhaps characterized by its close engagement with *sociological theory* (Cockerham, 2001) and greater flexibility in terms of epistemology and methodology.

The Development of Medical Sociology

Medical sociology emerged as a recognized and distinct subfield within sociology in the 1940s (Bloom, 2002). Initially, medical sociology was particularly dependent upon and influenced by medicine; medical research shaped the field, defining the topics that were to be studied. Medical sociology was "intended to help solve a clinical problem or policy issue, rather than develop theory or utilize it as a tool to further understanding" (Cockerham, 2001: 3); as such, it was a particularly *applied* endeavour.

In an influential early review of the state of medical sociology, Straus (1957) developed the distinction between sociology *in* medicine versus the sociology *of* medicine. Sociology *in* medicine is an applied sociology, motivated by a particular medical problem. Here, the sociologist collaborates with the health care system and functions as a part of it. They may work alongside a physician to study a disease process or the factors influencing a patient's recovery. Sociology *of* medicine has its primary emphasis on the sociology – the sociologist uses health issues to better understand society, social change, and other sociologically defined problems. For example, we can study medicine as an institution or as a social system, with its own symbols, norms, and sanctions.

For Straus, "the sociology *of* medicine is concerned with studying such factors as the organizational structure, role relationships, value systems, rituals, and functions of medicine as a system of behavior... this type of activity can best be carried out by persons operating from independent positions outside the formal medical setting" (1957: 203). Straus recognized a strain between these two versions of medical sociology, which "... tend to be incompatible with each other ... the sociologist of medicine may lose objectivity if he identifies too closely with medical teaching or clinical research while the sociologist in medicine risks a good relationship if he tries to study his colleagues" (1957: 203). This strain holds important implications for medical sociology's capacity to foster a *critical* stance on medicine, and raises methodological issues that we grapple with in contemporary research. These include the notions of objectivity and "over-rapport" (otherwise known as "going native", to use an anachronistic term) (Bryman and Teevan, 2005).

Over time, there have been some exceptions to this dichotomy. Straus (1957) himself pointed out that sociologists collaborating with psychiatrists often crossed back and forth between sociology *in* and *of* medicine. More recently, sociological research on the social determinants of health has also blurred Straus' distinction. Sociologists within this tradition work with the explicit goal of improving population health (a sort of sociology *in* medicine) but focus almost entirely on factors outside of the traditional health care system, often working with a critical perspective on the actual health effects of medical care – some going as far as to claim that health care is itself pathogenic (Illich, 1976).

As I will discuss in subsequent chapters, researchers working within the social determinants of health model see social conditions as *fundamental causes* of disease (Link and Phelan, 1995). In a way, this brings medical sociology full circle to its roots in Engels and Virchow more than 150 years ago (a notion that is explored in some detail in Chapter 4). The following chapter explores some of the most important theoretical debates that have taken place over the past 60 years in medical sociology, beginning with Talcott Parsons and the sick role.

3

Theoretical Contours

The major theoretical frameworks of structural functionalism, symbolic interactionism, and conflict theory have competed for influence within the field of medical sociology over the past 60 years. Different approaches have dominated at different times; for example, as we will see below, the structural functionalist medical sociology of Parsons was most influential in the 1950s. It subsequently gave way to research more closely aligned with symbolic interactionism in the 1960s. In the past 15 years, a medical sociology inspired by a cluster of approaches that are often grouped together and characterized broadly as "conflict theory" has focused on inequality as a social determinant of health and has fostered links with theoretical and empirical research in political economy and at the same time nurtured discussion between researchers employing positivist, interpretivist, and critical realist epistemologies. Research tied to the theoretical tradition of symbolic interactionism was central to some of the pioneering work in medical sociology of the 1960s, and continues to flourish.

My analysis of how these traditions have influenced the development of medical sociology highlights the notion that theories should not be seen as discrete models; they often interact and sometimes clash, and in doing so, change the fundamental nature of the field. Theories act as lenses through which we investigate the social world; some bring to our attention problems of inequity, while others bring forth issues of lived experience. In other words, theories enable researchers to view questions of health and illness from different perspectives and help us to identify a wide range of issues that influence patterns of health in society. The discussion below traces the general theoretical contours of the field by asking: What are the major theoretical perspectives of sociology that have influenced medical sociology, what roles have they played, and what influence do they currently have?

The Sick Role: Parsons and Structural Functionalism

The major theoretical perspectives are distinguished by the way they view or define society. The structural functionalist perspective, with its roots in the works of Auguste Comte (1798–1857), Herbert Spencer (1820–1903), and Emile Durkheim (1858–1917), is based on the notions of equilibrium and consensus. It sees society as a system of inter-related parts, and seeks to identify the functions (both manifest and latent) that these parts carry out (Craib, 1997).

Structural functionalist analysis rests on the idea of *functional necessity*. This was most clearly elaborated in Kingsley Davis and Wilbert Moore's (1945) analysis of the functional necessity of stratification, where they argued that differential rewards are required by society. Under this approach, a system of differential rewards (in other words, inequality in resources and prestige) is needed for the proper functioning of a social system, a notion with deep Parsonian roots. Their analysis begins with the observation that stratification is universal; no society is "classless" or unstratified. They then attempt to explain the universality of stratification with its functional necessity:

> As a functioning mechanism a society must somehow distribute its members in social positions and induce them to perform the duties of these positions. It must thus concern itself with motivation at two different levels: to instill in the proper individuals the desire to fill certain positions, and, once in these positions, the desire to perform the duties attached to them ... Inevitably, then, a society must have, first, some kind of rewards that it can use as inducements, and, second, some way of distributing these rewards differentially according to positions. The rewards and their distribution become a part of the social order, and thus give rise to stratification.
>
> (1945: 242–243)

For Davis and Moore, stratification therefore serves a vital societal function. They conclude

> Social inequality is thus an unconsciously evolved device by which societies insure that the most important positions are conscientiously filled by the most qualified persons. Hence every society, no matter how simple or complex, must differentiate persons in terms of both prestige and esteem, and must therefore possess a certain amount of institutionalized inequality.
>
> (1945: 243)

Their theory of stratification has been heavily criticized for ignoring factors such as inherited wealth, inter-generational family status, and class structure (Tumin, 1953; Waters, 1994), and is not widely accepted today. However, their work remains a classic example of the logic underlying the structural functionalist approach insofar as it relies on the concept of functional necessity and seeks to understand how a social system achieves equilibrium.

Along these lines, structural functionalism sees health as requirement of a properly functioning system; it is prerequisite for proper role performance. For instance, illness is *dysfunctional* in the sense that it interferes with people's capacity to carry out their prescribed social roles and obligations; as such, without some mechanism for legitimization, illness is deviance. It is the role of the medical system (or more precisely, the medical profession) to regulate this dysfunction by treating, curing, or preventing disease that may otherwise interfere with expected social actions and norms (Cockerham, 2004). For Gerhardt, "illness represents a threat to the social structure and its fabric of roles. It reverses the repression of emotional needs which produces role conformity, and it allows passivity and dependency which jeopardize 'healthy' competition in the labour market" (1979: 230–231). This theoretical lens therefore gives primacy to issues of social roles and mechanisms that shape those roles.

The American sociologist Talcott Parsons developed structural functionalism as a leading theory in sociology (Holton, 2008). Indeed, Parsons' publication of *The Social System* in 1951 was a landmark in the development of medical sociology as a theoretical subdiscipline. In *The Social System*, he developed a novel model of society, one where "social order and harmony are preserved by people acting in certain defined roles and performing certain functions" (Lupton, 2003: 7). For Parsons, illness is dysfunctional and therefore "deviant", as it interferes with the performance of normative roles. Indeed, he defined deviance as "behaviour which is defined in sociological terms as failing in some way to fulfill the institutionally defined expectations of one or more of the roles in which the individual is implicated in society" (1951: 610).

Consider an office clerk who misses work, or a student who fails to attend a final exam. Both are examples of individuals failing to perform their expected roles; on a basic level, both cases are examples of deviant behaviour. But what happens if their behaviour is a result of an illness of reasonable severity? Most of us would excuse the clerk and the student from their expected roles; the clerk may stay at home without fear of losing pay and the student may rightfully expect to be able to write a makeup exam. The structural functionalist position

> is to view illness as a potential state of 'deviance'; that is, failure to conform to societal expectations and norms in some way. Illness is considered an unnatural state of the human body, causing both physical and social dysfunction, and therefore a state which must be alleviated as soon as possible.
>
> (Lupton, 2003: 7)

To account for this potential problem, Parsons theorized the *sick role* – a normative social role with accompanying rights and obligations that sick people follow to legitimate their condition.

Parsons (1951) argued that there are four components to the sick role: (1) the sick person is exempt from "normal" social roles; (2) the sick person is absolved of personal responsibility; she or he is not to blame for their condition; (3) the sick person should try to get well; and (4) the sick person should seek technically competent help and co-operate with a physician. The first two components describe rights which the sick person is entitled to under the sick role. In the example that I described above, the sick role offers the office clerk and the student an exemption from their normal duties and they are not held culpable for their illness. The second two components describe obligations that accompany those rights; both the clerk and the student are expected to do all they can to get better and see a medical professional if their condition requires it.

With these four components of the sick role, Parsons believed he had discovered how society legitimates certain conditions as illness. If a person falls ill, they enter the medical system and they can fulfill the sick role – if they do not, their behaviour begins to verge on deviancy and falls outside of the medical system. Notice that the four components of the sick role act as a sort of self-adjusting mechanism; if the clerk and the student who fall ill do not try to get better (i.e., if they actively do things that lead to deterioration in their condition, or if they fail to seek and comply with a physician's instructions), the rights that accompany the sick role would be void, and the clerk or student would be seen as deviant, rather than ill. At its core, the sick role emphasizes the social context of illness. Holton notes that "[f]or Parsons, sickness was not only a biological state, but also a matter of social significance. One did not become sick independent of the social system, rather one was socially defined as sick" (2008: 143). This notion foreshadows later developments in medical sociology on the social construction of disease.

This approach also theorized about the social relationships related to health and illness. Parsons' notion of the sick role is above all concerned with the doctor–patient relationship and reflects a continuation of his work on the sociology of the professions (Gallagher, 1976). Lupton argues that under Parsons' sick role, the patient is placed

> . . . in the role of the socially vulnerable supplicant, seeking official verification from the doctor that she or he is not "malingering". The role of the doctor is seen as socially beneficent, and the doctor–patient relationship as inherently harmonious and consensual even though it is characterized by an unequal power relationship.
>
> (2003: 7)

In Chapters 6 and 7, I will examine how Parsons' views of the medical profession and the medical encounter have shaped subsequent research in these areas. Partly based on his conceptualization of the sick role, Parsons has been criticized for having an uncritical view of physicians and a simplistic understanding of the medical encounter.

It is important to note that Parsons' formulation of the sick role was primarily a theoretical construct; it was not based on extensive empirical investigation (Clarke, 2004). That is not to suggest that his work in this area is not valid; indeed, most medical sociologists – even if they disagree with the basic assumptions of structural functionalism – acknowledge the importance of the concept to the development of medical sociology. They would also acknowledge the theoretical importance of Parsons' work. For Pflanz and Rohde, "the foundation of our sociological understanding of illness has been laid by Talcott Parsons, no matter to which specific theoretical approach we may have subscribed" (1970: 645). Along these lines, Cockerham notes that

> Parsons' concept of the sick role is a clear and straightforward statement of four basic propositions outlining the normative pattern of physician utilization by the sick and their respective social roles. Parsons not only constructed the first theoretical concept directly applicable to medical sociology, but by utilizing the work of Durkheim and Weber, he did so within the parameters of classical social theory.
>
> (2001: 6)

Indeed, Parsons' sick role is essentially a Weberian *ideal type*; one informed by Durkheim's work on the function of moral authority (with doctors yielding the power of social control traditionally associated with priests) and by Freud's psychoanalytic theory. For example, Parsons was concerned with patients' motivation to recover from an illness and perhaps their conscious or unconscious desire to accrue "secondary gain" (Cockerham, 2004), what psychoanalysts label the "holding on" to illness because of real or perceived advantages (van Egmond, 2003). However, despite this strong theoretical lineage, the concept of the sick role needed empirical verification in order to have long-term utility in medical sociology.

Whilst Parsons himself did not test the sick role in an empirical manner, other researchers soon did. For example, Kassebaum and Baumann (1965) developed the *Dimensions of the Sick Role Scale*, a battery of twenty Likert-type statements that aimed to test the applicability of Parsons' concept among samples of sick people (see Text Box 3.1).

Text Box 3.1: Likert Scales

One of the most common ways of measuring attitudes in survey studies involves the use of Likert or Likert-type scales. Likert scales present the respondent with a statement, and the respondent is then asked to indicate their level of agreement to that statement using pre-set categories that usually range from 1 = "strongly disagree" to 5 = "strongly agree". Likert-type scales are similar in format, but instead of presenting statements, they can pose questions. For example, many surveys in medical sociology include Likert-type items to measure self-rated health. These may ask respondents: "In general, would you say your health is: 1 = excellent, 2 = very good, 3 = good, 4 = fair, or 5 = poor?" or "Compared to one year ago, how would you say your health is now? 1 = much better than one year ago, 2 = somewhat better now than one year ago, 3 = about the same, 4 = somewhat worse now than one year ago, or 5 = much worse now than one year ago". Scales such as these can be used quite effectively with large samples and can be used to identify differences between groups (Bryman and Teevan, 2005). Self-reported health status is widely used in medical sociology and social epidemiology, and has been found to be highly predictive of actual health status, including subsequent morbidity (Kennedy et al., 1998) and mortality (Idler and Benyamini, 1997). Although some researchers have raised questions regarding the validity (De Maio, 2007a; Sen, 2002) and reliability (Crossley and Kennedy, 2002) of self-reported health status measures in some settings, they remain an important and useful part of a sociologist's methodological toolbox.

More specifically, Kassebaum and Baumann (1965) sought to relate differences in the *Sick Role Scale* to differences in age, sex, ethnicity, socio-economic status, and clinical diagnosis. For Kassebaum and Baumann, "...the sick role, as described by Parsons, although a useful conceptual model for organizing normative expectations, may vary among different types of *patients*, that is, among persons occupying different positions in the social structure" (1965: 26). To test this notion, they enrolled a sample of 201 patients from an out-patient clinic of an urban teaching hospital in the United States. The patients ranged in age from 14 to 91 years; some had no formal schooling, whilst others had college degrees. Most were diagnosed with heart disease, diabetes, or psychoneurosis (a set of mental disorders typically not requiring hospitalization). Slightly more than half of the sample had been born in the United States. All of the patients had low to moderate incomes, one criterion for eligibility in the out-patient clinic.

They used factor analysis, a statistical technique for identifying groupings of items made by respondents, rather than *a priori* groupings made by the investigators, to collapse their 20 statements into the four clusters listed in Figure 3.1 – dependence, reciprocity, role-performance, and denial. In other words, factor analysis enabled the identification of latent concepts underlying the data.

Factor 1 – Dependence

Illness makes a person a burden on other folks around him.
The trouble with being ill is that you have to depend on other people.
There is some truth to the saying that illness is a punishment for sins.
The most important thing for a sick person to understand is that he needs outside help because he cannot help himself.
Sick people deserve more consideration than they usually get.
Most sick people are difficult to get along with.

Factor 2 – Reciprocity

People in general realize it is not the patient's fault that he is ill.
In general, people make allowances for the fact that a sick person isn't able to carry out his normal social responsibilities.
While a woman is sick, people don't blame her for not managing the home the way she normally does.
People in general are usually very kind and considerate to a person who is ill.
Most people do not blame a person for being sick.

Factor 3 – Role-Performance

People who are sick have a right to expect that others will help them.
In general, people demand too much from a person who is ill.
Often the only rest a busy person gets is when he is sick.
When a person is sick, he usually isn't expected to hold a job.

Factor 4 – Denial

Many people act sicker than they are just in order to get sympathy.
Most sickness is due to careless and wrong living habits.
How fast a sick person gets well is due more to his own efforts than to any particular medicine he is taking.
A person's health is his own responsibility just like any other part of his life.
Most people do not understand the problems a sick person has in his life.

Figure 3.1 The dimensions of the sick role scale

Source: Adapted from Kassebaum, G. G. and Baumann, B. O. (1965). Dimensions of the sick role in chronic illness. *Journal of Health and Human Behavior*, 6(1), 16–27.

Kassebaum and Baumann found that a respondents' score on these items (representing their agreement with the statement) was related to their age, sex, ethnicity, education, occupational category, and diagnosis. For example, "the tendency to score high on *Dependence* was most characteristic of older respondents, of men, of foreign-born patients, of those with low educational attainment, of those in blue-collar occupations, and of patients with psychoneurosis" (1965: 26). In addition, blue-collar respondents responded with greater agreement to *Role-Performance* items, suggesting that "different positions in the social structure are associated with different sick role expectations" (1965: 23). The results of the study suggested that low educational attainment – a measure of low social class – was perhaps associated with willingness to adopt sick role expectations.

The results held implications for the concept of the sick role and its use *in* medicine. As Kassebaum and Baumann point out,

> ...any attempt to describe sick role expectations in terms of behavior alone, without specifying a context, is necessarily inadequate....[However] a systematic investigation of the relationship between sick role expectations and response to different types of therapeutic programs would be of considerable utility to persons engaged in providing medical care...
>
> (1965: 27)

Overall, this empirical study developed Parsons' concept of the sick role in important ways; no longer was it a universal norm, but something that – along with health – was socially patterned. The empirical finding that willingness to adopt sick role behavioural expectations depended on social factors was arguably relevant for treatment regimens and patient education programs.

Twaddle (1969) and Berkanovic (1972) published qualitative studies which led to further criticism and refinement of the Parsonian sick role. Twaddle begins his report with an acknowledgement of the importance of Parsons' work, noting that "the study of illness behavior from a sociological perspective began in earnest with Parsons' formulation of the sick role" (1969: 105). He further noted that whilst the concept had been critically discussed by some (including Freidson (1970a)), it had yet to be adequately investigated using qualitative methods that asked participants to describe their experience of illness in their own terms. Twaddle conducted a series of 29 interviews with a subsample of males enrolled in a larger health study. The interviews focused on normative behaviour among individuals defined as "ill". With respect to the sick role, Twaddle observed that "in this sample, Parsons' formulation of the sick role successfully described the modal pattern of expectations and behavior for older, married, urban males *when each component was treated separately*. It was further found, however, that the *combined configuration described the response of only a minority*" (1969: 110, emphasis in original). In other words, support was observed for each of the four sick role components when they were analyzed in isolation; the complete sick role, with all four components, actually fit only a minority of the sample's experiences. Among his sample of men, Twaddle observed that the most contested component of the sick role was the exemption from normal roles, and that the least contested component was responsibility for the illness. In fact, Twaddle's qualitative study helped to generate seven possible configurations of the sick role (see Figure 3.2).

Exemption from normal roles	Responsibility for onset or continuation of illness	Cooperation with a treatment agent	Number of respondents
−	−	+	1
+	−	+	2
−	+	+	10
+	+	−	4
+	+	+	5
+	−	−	1
−	+	−	3

Figure 3.2   Expanded sick role configurations, based on Twaddle's empirical study

Notes: A "plus" (+) indicates a response consistent with Parsons' conceptualization, and a minus (−) reflects a response inconsistent with Parsons' conceptualization.

Source: Adapted from Twaddle, A.C. (1969). Health decisions and sick role variations: an exploration. *Journal of Health and Social Behavior*, 10(2), 105–115.

All of Twaddle's interviewees agreed with the third component of Parsons' formulation (being ill is undesirable and the patient has an obligation to want to get well). However, the other components of the sick role could be seen in myriad combinations; for example, one respondent disagreed with the sick role's components of exemption from normal roles and responsibility for onset or continuation of illness and agreed with the component dealing with cooperation with a treatment agent, such as a physician (see Figure 3.2). Twaddle did acknowledge that his small sample inhibited generalization, noting that "one can only wonder to what extent the findings reported here would apply to the wider population" (1969: 113). But despite this limitation, he argued that – instead of Parsons' *one* sick role, there are *many different* sick roles; that is, different people enact different patterns of behaviour in the face of an illness. This may, for example, depend on particular life circumstances and/or a range of sociological characteristics, including socio-economic position. This is an interesting example of empirical findings being used to redefine a theoretical construct.

Studies published in the 1970s continued the attempt to examine Parsons' sick role empirically and systematically. Empirical research in this case played a very important role in the development of the concept; above all, it enabled a critical analysis of its universality (Berkanovic, 1972). Segall notes that "the general tendency has been to accept uncritically the assumption that the pattern of expected behaviour described by Parsons is the same for all members of society" (1976b: 47). However, the early work of Kassebaum and Baumann summarized above suggested that the sick role may not have universal applicability.

Building on this notion, Segall (1976a, 1976b) and then Arluke et al. (1979) sought to empirically test socio-cultural variations in the perception of and willingness to adopt the sick role. Segall developed two additional Likert-type instruments – the *Perception of the Sick Role Scale* and the *Willingness to Adopt the Sick Role Scale* – and found little support for the overall sick role concept among a sample of 70 hospital patients from Toronto. Indeed, the majority of responses documented by Segall indicate a sense of anomie, or uncertainty regarding the rights and obligations of a sick person. Fully 69 per cent of participants in his study were uncertain about their agreement with the sick role's notion that the sick person should be exempt from responsibility for their incapacity to fulfill their regular obligations, and 53 per cent indicated being uncertain whether it was the sick person's obligation to seek medically competent help. The only dimension of the sick role that received strong support in Segall's (1976b) study was the sick person's obligation to try to get well, with 84 per cent of respondents in agreement. Segall hypothesized that Anglo-Saxon and Jewish respondents would differ in their perceptions of the sick role and their willingness to adopt sick role behaviour; however, his data revealed no statistically significant differences between these groups. He concluded the study with a call for methodological and theoretical refinement of ethnicity as a concept in social science research, and supporting the earlier findings of Kassebaum and Baumann, affirmed that "the evidence seems to indicate that the sick role (as conceived by Parsons) is not a unitary concept and empirically, the ideal model of the sick role is often not fully realized" (1976b: 50).

As part of a larger study of hospital volunteers, Arluke et al. explored the notion that Parsons failed to adequately account for "the empirical variety of expectations that people bring to the illness situation" (1979: 30) by collecting survey data from 490 recently discharged patients from two large New York City hospitals. Their self-administered postal survey used Segall's *Perception of the Sick Role Scale*, a Likert-type scale. They also collected information on a range of demographic and socio-economic factors, including sex, age, employment status, education, income, marital status, and religion. Their correlation and regression analyses (see Text Box 3.2) indicated interesting patterns; for example, education, sex, employment status, marital status, and religion did not influence levels of agreement with the sick role. But respondents with lower levels of income were most likely to agree to the second component of the sick role – that the sick person is not to blame for their condition. For Arluke et al., "these data all suggest that the class patterns we find in accepting the notion that illness

---

Text Box 3.2: Regression Analysis

Statistical research in medical sociology often involves regression analysis. Studies employing this technique usually have one "outcome" or "dependent" variable (e.g., an individual's probability of being in poor health, or a country's life expectancy) and attempt to model that outcome with a set of "explanatory" or "independent" variables. There are many different types of regression analysis, and they differ in that some are more appropriate than others for certain types of data, often depending on the level of measurement of the data. For example, logistic regression is used when the outcome measure is a dichotomy (e.g., 0 = respondent is not taking an antidepressant, 1 = respondent is taking an antidepressant), whereas ordinary least squares regression is used when the outcome measure is continuous (e.g., life expectancy at birth, measured in years). This type of analysis is most closely associated with positivism; yet as Olsen and Morgan (2005) and Porpora (2001) argue, regression analysis can be used quite effectively under a critical realist epistemology as well.

---

is not the responsibility of the sick person might be related to broader class differences in imputation of responsibility" (1979: 33–34). Research like this extended Parsons' theoretical concept; given the findings described above, the sick role could no longer be seen only from the perspective of social psychology (focused on individual beliefs and action) and instead, began to be seen as a normative behaviour shaped by divisions within society itself.

Parsons' sick role has been criticized from a variety of perspectives. Critiques have focused largely on the issue of responsibility. The second component of the sick role asserts that "the sick person is not responsible for his or her condition"; yet a well-known effect of the health promotion community's emphasis on *healthy lifestyles* is that of blaming the victim. In this view, *we know what it takes to be healthy*: don't smoke, don't overeat or indulge in unhealthy foods, don't consume too much alcohol, practice safe sex, and exercise. Indeed, the current emphasis on healthy living as a result of personal choices suggests that the second component of the sick role may not hold true in contemporary society. Instead of absolving the sick person from responsibility for their illness, we may instead think about illness as a stigma (Goffman, 1963; Scambler, 2004).

The sick role has also been criticized for being irrelevant to the experiences of those with chronic illnesses (e.g., cancer, asthma, and cardiovascular heart disease) (Cockerham, 2004). These conditions often require lifelong treatment and may even be asymptomatic – the sick role, with its focus on a temporary exemption from "normal" duties, says little about illness experience for chronic or re-occurring conditions. A recent empirical study on this issue examines how chronic back pain sufferers frame the delegitimation of their condition as an inability to achieve the sick role (Glenton, 2003). By focusing on a "contested" illness without a clear physiological cause (like back pain), the study extends our understanding of how the sick role works in everyday life, and importantly, how in some cases, individuals have to strive to *achieve* the sick role and gain its benefits. For Glenton,

> individuals who experience bodily suffering but who fail to gain acceptance for this suffering find themselves with illness but without sickness and can be described as inhabiting a liminal space, being both well and sick, and being neither...To achieve the sick role is to achieve recognition of one's suffering and is also a license to be exempt from particular duties for a given period of time. This exemption requires legitimation...[usually from a medical doctor].
>
> (2003: 2244)

Above all, this speaks of the importance we attach to the legitimation of illness experience by authority.

The methodology in the study was quite innovative. Glenton used qualitative content analysis of almost 500 contributions to an online discussion list where visitors wrote about their experience with chronic back pain. These data were supplemented by open ended, in-depth interviews with 19 back pain sufferers. In general, respondents lamented the lack of a clear diagnosis. The data emphasize the role of medical diagnoses as "proof of suffering"; an entry point to the benefits of the sick role. Respondents lamented the lack of clear diagnosis for chronic back pain. When a physical origin was detected, respondents reported a sense of relief – "proof to one's doctor and to one's social surroundings that one truly is in pain" (Glenton, 2003: 2246). The data also reflect patients' efforts to comply with sick role obligations; Glenton notes that several of the respondents expressed fear that the lack of available treatment could be seen as a sign that they were not serious about getting back to work, that they were malingering and not committed to their obligations.

Central to the responses was the struggle back pain sufferers endured to *achieve* sick role status. Glenton notes that

> while other patient groups may meet the identification of a disease with dismay, and many try to negotiate for another alternative, either because the disease in question has serious implications for the person's health or because it is associated with social stigma, back pain sufferers in this study and elsewhere often

welcome and encourage positive diagnostic tests and diagnoses, describing them in terms of relief, as vindication and as "proof" of their suffering.

(2003: 2249–2250)

Glenton concludes that "while the expectations and demands of the sick role are indeed ill-suited for people living with chronic back pain, the sick role concept appears to reflect the social obligations and expectations that are present in the minds of health professionals, colleagues, family members, and back pain sufferers themselves" (2003: 2245). Thus, whilst the sick role as a theoretical construct may be criticized, empirical studies have shown that the role very much exists and structures the health care encounter.

Lastly, Parsons' sick role has been criticized, along with the structural functionalist perspective in general, for neglecting issues of power and conflict. As the guardian of the sick role, the medical profession serves as an institution of social control, "using its power to distinguish between normality and 'deviance' " (Lupton, 2003: 7). In the years following the publication of *The Social System*, medical sociologists began to examine this notion under the concept of "medicalization" (see Chapter 6); however, it was not something that Parsons considered when writing on the sick role. It is also unclear how alternative approaches to health care are handled under the sick role – again, an issue of power and territoriality. Parsons, true to his structural functionalist perspective, also modeled the doctor–patient relationship as one of consensus and harmony. Critics, on the other hand, assert that the relationship is often a struggle for power, a contested relationship where organizational constraints (the time that a doctor has available to see a particular patient), patient history (previous experience with the medical system), and other factors (illness under consideration, insurance/cost considerations) influence the negotiation of the sick role. Indeed, Parsons' sick role pays no attention to differences in health care or doctor–patient communication based on age, gender, class, or ethnicity (Williams, 2005). Interestingly, the basis of all of these criticisms lies in the empirical world.

Parsons' work on the sick role in the 1950s reflects the historical dominance of the structural functionalist perspective in North American sociology. Despite criticism leveled against it, the concept has been at the centre of medical sociological research for the past 50 years, and continues to be used today. For example, the concept is used by researchers trying to better understand why some people dutifully comply with the instructions of their doctors and others do not, an issue with particular relevance in research on prescription medication non-adherence or non-compliance (Becker et al., 1974; Coambs et al., 1999; Conrad, 1985; Wilson et al., 2002). There remain important dimensions of the sick role open to empirical research, for example, in terms of the psychological benefits that accrue from it (Hamilton et al., 2003). In recent reviews, Shilling (2002), Cockerham (2004), and Williams (2005) argue that, despite criticisms against it, the Parsonian legacy in medical sociology is timely and relevant.

The development of the sick role was undoubtedly an important landmark in the development of medical sociology. It signaled the growth of the subdiscipline as a distinct area within academic sociology. At a theoretical level, it reflected the dominance that structural functionalism enjoyed across the discipline. Holton notes that

> . . . in Parsons' discussion of the sick role, we see both his general theoretical ambitions and his concern for concrete interactions of daily life at work. At one and the same time, he is challenging the idea that "the invading microbe" is the root cause of all sickness, while claiming for sociology a part in the fine-grained analysis of health and illness, within – not outside – society.
>
> (2008: 144)

However, with the exception of Merton's structural functionalist account of the socialization of medical students in *The Student Physician* (Merton, 1957b), no other major structural functionalist works were published in medical sociology during this period (Johnson, 1975). Overall, structural functionalism quickly lost support. For Cockerham, "structural-functionalism, with its emphasis on value consensus, social order, stability, and functional processes at the macro-level of society, had a short-lived period as the leading theoretical paradigm in medical sociology" (2001: 6). The perspective seems detached from the revolutionary changes which societies around the globe experienced in the 1960s; as a theoretical perspective, it was soon replaced by symbolic interactionism and conflict theory.

Medical Sociology's Expanding Theoretical Base

As we saw in the discussion above, Parsons' conceptualization of the sick role claimed new territory for medical sociology by bringing the particular roles enacted by patients and medical professionals within the research gaze of social scientists. However, his analysis, rooted in structural functionalism, was not without limitations, and researchers utilizing different theoretical positions soon rose in prominence in medical sociology. In particular, symbolic interactionism offered medical sociology an important new perspective on health and illness; research guided by symbolic interaction has influenced our understanding of the very meaning of these concepts. For example, symbolic interactionism has generated the idea that *disease* refers to particular pathologies of the body, whilst *illness* is the social meaning given to that pathology (and thus has opened extensive possibilities for cross-cultural and longitudinal research). As Schneider and Conrad, in *Having Epilepsy: The Experience and Control of Illness*, have pointed out: "We cannot understand illness experiences by studying disease alone, for disease refers merely to the undesirable changes in the body. Illness, however, is primarily about social meanings, experiences, relationships, and conduct" (1983: 205). Similarly for Freidson, it is clear "... that what is social about illness is analytically independent of what is biophysical. In its social form, illness is a meaning assigned to behaviour by the actor or those around him, and illness behaviour is ordered by that meaning" (1970a: 224). A focus on "understanding illness experiences" is central to the symbolic interactionist approach to medical sociology, and is often perceived as a fundamental break with the Parsonian approach to health. I hope to show, however, that there are good grounds for thinking that whilst the focus of the two approaches differs, they are ultimately overlapping and compatible.

At its core, the symbolic interactionist approach to medical sociology builds from Max Weber's (1864–1920) *verstehen* (subjective meaning, empathy, or "to understand") and his definition of sociology as "... a science which attempts the interpretive understanding of social action" (Weber, 1947 [1922]: 88). Craib's (1997) overview of Weber's sociology offers insight into these points. When applied to health issues, the symbolic interactionist framework gives primacy to particular questions, primarily those which accentuate people's understanding of their situation, and focuses on the notion that social reality is constructed on an everyday basis through the interaction of individuals (see Plummer, 1991). Methodologically, this tradition of sociological research has been most closely associated with qualitative research designs, particularly those relying on participant observation as a means of data collection.

This tradition influenced two of the major early medical sociologists: Anselm Strauss and Erving Goffman, whose works dominated post-Parsonsian medical sociology. Strauss, now most closely associated with *grounded theory analysis* (Charmaz, 1983), co-authored the classic study of medical school socialization *Boys in White* (Becker et al., 1961) with Howard Becker, the author of *Outsiders* (Becker, 1963) and leading thinker behind *labeling theory*. That theory posits that deviant behaviour is not a characteristic of the act in question, but rather the consequence of its definition as deviant by others. This framework has been particularly useful in medical sociology and influenced Thomas Scheff's classic *Being Mentally Ill* (1966), where he defined psychiatric symptoms as "residual rule-breaking" – that is, behaviour that violated social norms that did not fit existing culturally recognizable categories of violations. In this light, madness (much of Scheff's work is focused on schizophrenia) is a social construction; for Scheff, "mental illness in general – and schizophrenia in particular – are not neutral, value-free scientifically precise terms but are, for the most part, the leading edge of an ideology embedded in the historical and cultural present of the white middle class of Western societies" (1975: 6–7). Strauss also made important contributions to the sociology of death and dying, and examined the "negotiated order" of hospital work (see Cockerham, 2001).

Goffman began his research career in medical sociology, but he did not continue to work much in the area after the publication of his landmark books *Asylums* (1961) and *Stigma* (1963). Both works contributed important concepts to sociology's theoretical stock, including "total institutions", "moral career", "betrayal funnel", and "impression management". Methodologically, he developed the dramaturgical approach to sociology, which views the social world as theatre and people as if they were actors on the stage.

Asylums is a collection of essays based on Goffman's fieldwork at St. Elizabeth's Hospital, a Washington, D.C. institution housing 7,000 patients. The work is best understood in context; a period of revolutionary change in the field of mental heath. This was a period of deinstitutionalization, where the mental hospital lost much of its legitimacy. Goffman's observations and subsequent analysis did much to portray mental hospitalization as a dehumanizing experience. Kesey's (1962) *One Flew Over the Cuckoo's Nest* and Szasz's (1961) *The Myth of Mental Illness* were published around the same time.

Johnson describes Goffman's *Asylums* as a "methodological breakthrough which had important theoretical implications, at the same time as providing enough insights and hypotheses to keep an army of empiricists in ceaseless activity" (1975: 229). Indeed, Goffman's sociology was very much an integrated empirical and theoretical endeavour, and drew from qualitative methods in particular. Interestingly, quantitative survey-based research in the late 1960s through to the 1980s attempted to "test" Goffman's analysis. Mechanic notes that

> ...none of these studies has the theoretical brilliance of Goffman's work or the quality of his insight, but they consistently fail to replicate his view of the patient's experience. Most patients did not report feeling betrayed; many reported being helped by hospitalization, and viewed the hospital as a refuge from impossible problems and stresses. Moreover, some patients from disadvantaged backgrounds viewed the hospital experience as less coercive and less depriving than their usual life situation. The studies do provide evidence of stigma associated with mental illness but negate the profoundly negative conception of the experience depicted by Goffman.
>
> (1989: 148)

Goffman's analysis – like Parsons' – is particularly interested in social roles, and the rules that underlie them. However, Goffman's roots in symbolic interactionism centres his research gaze on the performance and negotiation of meaning that is embedded in interaction, a focus quite distinct from that of Parsons' structural functionalism, which above all, focused on consensus and system integration.

A very interesting interplay between theory and empirical data is evident in the dissonance between Goffman's observations and the patient survey studies that have subsequently been published in this area. For Mechanic, the issue "is not simply one of deciding whether the studies based on patient interviews and questionnaires support or disconfirm Goffman. It becomes necessary to inquire more deeply whether this type of evidence invalidates the theoretical 'ideal type' of mental hospitalization that Goffman developed" (1989: 148). Furthermore,

> Goffman's observations appear credible despite disconfirmation by surveys, because readers of his analysis find his depiction meaningful and convincing when they view themselves as the hypothetical patient in the context he describes. Thus Goffman conveys a certain kind of "truth" that cannot be dismissed easily. This type of contextual credibility is often persuasive, having the quality of *verstehen* embodied in the methodology of Max Weber.
>
> (Mechanic, 1989: 150)

In other words, Goffman's analysis of mental institutions created a Weberian ideal type – an analytical construct, which according to Weber: "... is formed by the one-sided accentuation of one or more of points of view, and by the synthesis of a great many diffuse, discrete more or less present and occasionally absent concrete individual phenomena ... In its conceptual purity, this mental construct cannot be found anywhere in reality" (Weber, quoted in Craib, 1997: 50). Studies relying on patient surveys and usually working with a positivist epistemology are arguably ill-suited for "testing" the validity of Goffman's analysis of the dehumanizing elements of institutional life, their fixed-response categories and hypotheses perhaps not appropriate for the context. Arguably, the asylum is a place where quantitative survey methods reach a limit; whilst they may continue to be used, the knowledge that is generated through these methods in that context may not be congruent with the knowledge that is generated through other methods and under different epistemologies. The validity or credibility of any of these approaches is an open question.

The subjectivity inherent in Goffman's participant observation methodology is important. It is something that must be acknowledged and understood if we are to make sense of his work. Later in life, Goffman himself lived through an episode of mental illness involving a person close to him; he is reported to have said that if he had written *Asylums* after this experience, his analysis would be quite different (Mechanic, 1989). What we have in *Asylums* is the interpretation of a mental hospital from the viewpoint of an independent-minded, middle-class university professor; a person who strongly valued the personal autonomy that was compromised by the strict routines of hospitalization (Mechanic, 1989).

Goffman's influence on medical sociology can also be implicitly seen in research on the medical encounter. This area of research owes a great deal to Goffman's work on "interaction order"; that is, "environments in which two or more individuals are physically in one another's response presence" (Goffman, 1983: 2). Goffman argued that this should be a central area of sociological research, noting that "it is a fact of our human condition that, for most of us, our daily life is spent in the immediate presence of others" (1983: 2). For Goffman, sociology ought to be concerned with identifying and understanding the rules and norms which govern any interaction order, be it in an asylum, a classroom, or at home. Based on this notion, medical sociologists have studied the interaction between medical doctors and patients, noting the structure of medical communication, and importantly, examining efforts by patients to challenge the authority of medical professionals in face-to-face interaction. From this perspective, we may pose the following question: what roles do individuals enact, and what scripts do they follow? How are scripts constructed, and what happens when actors deviate from them?

Along with Strauss and Goffman, Eliot Freidson's books *Profession of Medicine* (1970a) and *Professional Dominance* (1970b) are central works in the canon of medical sociology and represent significant contributions based on symbolic interactionism. Freidson's books made contributions to several important areas of medical sociology, including the analysis of medical doctors as a professional force and the illness experience, where he significantly extended Parsons' sick role. His analysis of professional power is discussed in Chapter 5. Here, I would like to briefly examine Freidson's writings on the sick role. He begins by noting that Parsons' formulation is "a penetrating and apt analysis of sickness from a distinctly sociological point of view" (1970a: 228). However, Freidson soon thereafter takes issue with Parsons' discussion; incorporating insights into stigma and identity from Goffman, Freidson develops an expanded classification of illness behaviour (see Figure 3.3).

Freidson explains that his classification is "based on the meanings that people impute to physical attributes or concrete facts whether or not the imputation is, in the professional view of doctors and judges, 'correct' " (1970a: 225), a clear signal of his ties to the tradition of symbolic interactionism. His framework distinguishes six different varieties of illness.[1] They differ by their ascribed legitimacy and the severity of the condition itself. According to Freidson, legitimacy can take one of three forms: (1) *conditional legitimacy*, where the person is temporarily exempted from normal obligations (this applies to acute health conditions, where a person can be expected to fully recover after treatment); (2) *unconditional legitimacy*, where the person is granted long-term or even permanent

Imputed seriousness	Illegitimate (stigmatised)	Conditionally legitimate	Unconditionally legitimate
Minor deviation	Cell 1: "Stammer" Partial suspension of some ordinary obligations; few or no new privileges; adoption of a few new obligations.	Cell 2: "A cold" Temporary suspension of few ordinary obligations; temporary enhancement of ordinary privileges. Obligation to get well.	Cell 3: "Pockmarks/Acne scars" No special change in obligations or privileges.
Serious deviation	Cell 4: "Epilepsy" Suspension of some ordinary obligations; adoption of new obligations; few or no new privileges.	Cell 5: "Pneumonia" Temporary release from ordinary obligations; addition to ordinary privileges. Obligation to cooperate and seek help in treatment.	Cell 6: "Cancer" Permanent suspension of ordinary obligations; marked addition to privileges.

Figure 3.3   Freidson's typology of illness

Source: Adapted from Freidson, E. (1970a). *Profession of Medicine: a Study of the Sociology of Applied Knowledge*. New York: Dodd, Mead. Reproduced with the permission of the University of Chicago Press.

exemption from normal obligations (this applies to chronic conditions and long-term disabilities); and (3) *illegitimacy*, where the person is not held accountable for their condition (and thus not culpable), but at the same time, is awarded few or no privileges. This is a situation of *stigma*; the person gains few, if any, privileges and concurrently takes up burdensome obligations. Freidson argued that such experiences were common for people with epilepsy.

For Freidson, "the *sick role*, as Parsons defines it, is only to be found in cell 5 of the table" (1970a: 239) (see Figure 3.3). This is where the condition is awarded legitimacy by the medical profession (i.e., it is something within the medical sphere) *and* it is a condition from which the patient may recover in the short-term. Freidson points out that the Parsonian sick role does not fit very well in the case of debilitating chronic illnesses (cell 6 in Figure 3.3), where a patient's exemption from normative roles may be permanent, writing that

> ...a chronically ill or permanently impaired person who "expects too much" or "makes too many demands" is likely to be rejected by others. In that case, legitimacy is not conditional on seeking help as it is for illness believed to be acute and curable. Rather, legitimacy is conditional on limiting demands for privileges to what others consider appropriate.

> (1970a: 235)

Freidson's writing on the sick role has interesting theoretical implications – it is a case where symbolic interactionism refines a structural functionalist concept. Here, the sick role is significantly modified by the reaction of other social actors; illness can only be understood as social interaction, and the sick role varies by ascribed legitimacy and the severity of the condition.

The rise of symbolic interactionist research in medical sociology – an area previously dominated by Parsons and structural functionalism – meant that the subdiscipline became a focal point of debate between two of sociology's major theoretical perspectives (Cockerham, 2001). Conflict theory soon entered the fray as well and moved us from a focus on individuals to a focus on populations.

Sick People or Sick Societies?

Thinking broadly about conflict theorizing, we can identify several varieties under this general framework. At the heart of this approach is, of course, Karl Marx (1818–1883) – who did not explicitly write about health, although much of his work has influenced contemporary research on health inequities and the political economy of health and illness. Along with Marx, the tradition of conflict theory brings into focus the diverse works of Ralf Dahrendorf, Lewis Coser, Randall Collins, David Lockwood, and Jürgen Habermas and the Frankfurt School (Stones, 2008; Turner, 1991). Interestingly, questions of health and illness featured in none of the major works by these theorists – perhaps reflecting sociology's hesitation to enter the realm of medicine and the early dominance of sociology-in-medicine in the field. Indeed, whilst conflict theories have been particularly important in the development of social theory, their role in medical sociology has been questioned (Cockerham, 2001).

My own perspective is that researchers working within the conflict theory perspective – particularly approaches with Marxist roots – have been very influential in medical sociology. Indeed, much of today's research on health inequities traces its lineage, at least implicitly, to Engels and his classic treatise on the *Condition of the Working Class in England*. As discussed in Chapter 2, Engels and his contemporary Virchow developed a perspective on health that identified societal factors as determinants of disease, a notion that is at the crux of contemporary research on health inequities. It is worth noting that this is an aspect of health that is temporally prior to the moments focused on by symbolic interactionists when they analyze the differences between disease and the social meaning given to the pathology; in this sense, symbolic interactionist and conflict approaches to health and illness bring our attention to different phases of a health – disease spectrum.

Marxist models of class division have greatly shaped research on the political economy of health. In *Medicine Under Capitalism* (1976) and *Crisis, Health and Medicine: A Social Critique* (1986), Vicente Navarro examined how the fundamental pursuit of profit by the capitalist system *produces* disease – for example, people suffer due to chemical, biological, or physical agents in the workplace or indirectly, through stress and alienation. Today, much of the research published in the *International Journal of Health Services* continues to examine these issues (Navarro is the editor of the journal). Navarro continues to publish regularly in the field of medical sociology, and his more recent writings have focused on the political context of health inequities (Navarro, 2002b; Navarro et al., 2003; Navarro and Shi, 2002), a critique of the concept of social capital (Navarro, 2002a), and more widely, globalization (Navarro, 1999).

Most recently, Richard Wilkinson – in numerous publications, including *Unhealthy Societies: The Afflictions of Inequality* (1996), *Mind the Gap* (2000), and *The Impact of Inequality* (2005) as well as articles in *Social Science & Medicine*, the *British Medical Journal*, and the *American Journal of Public Health* – has outlined a hypothesis linking a society's level of income inequality to its level of population health. The hypothesis claims that an individual's health is influenced not only by their own level of income, but by the level of inequality in the area in which they live. As discussed in the following chapter, this hypothesis has important underlying (yet often unacknowledged) links to social theory, including Durkheimian notions of social integration and social cohesion as well as a conflict theory perspective on status, power, and class. Coburn (2004) has explored Wilkinson's income inequality hypothesis from the perspective of political economy, and in doing so, has generated significant debates between the (neo-) positivism of Wilkinson and social epidemiology with the critical realism espoused by contemporary writers on globalization and neo-liberalism. Similarly, Muntaner (2003) has provided thoughtful discussion on how Wilkinson's analysis could be strengthened by a renewed focus on not just income inequality, but on Marxist notions of class exploitation as well. The debates embedded within the literature on Wilkinson's income inequality hypothesis provide us with important lessons about the nature of empirical/theoretical connections in medical sociology in general and, in particular, how a researcher's decision to include or exclude variables from an analysis (a decision always based on both theoretical and empirical grounds) can significantly alter the kinds of messages that arise from the work. Debates surrounding Wilkinson's hypothesis also clearly signal the influence of the importance of conflict theories in medical sociology.

In contrast, Cockerham, in a recent analysis of the relationship between medical sociology and sociological theory, argues that conflict theory "has failed to date to establish a major foothold in medical sociology" (2001: 9). Aside from a brief acknowledgement that conflict theory can be brought to bear on questions of politics and health care reform, Cockerham argues that

> there are inherent limitations in the use of conflict theory in medical sociology. While some health situations are affected by conflict-related conditions, others are not. People may maintain their health or become sick and these outcomes can have little or nothing to do with conflicts, politics, interest-group competition, class struggles, and the like.
>
> (2001: 10)

He goes on to claim that the "greatest potential of conflict theory for medical sociology thus lies in its non-Marxist aspects, as interest-group competition in welfare states proves more relevant for health concerns than class struggle" (2001: 11). This is a controversial assessment; and indeed, not one shared by other writers who have analyzed the link between medical sociology and social theory (Bourgeault, 2006; Gerhardt, 1989; Lupton, 2003). Indeed, the medical sociological literature is replete with research informed or inspired by conflict theory; along with Vicente Navarro and Richard Wilkinson (who is ignored altogether by Cokerham), we have, for example, Ivan Illich.

Illich's *Limits to Medicine* offers a devastating critique of contemporary medical practice in general and the process of medicalization in particular. His analysis begins with the position that "the medical establishment has become a major threat to health" (1976: 3) and he famously noted, as we saw in Chapter 1, that "medicine is but a device to convince those who are sick and tired of society that it is they who are ill, impotent, and in need of technical repair" (1976: 9). For Illich, medicine, as practiced in industrialized countries, only obscures the political conditions that cause sickness. Central to his analysis is the concept that medical practice is *iatrogenic* – that is, it actually creates disease and illness through its normal operation. Illich identified three types of iatrogenesis

> [It is] clinical, when pain, sickness, and death result from the provision of medical care; it is social, when health policies reinforce an industrial organization which generates dependency and ill health; and it is structural, when medically sponsored behaviour and delusions restrict the vital autonomy of people by undermining their competence in growing up, caring for each other and aging.
>
> (1976: 270–271)

His analysis has significant contemporary echo; indeed, clinical iatrogenesis is widespread, for example, as demonstrated in the current debates surrounding the efficacy and effectiveness of pharmacological treatments for mood disorders (Blech, 2006; Moynihan and Cassels, 2005).

Illich's analysis is fundamentally a lament over the health effects of life in industrialized, highly bureaucratic societies – a concern that he shared

with Weber. Illich saw the process of medicalization as one that disem-
powered people, and that leads to a decline in personal freedom. Illich
warns: "[o]nce a society is so organized that medicine can transform people into patients because they are unborn, newborn, menopausal, or at
some other 'age of risk,' the population inevitably loses some of its autonomy..." (1976: 78). This concern is shared with other researchers engaged
with conflict theory. However, where Illich and other conflict theorists
such as Navarro (1975) diverge is with respect to strategies for change.
For Illich, the only way to combat medicalization is to de-bureaucratize
and de-professionalize the practice of medicine; his is a radical (anarchist) position which sees efforts to reduce unequal access to medical
treatment by ensuring universal access to health care as *regressive* and
counter-productive.

Conflict theory – particularly of the Marxist variety – has made a profound contribution to our understanding of global health issues, health
inequities, the power of the pharmaceutical industry, and health care
reform. Conflict theory has been particularly useful in the analysis of
health care as a private commodity, something to be purchased under market mechanisms rather than a public good, guaranteed by citizenship or
human rights. However, its contribution has at times been more implicit
than explicit, and some commentators have noted that conflict theory's
use in medical sociology has at times also been contradictory. For example, Lupton notes that under the conflict theory perspective, "medicine is
typically criticized for being both overly expansionist and exclusionist (of
the underprivileged), and illness is seen as being caused by both deprivation
and medical domination" (2003: 10).

The political economy branch of medical sociology has also been criticized for failing to recognize or acknowledge the significant improvements
to living conditions, life expectancy, infant mortality rates, and medical
treatment that most countries – even those low on the United Nations'
Human Development Index – have experienced over the past 100 years
(Lupton, 2003). However, I would suggest that this is an unfair criticism.
Working within a political economy-based conflict perspective, Raphael
et al. (2004) acknowledge that significant improvements in health status
have occurred in all industrialized nations since 1900. Indeed, profound
improvements in health status have occurred in most places in the globe
since 1900 (with some significant exceptions in recent decades, particularly as a result of HIV/AIDS in sub-Saharan Africa (Mathers and Loncar,
2006)). Whilst much of this improvement is attributable to factors outside
of the health care system (and instead, can be traced to improvements in
sanitation, housing, nutrition, and access to potable water), health care
services are by no means devoid of importance among conflict theorists
(with a notable exception, as noted earlier, being Illich, who focused on its
iatrogenic effects). Disagreement clearly exists about the status and prestige

that should be awarded to medical services; these debates show that conflict theories can be both critical of the expansionist/iatrogenic properties of modern biomedicine and at the same time be used to highlight issues of inequitable access to effective treatments. Conflict theorists can emphasize the point of overall improvements in health status – because it is precisely those improvements that make the remaining (and in some places and cases, growing) inequities so problematic. Farmer, a first-hand witness to the effectiveness of treatments for tuberculosis and HIV, has expressed this most clearly: "... one can be impressed by the power of modern medicine and yet dejected by our failure to deliver it equitably" (1999: 264–265).

The statistics on health inequities are indeed striking. At a global level, life expectancy data indicate that the richest nations have life expectancies of about 80 years. Yet people born in the poorest nations in the world experience life expectancies of half that amount – about 40–45 years (Coburn, 2006), with life expectancies in some African countries now dipping below 40 (UNDP, 2007). It is this global pattern of inequity that has at the same time outraged and inspired researchers working under a conflict theory paradigm. Much like Virchow and Engels (and Marx), conflict theorists attempt to identify underlying structural forces that result in these disparate statistics, and engage with policy issues. For example, Coburn writes: "degrees of inequality are clearly influenced by international, national and local political policies which are amenable to change. We can either ignore these processes or seek to understand and begin to change them" (2000: 144). This reflects (following Marx's dictum) an underlying commitment to not only describe the world, but to change it.

Much feminist social theory has conflict theory roots, and like other conflict theories such as Marxism, has informed the development of medical sociology. A notable example of this tradition is Doyal's (1995) *What Makes Women Sick: Gender and the Political Economy of Health*. Feminist medical sociology has contributed in significant ways to research on medicalization, with a landmark study published by Oakley (1984) on pregnancy. Her work developed a feminist analysis of childbirth and examined mechanisms that establish and expand medical dominance over women (also see Barker, 1998). In other words, this work frames much of Western medical practice as a patriarchal force interested in extending control over women's bodies (Ballard and Elston, 2005). Additionally, as shown in Chapter 7, feminist notions of gender as performance (with an implicit link to Goffman's dramaturgical sociology) have made significant contributions to how we understand the medical encounter.

This is not only seen in relation to pregnancy, but also with the menopause (McCrea, 1983), which in the past 30 years has also been "medicalized". Ballard and Elston note: "... as a result of medical definitions of the menopause as a 'deficiency disease', many women came to feel morally obliged to accept medical intervention in order to prevent future ill-health" (2005: 232). Their comment reveals important links between feminist-inspired medical sociology and insight derived from the writings of Michel Foucault, particularly his work on surveillance and more recent writings on risk (see Chapters 6 and 7).

Refocusing: From Roles and Populations to Discourse

The philosopher Michel Foucault has had a profound influence in the development of medical sociology and is the last of the major theorists that I would like to introduce in this chapter. His work has generated insight into the relationship between knowledge and power, and how these are embedded within the language and thoughts of individuals (Cowley et al., 2004). In Foucault's analysis, knowledge and power are positioned as being so closely connected that an extension of one means an expansion of the other; Foucault used the term "power–knowledge" to express this unity. For Foucault

> We should admit rather that power produces knowledge…that power and knowledge directly imply one another; that there is no power relation without the correlative constitution of a field of knowledge, nor any knowledge that does not presuppose and constitute at the same time power relations. These "power-knowledge relations" are to be analysed, therefore, not on the basis of a subject of knowledge who is or is not free in relation to the power system, but, on the contrary, the subject who knows, the objects to be known and the modalities of knowledge must be regarded as so many effects of these fundamental implications of power-knowledge and their historical transformations.
>
> (1977: 27–28)

Above all, Foucault's account of power–knowledge brings our attention to discourse, and how it reflects power–knowledge relations. He gives us an important example of this in his landmark book *The Birth of the Clinic*, where Foucault (1994 [1973]) distinguished "medicine of the species" and "medicine of social spaces". The former refers to classification, diagnosis, and treatment of disease and defines the human body as an object of study, whilst the latter characterizes preventive public health measures. In doing so, Foucault conceptualized medicine as a type of perception (the "clinical gaze") which gave ontological primacy to the body and its parts, at the expense of the person. He describes the medical gaze: "In order to know the truth of the pathological fact, the doctor must abstract the patient…in relation to that which he is suffering from, the patient is only an external fact; the medical reading must take him into account only to place him in parentheses" (1994 [1973]: 8). This gaze not only describes the interaction between physician and patient, but it also establishes power – a power that produces authority as well as knowledge. Samson notes that observations derived from the clinical gaze

> eventually form the basis for the medical categorization of illness, [and] ignore the individual patient as a person. As soon as definitions, categories and taxonomies are formalized in texts and taken to be sources of authority, medical power is expressed in the routines, rituals and bureaucracies of hospitals and clinics.
>
> (1999: 9)

Foucault's analysis of the clinical gaze shows how biomedicine became established as the authoritative "truth" on matters of health and illness; how we think about disease is shaped by the clinical gaze. In this way, the clinical gaze is both a consequence and a driver of what we now call biomedicine – an approach to healing firmly rooted in mechanistic models of the body which relies on scientific reason to identify how pathogens influence bodily systems to produce disease. As we saw in Chapter 2, this atomistic model of medicine is also one of Virchow's legacies.

Similarly, in his book *Madness and Civilization*, Foucault (1965) used historical analysis (which he defines elsewhere as a "genealogy" or an "archaeological method") to examine how medical discourse surrounding madness led to the development of psychiatry as a system of knowledge and a way to exert disciplinary power over populations. He noted that whilst how society treats "lunatics" has changed dramatically over time, "modern" systems of treatment may best be understood as evermore powerful techniques of surveillance, based on the internalization of societal norms and subtle, indirect ways of regulating individuals (Turner, 1995). For example, Foucault's analysis examines how the surveillance of human sexuality subjected intimate bodily activities to institutional monitoring and control and is at the root of extensive literatures on so-called surveillance medicine and, more recently, the sociology of the body.

Foucault referred to this notion of regulation as "panopticism" (after the Panopticom, a type of prison designed by Jeremy Bentham which allowed observers to see all prisoners but kept the prisoners from knowing when they were being watched). From this perspective, medicine is but one of many mechanisms through which control manifests. In *Discipline and Punish*, Foucault writes of "disciplinary projects" that began to come together in the nineteenth century and situates these projects "in the psychiatric asylum, the penitentiary, the reformatory, the approved school and, to some extent, the hospital" (1977: 199) and questions: "Is it surprising that prisons resemble factories, schools, barracks, hospitals, which all resemble prisons?" (1977: 228).

Foucault's notion of knowledge/power has greatly influenced work on medicalization, particularly the writing of Deborah Lupton (see Chapter 6), who sees in Foucault's theorizing both an anchor and a critique of the concept. And in Chapter 7, I examine the work of Nicholas Fox, who has developed a post-structuralist ethnographic study of the medical encounter. Building from the work of Foucault (and other post-structuralist/post-modern theorists), Fox notes that "post-structuralism has led to a radical re-thinking within social theory of the nature of power" (1993: 17–18); this re-thinking has involved a shift of attention towards the concept of *discourse*. His writing on this notion is very instructive and is worth quoting at length:

> The distinctive character of such an approach is perhaps worth exploring. Structuralist, both functionalist and marxist, perspectives reify "organisations" as things, treating the structures they uncover as *sui generic* realities. For the post-structuralist, so to do is to confuse the model or method of social analysis with organization itself: if you look for a system, you will find one. Interactionist and phenomenological perspectives on organization have explored how the social world becomes routinised in practice through actors' taken-for-granted assumptions about their environment, while ethnomethodologists seek to show how actors use organizational rules to validate their activities. These perspectives have this in common with postmodern social theory: they reject the notion of organizational structure as reality. But whereas for traditional idealist approaches rules and routines reflect consensus, negotiation and shared world-views, in the postmodern study of organization, routine is not the outcome of a shared world-view, but the opposite: the imposition of control and constraint by the empowered, through techniques of power mediated by discourse.
>
> (1993: 18)

This is a powerful development of Foucault's writings on discourse. Fox's analysis is based on ethnographic data and conversation excerpts and focuses on the discourse that takes places between surgeons and their patients shortly after the operation has taken place. Following Foucault, Fox is particularly concerned with how discursive structures dominate interaction between surgeons and patients, and how surgeons shape and control post-operative discourse in such a way that their claim to be healers is privileged. This hegemonic discourse – central to the medical encounter – is, for Fox, best analyzed through post-structuralist "deconstruction", wherein "the ideological claims of text are exposed, the very things which the author of discourse would deny come to be seen as the bedrock without which the discourse would founder" (1993: 38). This analysis of "micropolitics" owes much to the Foucauldian framework of knowledge/power. In Chapter 7, I examine the differences between this approach to the medical encounter and the approach espoused by Parsons.

Conclusion

Medical sociology has developed over the past 60 years into an arena of rich theoretical debate. As we saw in Chapter 2, the origins of the field can be traced to the pioneering work of Engels and Virchow – writers who saw the social seeds of disease and analyzed health issues through the prism of social inequality. That perspective still holds significant influence, particularly in contemporary research on health inequities, as we will see in the next chapter. This chapter traced the major theoretical contours of the discipline, centring our gaze primarily on the work of Parsons on the sick role – in many ways, medical sociology's core theoretical construct.

Arguably, it is debate over the merit and limitations of Parsons' sick role that has allowed medical sociology to develop a rich mix of theoretical positions. As we saw in this chapter, Freidson's symbolic interactionist critique of Parsons yielded a major development for the field, and enabled us to see the sick role from a different perspective. Goffman's work in *Asylums* and *Stigma* also center on sick roles – and therefore may be seen as an extension of Parsons' original framework (and clearly Goffman's work on stigma influenced Freidson's typology of illness). Conflict theorists, and their focus on health inequities, arguably are also centred on the sick role – but in most cases, the emphasis moves from sick people to sick populations. And Foucault's analysis of knowledge/power shows how the very ways we think about disease are intertwined with regimes of social control.

4
Health Inequities

Medical sociology's focus on health inequities was clearly displayed in the revolutionary prose of Engels and Virchow in the 1840s. Interest in health inequities remains a vital part of the field today, and although contemporary empirical research looks quite different than Engels' or Virchow's, researchers in this area continue to work in hopes of reducing unnecessary morbidity and mortality by identifying fundamental causes of poor health. Research in this area has followed Mills' conceptualization of sociology and regularly frames health not only as a personal trouble but also as an underlying public issue. In this way, disease ceases to be only a personal experience – something to be treated on an individual-case basis, and becomes a social phenomenon, one shaped by history, economics, culture, and politics. This is a legacy of the foundational writings of Engels and Virchow, both of whom directed our attention to not only the *social patterning of disease*, wherein the poor and disadvantaged are most likely to suffer from health problems, but also to the *social production of disease*, whereby the very way in which we organize our societies has an effect on our health status.

This perspective draws our attention to factors outside of the traditional health care system as determinants of health. Such factors have traditionally included housing conditions, employment, the availability of nutritious food, neighbourhood patterns of trust, and the existence of affordable and efficient public transportation. However, the most studied social determinant of health has been socio-economic status (SES), a factor that is associated with each of the 14 major cause-of-death categories of the influential International Classification of Diseases (Link and Phelan, 1995) and that underlies empirical and theoretical research on the social gradient in health (De Maio, 2007a; Ecob and Davey Smith, 1999; McDonough et al., 1997; Singh-Manoux et al., 2002).

Research using SES as a causal factor in health research has involved an important distinction between *distal* (also referred to as fundamental) causes of illness and *proximal* causes such as elevated blood pressure. In an influential paper published in the *Journal of Health and Social Behavior*, Bruce Link and Jo Phelan developed this model and posited that SES is a fundamental cause of illness; an all-important distal "risk factor". According to Link and Phelan,

> . . . a fundamental cause involves access to resources, resources that help individuals avoid diseases and their negative consequences through a variety of mechanisms. Thus, even if one effectively modifies intervening mechanisms or eradicates some diseases, an association between a fundamental cause and disease will reemerge. As such, fundamental causes can defy efforts to eliminate their effects when attempts to do so focus solely on the mechanisms that happen to link them to disease in a particular situation.
>
> (1995: 81)

Their paper is a critique of the view – commonly held among epidemiologists – that SES matters simply because it is a *proxy* measure for other, more biological, determinants that are causally closer to disease and may be avoided through individual-level behaviour change (e.g., cigarette smoking). Link and Phelan forcefully argue that this conceptualization resonates with Western values and beliefs systems by giving primacy to the individual and his or her actions. They also note that the understanding of SES as simply a proxy measure is consistent with the dominant biomedical model of disease. This is because whilst a social patterning is acknowledged, it is *explained* by underlying biological pathways or associations. As a result, the power of medicine remains unchallenged, and policies aiming to reduce inequities or improve population health in general can thereby focus on the link between the actions of individuals and their health. Link and Phelan decry

> All too frequently, even those of us who believe that social conditions are important for health are lulled into thinking that the best way to understand and ultimately address the effects of social conditions is to identify the intervening links. . . . But the concept of a fundamental cause sensitizes us to the possibility that fundamental social causes cannot be fully understood by tracing mechanisms that appear to link them to disease. To be sure, a focus on mechanisms can help identify variables more proximal to health, and if such risks are addressed, the health of the public can be improved. However, in the context of a dynamic system in which risk factors, knowledge of risk factors, treatments, and patterns of disease are changing, the association between a fundamental social cause and disease will endure because the resources it entails are transportable to new situations. If one genuinely wants to alter the effects of a fundamental cause, one must address the fundamental cause itself.
>
> (1995: 88)

As we will see below, their argument has crucial implications for how we conceptualize health and illness, how we research health inequities, and how we attempt to transfer health-related social research findings to the public policy sphere.

How do Social Researchers Study Health Inequities?

Medical sociologists examine health inequalities using myriad methodological and theoretical approaches. An important branch of this work is based on the statistical analysis of large-scale datasets. This kind of research has made important contributions to our awareness of (a) the extent of health inequities, and (b) the factors that are associated with, and perhaps even cause, poor health outcomes. For example, in Britain, statistical analysis has shown that a man born into the highest socio-economic group can expect to live 9.5 years longer than a man born into the lowest socio-economic group (the gap is slightly smaller for women, at 6.4 years) (Coburn, 2006; Marmot, 2004). Even larger gaps exist within the United States (Singh and Siahpush, 2006). A key factor which some medical sociologists think may underlie these patterns is income inequality – what Link and Phelan would call a fundamental cause of disease. For example, Kahn et al. (2000), in a statistical analysis of US survey data, found a 30 per cent greater risk of reporting depressive symptoms among women living in areas of high income inequality. Much of the research of this type reflects a positivist epistemology and quantitative methodology, but medical sociological work on health inequalities is not confined to positivist statistical analysis. Indeed, the most recent advances in this area are a result of analyses driven by critical realism – an epistemology that posits that knowledge is not limited to that which can be directly measured, but that it also contains that which exists underneath the surface of observable phenomena and that can only be ascertained through theoretical reasoning (Coburn, 2004). Whilst open to quantitative research strategies and statistical analysis (Porpora, 2001), critical realism places emphasis on "generative mechanisms" that exist beneath the surface of the phenomena we can measure with positivist methods (see Scambler, 2001).

A rich tradition of interpretivist ethnographic research also exists in this area. Such studies foster an in-depth understanding of the lived experience of poor health. For example, Laurie Abraham's *Mama Might Be Better Off Dead* (1993) provides readers a vivid account of what it means to live under the dual pressures of poverty and ill health. Working with an interpretivist epistemology, studies such as Abraham's (which is discussed in some detail at the end of this chapter) enable us to see the world from the perspective of others; in doing so, they generate potentially life-saving ideas on how to improve health services and foster possibilities for truly participatory research designs that work with communities, not merely study them.

Regardless of methodology or epistemology, medical sociological work on health inequalities is characterized by an interest in the structural conditions which lead to poor health; this focus is clearly a part of quantitative research on the social gradient in health as well as qualitative research on the lived experience of health problems. This implies the need for a wide-ranging research gaze. As Bartley notes,

> It is a long way from Enron to the coronary arteries. The task of relating what goes on at the levels of global business and politics to health and disease is rather daunting. However, this is no excuse to not take it seriously: health inequality research is going in this direction....
>
> (2003: 109)

In other words, medical sociological research on health inequality can be characterized by its ambitious attempt to bridge political economy and health sciences.

Work in this area has used the Foucauldian construct of *embodiment* (Freund, 2006; Krieger, 2005), which may be defined as the process whereby "social influences become literally embodied into physio-anatomic characteristics that influence health and become expressed in social disparities in health" (Krieger and Davey Smith, 2004: 92). Ontologically, this results in a perspective that recognizes human beings as both social beings and biologic organisms; the task for medical sociologists and social epidemiologists is to theorize and research the complex connections between the two. For Krieger and Davey Smith,

> The construct of embodiment also invites us to consider how our bodies, each and every day, accumulate and integrate experiences and exposures structured by diverse yet commingled aspects of social position and inequality. It can assist us with thinking through, systematically, what any given investigation measures, what are likely to be important unmeasured covariates, and what are relevant time frames...With such knowledge, we better understand the meaning and limitations of the analytical findings any given study generates, plus potentially spark new hypotheses.
>
> (2004: 99)

An important example of how embodiment may act as an organizing concept is given to us by research on income inequality and health.

Income Inequality as a Social Determinant of Health

The study of the health effects of inequality is a relatively new topic in medical sociology. Although the field has a strong tradition of concern with social inequalities in health, it is only now beginning to examine social inequality *itself* as a key social determinant of health (Kawachi and Kennedy, 2002; Kawachi et al., 1999c; Wilkinson, 1996). Indeed, previous social scientific work on health acknowledges the fact that material deprivation is a relative, not an absolute, concept (following the work of Townsend (1970), Runciman (1966), and others), yet it has tended to focus on material, or absolute, deprivation as the cause of poor health. According to Quick and Wilkinson,

> ... in relation to health, discussions of the effects of poverty still tend to focus exclusively on the material deprivation it causes. There is a steady stream of otherwise excellent reports focusing on matters such as the prevalence of damp housing among the poor, the deterrent effect of charges for health services on take-up, and on the difficulty of shopping for a healthy diet on social security benefits. Such issues have been the traditional focus of those concerned with inequality in health.
>
> (1991: 6)

In contrast, the emerging literature on the health effects of inequality sees inequality itself as a source of poor health. At its centre is the work of Richard Wilkinson, who in numerous publications (Wilkinson, 1990, 1992, 1996, 1999b, 2000, 2002, 2005; Wilkinson and Pickett, 2006, 2009) has built upon the economic work of Preston (1975) and Rodgers (1979) by developing a model based primarily on psychosocial mechanisms to account for how inequality affects health status in societies that have undergone the epidemiological transition (the point at which infectious diseases decline in importance and a country's leading causes of death are non-infectious, or chronic, in nature).

The result, for Wilkinson, is that "the crucial determinants of population health and of health inequalities in most of the developed world turn out to be less a matter of medical care or the direct effects of exposure to hazardous material circumstances, as of the effects of the social environment as structured by social hierarchy" (1999a: 492). In this view, the quality of the social fabric, of which equity in income distribution is an important element, is related to population health "partly from the way a more unequal, more hierarchical, society increases people's sense of inferiority, shame and incompetence" (1999a: 496). In the quoted passage Wilkinson refers to "the developed world" (a term that is used somewhat vaguely in much of his work), but his analysis has usually been applied to countries with a gross domestic product (GDP) per capita of at least US$5000.

A good working definition of Wilkinson's income inequality hypothesis is that an individual's health is influenced not only by their own level of income, but by the level of inequality in the area in which they live. This is illustrated in Figure 4.1.

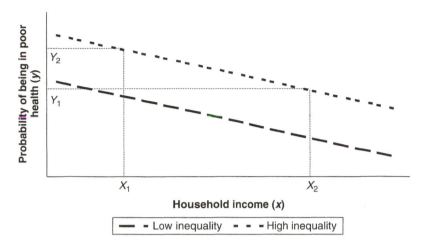

Figure 4.1 The income inequality hypothesis

Notice that Figure 4.1 depicts two downward-sloping lines. This reflects the pattern of a social gradient, wherein health improves as income increases. The figure also illustrates Wilkinson's hypothesis: For any level of household income (x), the probability of being in poor health (y) is lower if one lives in a region of low income inequality. For example, with household income of x^1, one would have a probability of being in poor health of y^1 or y^2, depending if one lived in a region of low or high income inequality. Since for any level of x, y^1 is less than y^2, population health is better in areas of low income inequality. Figure 4.1 also suggests that if one were to achieve a health status of y^1, one could do so by making x^1 and living in an area of low income inequality, or by increasing their own household income to x^2 and living in an area of high income inequality. The difference between the two downward-sloping lines represents the additional health burden associated with being "exposed" to a high level of inequality. This is, of course, a very simplified model – the relationship between income and health is not typically linear but instead follows a pattern of diminishing returns (Backlund et al., 1996; Ecob and Davey Smith, 1999), and "health" in this example has been purposefully left undefined. There is also reason to believe that the lines in the graph need not be parallel; that is, inequality may have a more significant burden on some parts of the socio-economic spectrum than others.

The foundation of the Wilkinson hypothesis is the notion that income matters as a social determinant of health *within* but not *between* industrialized countries (Wilkinson, 1996). Within-country inequalities in health are characterized by "the social gradient in health" (Adler et al., 1994), the ubiquitous relationship between income and health that runs throughout

~> the income spectrum. A long-standing tradition of medical sociology, particularly in Britain, has examined the relation between income (or social class) and health (see Davey Smith et al., 2001; Townsend and Davidson, 1982). These inequalities, importantly, do not display a standard "threshold effect" (i.e., it is not simply a distinction between the poor and the non-poor). According to Daniels et al.,

> ...the fact is that health inequalities occur as a gradient: the poor have worse health than the near-poor, but the near-poor fare worse than the lower middle class, the lower middle class do worse than the upper middle class, and so on up the economic ladder. Addressing the social gradient in health requires action above and beyond the elimination of poverty.
>
> (2000: 29)

The social gradient in health, or the notion that income matters as a determinant of health within countries, is a key pillar of the Wilkinson hypothesis.

Another pillar is the observation that, amongst so-called developed countries, it is the most equal countries, and not the richest countries, that are the healthiest. At an international level, the relationship between income and health is positive and significant (see Figure 4.2 for an analysis using male life expectancy at birth; the relationship is similarly positive using female life expectancy at birth).

As shown in Figure 4.2, GDP (a general, although imperfect, measure of societal wealth) is significantly correlated with population health, operationalized either as male or female life expectancy at birth. In other words, as GDP per capita increases, population health tends to improve. Figure 4.2 also highlights the substantial variance we can observe in life expectancy around the world, with the very poorest countries in the world experiencing life expectancies lower than 40 years.

But Wilkinson's analyses go beyond this stage: when one looks only at the advanced industrialized countries, it is no longer the richest that are the healthiest. Indeed, Figure 4.2 indicates a threshold effect, since above levels of approximately US$5000 GDP per capita further increases in life expectancy are not associated with further improvements in population health.

Figure 4.3 replicates the analysis from Figure 4.2, but includes only the 11 industrialized countries used by Wilkinson in his early analyses.

Limiting the analysis to these 11 countries results in a non-significant correlation between male life expectancy at birth and GDP per capita (the relationship is similar using female life expectancy at birth). Alternatively, Figure 4.4 presents the correlation between male life expectancy at birth and a country's income distribution, operationalized as the Gini coefficient (see Text Box 4.1).

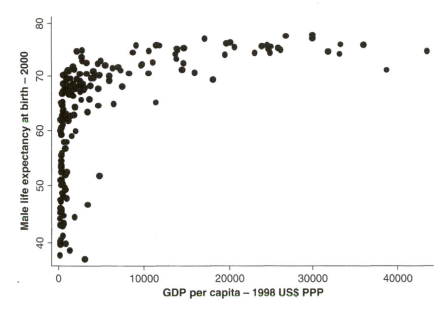

Figure 4.2 The relationship between male life expectancy and GDP per capita ($r = 0.55$, $p < 0.001$)

Source: Author's analysis of World Bank (2001) data.

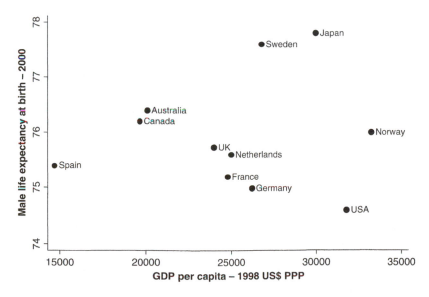

Figure 4.3 The relationship between male life expectancy and GDP per capita – selected countries ($r = 0.08$, $p = 0.80$; not significant)

Source: Author's analysis of World Bank (2001) data.

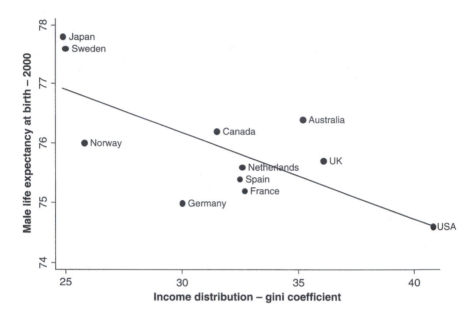

Figure 4.4 The relationship between male life expectancy and income inequality – selected countries ($r = -0.71$, $p < 0.05$)

Source: Author's analysis of World Bank (2001) data.

Text Box 4.1: *The Gini Coefficient*

By far the most popular measure of income inequality, the Gini coefficient (Atkinson, 1975; Campano and Salvatore, 2006; Champernowne and Cowell, 1998; Gillis et al., 1996) is derived from the Lorenz curve framework illustrated in Figure 4.5. The Lorenz curve shows the percentage of total income earned by cumulative percentage of the population. In a perfectly equal society, the "poorest" 25 per cent of the population would earn 25 per cent of the total income, the "poorest" 50 per cent of the population would earn 50 per cent of the total income and the Lorenz curve would follow the path of the 45-degree line of equality. As inequality increases, the Lorenz curve deviates from the line of equality; the "poorest" 25 per cent of the population may earn 10 per cent of the total income; the "poorest" 50 per cent of the population may earn 20 per cent of the total income, and so on.

One of the appealing properties of this framework is that it can be used to generate a single summary statistic of the income distribution, the Gini coefficient. The Gini coefficient is equivalent to the size of

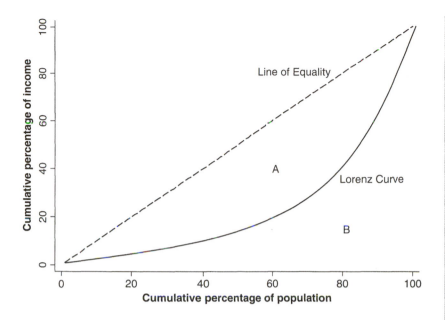

Figure 4.5 The Lorenz curve framework (hypothetical data)

the area between the Lorenz curve and the 45-degree line of equality divided by the total area under the 45-degree line of equality. In Figure 4.5, it is depicted by area A divided by area A + B. The Gini coefficient can be presented as a value between 0 and 1 or between 0 and 100. A coefficient of 0 reflects a perfectly equal society in which all income is equally shared; in this case, the Lorenz curve would follow the line of equality. The further the Lorenz curve deviates from the line of equality, the higher will be the resulting value of the Gini coefficient. A coefficient of 1 (or 100) represents a perfectly unequal society wherein all income is earned by one individual.

The Gini coefficient's main weakness as a measure of income distribution is that it is incapable of differentiating different kinds of inequalities. Lorenz curves may intersect, reflecting differing patterns of income distribution, but nevertheless resulting in very similar Gini coefficient values (Atkinson, 1975; Cowell, 1995). This troubling property of the Lorenz framework complicates comparisons of Gini coefficient values and may confound tests of the income inequality hypothesis. Along with this limitation, researchers working with the Gini coefficient need to be aware that it is most sensitive to inequalities in the middle part of the income spectrum (Ellison, 2002; Hey and Lambert, 1980). This may be appropriate in many studies, but in

---

Text Box 4.1: (Continued)

some cases, researchers will have valid reasons to emphasize inequalities in the top or bottom of the spectrum (Wen et al., 2003). Despite these limitations, the Gini coefficient has been used extensively in the public health literature (Beckfield, 2004; Blakely et al., 2003; De Vogli et al., 2005; Lopez, 2004) and it remains the most popular measure of income inequality. Yet, because it is highly sensitive to inequalities in the middle of the income spectrum, the Gini coefficient is not "neutral" or value-free (Gwatkin, 2000). Because of this property, the Gini coefficient is best seen as simply *one of the many* strategies available for the operationalization of income inequality.

Source: De Maio (2007b). Income inequality measures. *Journal of Epidemiology & Community Health*, 61(10), 849–852. Reproduced with the permission of BMJ Publishing.

For these 11 countries, there is a significant negative correlation between male life expectancy at birth and income inequality (see Figure 4.4). Findings such as these led Wilkinson to claim that it is "the most egalitarian rather than the richest developed countries which have the best health" (1996: 75).

Over the past ten years, a large literature has emerged which investigates Wilkinson's income inequality–health hypothesis (for recent systematic reviews, see Deaton, 2002; Lynch et al., 2004; Subramanian and Kawachi, 2004; Wilkinson and Pickett, 2006), and in turn, several versions of the hypothesis have been formulated. The hypothesis illustrated in Figure 4.1 corresponds to the "stronger" version of the hypothesis, because it suggests that the health effects of income inequality apply to the entire population, not just some parts of the socio-economic spectrum, or specific social or demographic groups, as posited by the "weaker" version of the hypothesis.

Findings from the United States (where the majority of studies on the income inequality–health hypothesis have been carried out) suggest that people living in states with high income inequality experience a 10 to 14 per cent increased risk of mortality (Lochner et al., 2001) and between a 10 to 54 per cent greater chance of self-reported poor health (Blakely et al., 2001, 2002; Kennedy et al., 1998; LeClere and Soobader, 2000; Shi and Starfield, 2000; Soobader and LeClere, 1999; Subramanian et al., 2001). In terms of Figure 4.1, these statistics would represent the difference between y^1 and y^2. As previously noted, Kahn et al. (2000) found a 30 per cent greater risk of reporting depressive symptoms among women living in areas of high income inequality. Another recent study found that for every point rise in the Gini coefficient the risk of reporting poor health increased by 4 per cent (after controlling for individual-level factors such as age, gender, education, and household income) (Lopez, 2004).

Results from studies in other parts of the world have yielded mixed findings, leading most researchers in this field to acknowledge the need for further empirical and theoretical work on the hypothesis (Subramanian et al., 2003a; Subramanian and Kawachi, 2003; Wen et al., 2003). A Chilean study that used sophisticated statistical techniques found that respondents from communities with high income inequality were 22 per cent more likely than respondents from communities with low income inequality to be in poor health (controlling for age, sex, ethnicity, marital status, education, employment status, type of health insurance, and household income) (Subramanian et al., 2003b). In contrast, a Japanese study by Shibuya et al. (2002) produced mixed results. Using a nationally representative survey, they found that people living in a high inequality prefecture had a 14 per cent greater chance of reporting poor health. However, this relationship did not retain statistical significance after controlling for individual level variables such as household income, age, marital status, and sex. When comparing studies such as these, however, it is important to recognize their context: Chile's Gini coefficient is one of the highest in the world, whilst Japan's is only of the lowest.

More recently, Hou and Myles, in a study using the Canadian National Population Health Survey, observed similarly mixed results. They found that "on average, the less affluent have better health outcomes when they share neighbourhoods with more affluent, better educated, individuals" (2005: 1566). This suggests that inequality *per se* may not be pathogenic; Hou and Myles posit that "the poor derive *positive* externalities from sharing neighbourhoods with more affluent families as a result of richer institutional resources and/or 'learning effects' " (2005: 1558). This is contradictory to the original income inequality hypothesis, and in many ways represents a "trickle down" model of inequality, wherein inequality is not inherently harmful to the poor, because they may share in better institutional resources that may accompany the presence of affluent residents in the community (clearly assuming that at least parts of these resources are shared communally).

In a study of region-level income inequality and the prevalence of common mental disorders[1] in Britain, Weich et al. (2001) found a 31 per cent greater chance of high income individuals living in areas of high income inequality reporting a common mental disorder, compared to high income individuals living in areas of low income inequality. However, no such relationship was observed for middle- and low-income respondents (Weich et al., 2001). These findings also differ from Weich et al.'s (2002) study of region-level income inequality and self-rated health in Britain, which found that the health effects of income inequality were most pronounced amongst low-income people, to the extent that they experienced a 55 per cent greater risk of reporting being in poor health if they lived in areas of high income inequality.[2] These studies indicate that the way in which researchers operationalise the concepts under study can have profound implications on the results generated by that study; a notion recently supported by my own analysis of income inequality and health in Argentina (De Maio, 2008a).

The last few years have seen continued research productivity in this area. Pickett et al. (2005) observed significant correlations between obesity and diabetes mortality with income inequality in a sample of 21 developed countries, and Ram (2005) found a significant relationship between state-level income inequality and mortality in the United States. This suggests that the scepticism raised about the income inequality hypothesis needs to be reconsidered, findings echoed by Zimmerman and Bell's (2006) US analysis and my studies of Argentine data (De Maio, 2007a, 2008a). At the same time, De Vogli et al. (2005) presented evidence from Italy and 21 wealthy countries in favour of the income inequality hypothesis. Cantarero et al. (2005) found an income inequality effect on life expectancy and child mortality using data from the European Community Household Panel Survey. Harling et al. (2008) observed a relationship between income inequality and tuberculosis in South Africa. Yet this latest wave of studies has not quelled the debate on the income inequality hypothesis, and a number of compelling questions remain. Many of these are statistical in nature (e.g., how to appropriately "test" the Wilkinson hypothesis, which type of regression model is best suited for the analysis, how variables should be operationalized and coded, and which variables should be included in the analysis), but many are centred on theory, in an attempt to understand why income inequality may affect health.

Pathways Linking Income Inequality to Health

What are the pathways which might link income inequality (an environmental, or area, characteristic) with health status (a property of individuals)? The emerging answer relies on evidence from a wide range of academic fields of study, including sociology, biology, psychology, and other health sciences. The four major pathways are illustrated in Figure 4.6 and are described below. It is important to note, however, that these pathways are not mutually exclusive; indeed, they can be expected to operate in conjunction with one another, though the relative importance of these pathways will vary for different groups in different places at different times.

Pathway I asserts that the relationship between income inequality and population health rests primarily on psychosocial mechanisms. This is the pathway favoured by Wilkinson and other influential writers in this field, including Sir Michael Marmot (Marmot, 2004; Marmot and Siegrist, 2004; Marmot and Wilkinson, 2001), and is highly integrated with

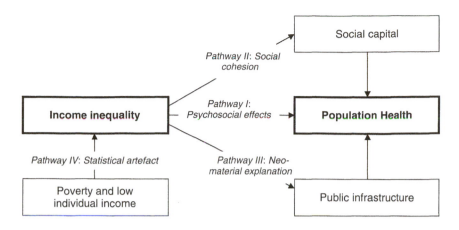

Figure 4.6 Pathways linking income inequality to health

theoretical and empirical research on the social gradient in health (Bartley, 2004; Elstad, 1998). The crux of this pathway has been best expressed by Marmot: "the psychological experience of inequality has profound effects on body systems" (2004: 7) and by Mel Bartley: "perhaps it is not the amount of money you earn, but how you feel about the status that this gives you in society, that influences your health. This might in turn be influenced by how many people earn a lot more than you do" (2004: 13). In general, these psychosocial mechanisms reflect the biology of chronic stress and the psychology of relative deprivation.

More specifically, the psychosocial pathway linking income inequality to population health draws from two related strands of the biology of chronic stress: (1) the allostatic load model (McEwen, 1998), and (2) the "fight or flight" syndrome (Brunner, 1997). Both strands of research examine the critical question of how unhealthy environments translate into disease, and both strands examine bodily changes as a response to stress. Central to this model is the role of cortisol, a stress hormone, and adrenalin (epinephrine). To fully understand the income inequality–health hypothesis, it is worth examining the role of these bodily systems in some detail.

In times of perceived danger, the body activates defences through the nervous and endocrine systems. The sympathetic nervous system is linked to all of the major organs; when activated, it releases adrenalin and other hormones to increase bodily action (e.g., the heightening of sensation and awareness). It increases the heart rate and channels blood supply to the muscles. In contrast, the parasympathetic nervous system is activated during times of sleep and relaxation, and functions to decrease the heart rate and divert blood from muscles towards system-maintenance processes (Wilkinson, 2000). The endocrine system functions by secreting hormones such as cortisol into the bloodstream, which increases blood sugar levels by counteracting the effects of insulin. Other bodily stress responses include the release of prolactin, a hormone which functions to inhibit reproductive processes, as well as the inhibition of insulin. According to Wilkinson,

> these responses all ensure that energy is kept for use instead of being stored for future needs.... [However] serious consequences for health arise when anxiety and physiological arousal are sustained or recur frequently over weeks, months or years. The feedback mechanisms – which should return the systems to normal – can be damaged by sustained periods of arousal.
>
> (2000: 40)

Indeed, the long-term effects of a sustained state of alarm include the deterioration of immune system functioning.

The allostatic load model (McEwen, 1998) is a function of the working of the nervous system, the hypothalamic-pituitary-adrenal axis (HPA), and the cardiovascular, metabolic, and immune systems (Wilkinson, 2000). It is roughly defined as the wear and tear that results from chronic overactivity or underactivity of allostatic systems. Wilkinson notes that the indications of allostatic load are

> ...higher blood pressure, insulin resistance, central obesity and raised basal cortisol levels. The higher the load, the greater the risks of cardiovascular disease, cancer and infection, and the faster the decline in mental functioning in old age (because the hippocampus, which is central to learning and memory, is very sensitive to cortisol).
>
> (2000: 42)

The key notion here is that as the allostatic load increases, in effect, the body experiences a state of permanent anxiety and physiological arousal. For Wilkinson, these are by-products of living in a situation of marked inequality. This is particularly damaging and has serious health consequences – effects which Wilkinson labels "analogous to more rapid ageing" (1999a: 493).

The second strand of research underlying this model of the biology of chronic stress refers to the fight-or-flight syndrome. This model also seeks to explain bodily effects of stress, but it emphasizes acute periods of anxiety. Key to this model is the role of adrenalin (epinephrine); according to Smith,

> ...when a person is confronted with an external threat and its accompanying stress, epinephrine (adrenalin) levels may be elevated, allowing the body to perform at higher levels. Elevated adrenalin may provide simultaneous challenges for blood pressure, heart rate and the immune system. Such fluctuations may be ideal for short-run responses, but frequent and cumulative episodes may be quite harmful and ultimately lead to disease.
>
> (1999: 162)

The central argument is that social inequality is associated with chronic, low-level stress; a situation which results in an increased allostatic load, but also acute periods of high-level stress, which triggers the fight-or-flight response. Theoretically, these effects influence the health of not just the poor, but the middle and upper classes as well (as illustrated in Figure 4.1). Kawachi and Kennedy call this a "spillover" effect: "income inequality induces 'spillover' effects on quality of life, even for people not normally affected by material wants" (1997: 1037). These and other aspects of the biology of chronic stress point to important links between our subjective understanding of our environment – whether or not we see ourselves to be in physical danger, or if we are in a situation of shame, inferiority, or subordination – and bodily changes that have documented effects on our health.

A second tier of evidence linking income inequality to health through psychosocial mechanisms comes from the social psychology of relative deprivation and the concept of self-efficacy. Building on earlier research on stress, the concept of self-efficacy refers to "the extent to which people see themselves as being in control of the forces that importantly affect their lives" (Pearlin et al., 1981: 339), and is largely synonymous with concepts such as mastery and a strong internal locus of control. Its opposite concepts include fatalism, a strong external locus of control, and powerlessness (Elstad, 1998). Interestingly, the social psychological concept of self-efficacy is closely related to the Marxist term of alienation. Gecas writes that under conditions of alienation,

> the sense of self-efficacy is frustrated or inhibited because of a disjuncture between action and self, wherein work activity is no longer a reflection and affirmation of self. At the heart of the problem of alienation for Marx was the issue of control, that is, the extent to which the individual has control over his/her labor.
>
> (1989: 296)

In the case of income inequality, the hypothesised pathway in this case sees decreased self-efficacy and increased alienation in areas of inequality. The health effect can then be attributed, at least in parts, to well-researched pathways linking self-efficacy to individual functioning, including health (Gecas, 1989).

The crucial link in this argument is the extent to which income inequality is associated with increased levels of relative deprivation and thus lower levels of self-efficacy among the population. For Wilkinson, the evidence suggests a strong relationship exists: "as income inequality increases, the quality of the social environment seems to deteriorate: trust decreases and hostility and violence increase. In other words, as hierarchical dominance becomes stronger, egalitarian social relationships weaken" (2000: 62).

Pathway II links income inequality to population health via social capital (Coleman, 1990; Fukuyama, 1995; Kawachi et al., 1997; Putnam, 2000), a term whose conceptual and operational definition has generated much debate in the sociological literature (Cooper et al., 1999; Navarro, 2002a; Pevalin, 2003; Pevalin and Rose, 2003; Portes, 1998). For some researchers, including Putnam (2000), social capital is an ecological, or community-level variable; that is, it is a characteristic of social organizations and groups (Lochner et al., 1999) and may roughly be thought of as the quality of social networks within a particular region. For others, including Bourdieu, social capital

> ... resides in the relationships between actors within the group and access to that capital is not available to actors outside the group. In this way the capital lies outside the individual per se but by an individual being or becoming part of a group that individual may access the capital.
>
> (Pevalin and Rose, 2003: 3)

These differing conceptualizations of social capital also imply that different mechanisms might link social capital to health. Taking the more individualistic definition of social capital as the property of individuals, a large body of literature has documented the pathogenic effects of social isolation. For example, it is widely accepted that socially isolated individuals are at increased risk of mortality from a number of causes (Berkman, 1995).

In contrast, seeing social capital as the property of groups, or geographical areas, suggests that different mechanisms may be at play. Myriad links have been identified in the literature, including (1) effects on health behaviours (i.e., areas with high level of social capital will enable the adoption of physical activities; such areas will be more likely to have public parks and recreational areas), including the diffusion of health information (e.g., neighbourhoods with high levels of social capital will have established effective communication channels); (2) effects on the access and use of local services and amenities; (3) effects via psychosocial mechanisms; and (4) effects through mechanisms of social control (i.e., areas of high social capital may be more effective at reducing crime, violence, and anti-social behaviour) (see Figure 4.7).

All four mechanisms linking social capital to health hint at the notion of *collective efficacy* (see Kawachi et al., 1999a). Overall, an impressive body of literature confirms that social capital affects the health of individuals, when measured at the compositional level; however, evidence of the health effects of social capital at the contextual level are very mixed at the moment (Mohan et al., 2004). Yet overall, the health effects of social capital appear to be quite important. For Putnam, social capital serves "as a physiological triggering mechanism, stimulating people's immune systems to fight disease and buffer stress" (2000: 327). And furthermore,

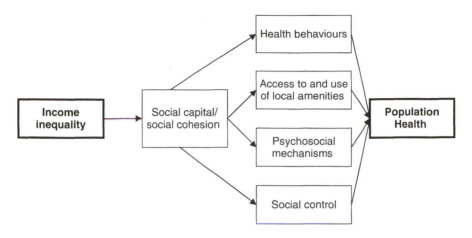

Figure 4.7 Mechanisms of the social capital/social cohesion pathway

> … mounting evidence suggests that people whose lives are rich in social capital cope better with traumas and fight illness more effectively. Social capital appears to be a complement, if not a substitute, for Prozac, sleeping pills, antacids, vitamin C, and other drugs we buy at the corner pharmacy.
>
> (2000: 289)

The connection between this pathway and the psychosocial pathway discussed previously is strong. However, the social capital pathway emphasizes the importance of social organization and social cohesion far more than the psychosocial pathway. The basic argument is that areas of high income inequality are likely to be areas of low social capital, low social cohesion, and therefore high social conflict. The idea is that if you live in a very unequal neighbourhood, you may be less likely to know and trust your neighbours, and you may be less likely to obtain help from them if needed.

The third major pathway linking income inequality to population health relies on neo-material mechanisms (neo-material, rather than material, to differentiate the material factors relevant today from the material factors determining patterns of morbidity and mortality in the past – for example, inadequate systems for sewage management). This explanation asserts that income inequality is associated with systematic underinvestment in social infrastructure (e.g., education, health services, transportation, the availability of nutritious food, occupational health controls, and housing) (Kahn et al., 2000). According to Lynch et al. (2000), the neo-material explanation sees income inequality as a result of historical, cultural, political, and economic processes which manifest themselves by influencing public infrastructure. In other words, "political units that tolerate a high degree of income inequality are less likely to support the human, physical, cultural, civic, and health resources needed to maximize the health of their populations" (Daly et al., 1998: 319) – suggesting an important overlap with the health effects of social capital.

Proponents of the neo-material explanation of the health effects of income inequality also argue that the psychosocial explanation ignores context; that is, it does not examine factors which are intrinsically related to income inequality, such as race and gender inequalities, class relations (Muntaner and Lynch, 1999; Muntaner et al., 1999, 2001), and neo-liberalism (Coburn, 2000, 2001b, 2004). Muntaner et al., perhaps the strongest "friendly" critics of Wilkinson's work, worry that the focus on psychosocial mechanisms and the effects of social capital may lead public health researchers to

> ...take a step back from the structural sources of inequalities – after all, if they are not an integral part of our theories of health inequalities and are so difficult to change, then perhaps an achievable alternative is to retreat to mass psychotherapy for the poor to change their perceptions of place in the social hierarchy.
>
> (2000: 116)

Interestingly, Wilkinson has responded by emphasizing that "rather than the psychosocial taking us into individualism, it [the psychosocial pathway] shows instead that the psychosocial welfare of populations is powerfully affected by structural factors" (1999a: 496). In this sense, the neo-material explanation can be seen as *both* a critique and a complement to the psychosocial explanation. It is a critique because it questions the psychosocial explanation's interpretation of the social gradient, and it is a complement in the sense that few would argue that the explanations are mutually exclusive. Indeed, proponents of the neo-material explanation have intensely advocated seeing the two pathways as reinforcing (Coburn, 2000, 2001a, 2004).

The fourth explanation does not actually explain why income inequality might affect health status; instead, it suggests that the observed association between income inequality and health is a statistical artefact – a mathematical trick, rather than a reflection of a real relationship. This explanation raises the problems of ecological fallacy – the inappropriate inference of relationships at the individual level from relationships observed at the population level (Diez-Roux, 2002; Pearce, 2000; Robinson, 1950). This is important because we are drawing inferences at the individual level (someone's health) from population-level information (the level of inequality in their area). This critique is most clearly discussed in the work of Gravelle (1998) and Ellison (2002). The argument behind this explanation builds upon the observation that the social gradient in health is not exactly linear;

the income–health relationship is more accurately described as curvilinear (e.g., exhibits diminishing returns to increases in income). This has important implications: the curvilinear relationship between income and health at the individual level may create "artefactual" associations between income inequality and population health at the ecological level (Ellison, 1999).

Senn (1998) has argued that this explanation is a far simpler model than Wilkinson's income inequality hypothesis, and as such, should be preferred unless convincing evidence emerges to support the more complex narrative. However, the statistical artefact explanation – whilst logically appealing – has been strongly criticized in the literature (Wildman, 2001; Wilkinson, 2002). Indeed, a data simulation study conducted by Wolfson et al. (1999) has shown that Gravelle's argument cannot account for all of the observed relationship between income inequality and population health. The statistical artefact explanation also does little to acknowledge the growing literature on "place" effects (Diez-Roux, 2001; Frohlich et al., 2001; Macintyre et al., 2002; Veugelers et al., 2001; G. H. Williams, 2003); that is, the notion that the social determinants of health cannot be reduced solely to the characteristics of individuals and that contextual effects do matter.

Conceptual Links to the Theoretical Literature

Substantial links between the income inequality–health hypothesis and larger social theory are present in the published work in this area. This section examines the links with theoretical discussions on social capital (linking back to Durkheim), class (recalling Marx), and social comparisons (engaging with Merton and Thorstein Veblen).

Durkheim's contribution

The concept of social capital and the underlying concept of social cohesion are at the heart of the income inequality hypothesis. Wilkinson sees levels of social cohesion as one of the key social manifestations of inequality; in unequal areas, we are unlikely to know our neighbours, to trust them, and as such we are less likely to call on them for help. However, this is something that very few studies on the income inequality hypothesis explicitly measure; income inequality in many ways is taken as a proxy measure for this concept.

Busfield (2000) and G. H. Williams, (2003) argue that Wilkinson's work is reminiscent of Durkheim's classic study of suicide, where social solidarity (i.e., what Wilkinson and others in this field label "social cohesion" or "social capital") was a key explanation for differing rates of suicide between European nations (Durkheim, 1951 [1897]). Indeed, Durkheim's

contribution to sociological theory in many ways is centred on his conceptualization of social solidarity, particularly the distinction developed
in *The Division of Labour in Society* (1984 [1893]) between mechanical
and organic solidarity. Mechanical solidarity refers to a characteristic of
pre-industrial societies where strongly held and shared beliefs and values integrated relatively homogeneous, undifferentiated collectives, and
organic solidarity refers to a characteristic of societies having greater
division of labour, where the "collective consciousness" was weaker and
integration was the result of mutual interdependence among individuals –
a market. In *Suicide* – arguably his most important work – Durkheim used
the concept of social solidarity to explain suicide rates, noting that too
much integration may lead to altruistic suicide and too little to egotistic
suicide, a condition of anomie characteristic of the modern world (Lukes,
1985; Pope, 1998).

Turner (2003) has suggested the focus on social capital in health
inequality research reflects a Durkheimian "revival"; but importantly, he
also notes that "this dependence on Durkheim is rarely acknowledged"
(2003: 4). This revival is primarily attributed to the popularity of Putnam's
work on social capital, where the connections with Durkheimian notions of
social integration and regulation are acknowledged. Putnam notes: "Self-
destruction is not merely a personal tragedy, he [Durkheim] found, but a
sociologically predictable consequence of the degree to which one is integrated into society... Social connectedness matters to our lives in the most
profound way" (2000: 326). Turner goes on to suggest that a key contribution of medical sociological work on income inequality, social capital, and
health has been to correct the view that Durkheimian sociology "is remote
from the social and political conflicts of modern society" (2003: 18). He
notes that there is thus "poetic justice that there should be a Durkheimian
revival against the global consequences of economic neo-liberalism on
health and well-being" (2003: 8).

Indeed, Durkheimian notions of social integration are embedded within
studies of the Wilkinson income inequality hypothesis. As we have already
seen, social integration is at the crux of Pathway II (see Figure 4.6); for
Turner,

> ...sociological research has returned to the issue of income inequality as an
> explanation of sickness, but has set these income inequalities within the broader
> context of social integration and cohesion.... *In this radical epidemiology*, sick-
> ness is a function of high inequality and low social cohesion. The biological
> and psychological connections between individual health outcomes, social par-
> ticipation and economic inequality remain somewhat obscure, but one can
> reasonably assume that a sense of self-worth is a consequence of supportive
> social environments that have beneficial consequences for the human body.
> (2003: 14, emphasis added)

In most cases, empirical studies in this area have (following Putnam's work in *Bowling Alone* and Durkheim's in *Suicide*) operationalized social capital as an aggregate-level concept – that is, it is a property of communities rather than individuals. Typically, measures of trust and membership/participation in community groups are used. Kawachi et al.'s (1997) study of social capital and self-rated health is indicative in this case: they used the US General Social Survey items on civic trust ("Generally speaking, would you say most people can be trusted?"), collective perceptions of reciprocity ("Would you say that most of the time people try to be helpful, or are they mostly looking out for themselves?"), and membership in voluntary organizations and aggregated the data to the state level. Thus, the contextual levels of social capital were derived from individual-level responses (synonymous with the derivation of area-level income inequality from household-level data on income).

Forbes and Wainwright criticize the prevailing conventions on the operationalization of the concept of social capital, pointing out that social capital is a multi-faceted concept whose conceptual definition has been elusive. However, they go on to argue that Kawachi et al.'s (1997) operationalization of social capital as group membership and feelings of trust "cannot be regarded as valid measures of social capital except perhaps at a very superficial level. It is difficult to see how any theoretical claims based on these data can extend beyond the immediate properties of the variables contained within the original survey" (2001: 804). In another paper they provocatively argue that Kawachi et al.'s use of survey data results in "an entirely superficial and socially meaningless level [of analysis]" (Wainwright and Forbes, 2000: 262). The question at hand is how to make the leap from Durkheim's notions of social integration to contemporary research using survey data and quantitative methods; Forbes and Wainwright argue that it cannot be done, whilst Wilkinson, Kawachi, and colleagues suggest that it can be.

This debate – not yet settled, of course – has led to further refinement of social capital as a theoretical construct. Indeed, debates over conceptualizations of social capital have led to the notion that different mechanisms might link social capital to health. For example, as noted, it is widely accepted that socially isolated individuals are at increased risk of mortality from a number of causes (Berkman, 1995). In contrast, if we see social capital as an aggregate-level variable, or the property of groups or geographical areas, other images emerge. According to Kawachi et al.,

> ... the mechanisms linking social capital to health might be different from those linking social networks to individual health.... it is important to distinguish between the *contextual* effects of living in an area depleted of social capital and any *compositional* effects of social capital.
>
> (1999a: 1190, emphasis in original)

The debates over social capital and health, however, are nowhere near being resolved. The political economy perspective has added further complexity to the discussion by critiquing the tendency to conflate political, cultural, and economic groups under the generic concept of social capital (Muntaner et al., 2000).

Despite important disagreements about its conceptual and operational definition, the concept of social capital (and social cohesion) is central to Wilkinson's relative income hypothesis; it is an essential pathway through which income inequality may affect health status and it is a clear example of the continuing importance of Durkheim's classic work. Indeed, whilst his main focus is on the psychosocial explanation, Wilkinson does also stress the importance of social capital. However, in contrast to Putnam (2000), Wilkinson asserts that income inequality, not social capital, is the relevant factor in the causal chain to population health. In other words, regions of high income inequality are likely to be regions with low social capital – but to focus only on social capital would be to miss an important, and ultimately more fundamental, driver of population health.

The contribution of Marxist perspectives of class

Muntaner (2003) offers an informative critique of Wilkinson's income inequality model from a Marxist perspective. He begins his analysis with an acknowledgement that Wilkinson's model is indeed to be praised; he asserts that Wilkinson's model provides a truly social approach to understanding the effects of inequality, "avoiding the idealist heritage of US functionalist sociology and the methodological individualism of rational choice theory" (2003: 551). From this perspective, an advantage of Wilkinson's model is that it provides an alternative to previous frameworks that emphasized individual health behaviours or at most socio-economic status as determinants of health inequities. However, his analysis then turns to critique when it emphasizes – as does Coburn (2004) – that the Wilkinson hypothesis is ultimately theoretically weak, as it ignores class processes. Muntaner claims that

> The emerging income inequality/social capital hypothesis threatens to destroy the possibility of an integrated race, gender, and class research program in social epidemiology at the altar of a theoryless empiricism in which "race", "class," or "gender" enter in the analysis only as an individual attribute ... More and better studies on income inequality and health will never deal with the theoretical need to explain how income and other forms of economic inequality are generated through class-, gender-, or race-related processes.
>
> (2003: 553)

Muntaner proposes that instead of centring the hypothesis on income inequality, alternative measures, including indicators of class exploitation should be used. One such measure would consist of the ratio of total value added in the manufacturing sector to wages and salaries in the manufacturing sector (see also Muntaner and Lynch, 2002); he suggests such a measure would be "preferable because it refers to an explicit social process whereas Wilkinson's income inequality concept does not" (2003: 552).

Muntaner's insights into the role of class in the income inequality–health literature are deeply steeped in social theory. Consider the following passage:

> Marxian class-based explanations are preferable because they expose the social mechanisms of exploitation in a way that income distribution models cannot. In this way, Marxian class analysis of the labor process is even deeper than Weberian class analysis as the former links exchanges in the labor market and production through the concept of exploitation, while Weberian class analyses keep labor market exchanges and production separate. Such a Weberian approach is evident in social epidemiology, where research into the health effects of work stress and work organisation have been conceptualized as independent of class.
>
> (Muntaner and Lynch, 1999: 67)

In Chapter 3, I considered Cockerham's assertion that conflict theory, and particularly Marxist conflict theory, had little to offer medical sociology. The exchange between Wilkinson, Muntaner, and Coburn clearly show otherwise – here we have a theoretical model (income inequality–health) being tested using myriad research designs directly benefiting from alternative conceptualizations of class, conceptualizations largely derived from classical sociology. In effect, long-standing debates between Durkheimian, Marxist, and Weberian strands of sociology have emerged in this area of medical sociology, with the effect of enriching both this particular research question and the wider body of sociological literature.

Ultimately, Muntaner and Coburn urge medical sociologists to recognize the intrinsic value of critical realism and call for a more comprehensive, theoretically informed research program that examines not only the health effects of income inequality, but its causes as well. Reminiscent of Link and Phelan's call for researchers to study fundamental causes of disease, the Muntaner, Coburn, and Wilkinson debates have caused medical sociology as a whole to re-examine its dominant theoretical, epistemological, and ontological positions.

Reference groups and social comparisons

A third major body of theoretical literature that underlies Wilkinson's income inequality hypothesis deals with social comparisons. This was an area of sociology central to Robert K. Merton, a noted student of Parsons (Sica, 2008). It is also a theme that has flourished in the field of social psychology (Buunk et al., 1997; Diener and Fujita, 1997). For Wilkinson, income matters to health partly because of its status-signifying properties; indeed, he claims that income differences matter mostly insofar as they map onto status differences:

> ... where income is related to social status, as it is within countries, it is also related to health. Where income differences mean little or nothing for people's position in the social hierarchy (such as those between countries), income makes little difference to health. This strongly suggests that psychosocial pathways are important: it is hard to believe that relative income is related to health unless those affected have some perception of their relative income or social position.
>
> (2000: 11)

Furthermore, he notes that

> we know ourselves partly through the eyes of others. As we monitor ourselves in relation to others, part of our experience of ourselves is our imagined view of how others see us. This ability is one of the foundations of human social life and close to the core of what we mean when we call ourselves "social beings".
>
> (2000: 52)

Although not explored by Wilkinson, there are strong implicit links between his observations and the writings of Goffman and the symbolic interactionist tradition.

The reliance on vaguely defined reference groups has been strongly criticized in the literature. Coburn, criticizing Marmot and Wilkinson, notes

> ... [they] talk frequently about "relative status" – yet they measure mainly income inequality. But income inequality as objectively measured, surely has a somewhat contingent relationship with "perceived status" which is the factor presumed to be important. Moreover, the authors never state or measure "who are the Joneses" that is, to whom do individuals and groups compare themselves?
>
> (2001b: no pagination)

Indeed, Wilkinson never explicitly develops a theory of how social comparisons occur. He cites convincing evidence that social comparisons *matter*, yet the process of how they occur is left unspecified. No specific reference groups or *reference individuals* (see Merton, 1968) are identified. What Wilkinson presents is what he interprets as the *result* of social comparisons: the social gradient in health. In other words, the process by which social comparisons occur is not the focus of Wilkinson's work. Instead, physiological pathways through which social comparisons *could* affect health status are identified, and evidence of social gradients are explored.

The underlying theory, in this case, needs substantial development. However, at least two elements of that theory have been already been identified. First, Kawachi et al. (1999c) point to Bourdieu's (1984) work on aesthetic taste as expressions of hierarchical structures (and a tool for maintaining such structures). Second, Thorstein Veblen's (1994 [1899]) writings on conspicuous consumption are also relevant; indeed, Wilkinson's model suggests that the ubiquitous need for social comparisons fuels conspicuous spending, weakens social bonds between neighbours, and ultimately, damages health.

We have here different layers of theoretical engagement at play. On one level, the literature on the health effects of income inequality has explicit connections with theoretical concepts such as social capital. And notably, empirical work in this area has fed back to the wider theoretical literature: it has contributed empirical evidence regarding the dynamics of social capital and has advanced methodological debates on its measurement. In terms of class, it has brought the works of Marx and Durkheim to the forefront of medical sociology and social epidemiology, thus contributing to and extending historical (and unresolved) debates.

On a second, more abstract and arguably more important level, the literature on the health effects of income inequality has only just begun to acknowledge the limitations of its positivistic/empiricist roots and is beginning to discuss how critical realism may be brought to bear on the income inequality–health relationship (S. J. Williams, 2003).

Epistemological Lessons

These have been most strongly emphasized by the "neo-material" theorists such as Muntaner. For example, neo-materialists criticize Wilkinson's neglect of the sources of inequality. Lynch et al. note: "We do not deny negative psychosocial consequences of income inequality, but we argue that interpretation of links between income inequality and health must begin with the structural causes of inequalities, and not just focus on perceptions of that inequality" (2000: 1202). Coburn, drawing on the political economy tradition of Navarro (2002b), notes that

income inequality is itself the consequence of fundamental changes in class structure which have produced not only income inequality but also numerous other forms of health-relevant social inequalities. Welfare measures in turn reflect basic social, political and economic institutions tied to the degree to which societies take care of their citizens or leave the fate of citizens up to the market i.e., neo-liberalism. Income inequality is a consequence, not the determinant.

(2004: 43)

He has forcefully criticized the trend in medical sociology to not question the origins of social inequalities:

> While numerous researchers have explored methods of ameliorating the effects of poor social conditions on the health of the underprivileged...hardly any have asked about the possible causes of inequality itself. Yet, examining the causes of social inequalities, and not simply their effects, changes our understanding of the causal sequences involved in the income inequality/health status relationship.
>
> (2001a: 50)

For Coburn, the health effects of income inequality are important but should be examined through the wider lens of political economy rather than epidemiology; he calls for an increased role for *critical realism* and for a diminished role for *positivism*. This says something fundamental about the nature of medical sociological research on health. It began with Engels' classic treatise on the conditions of the English working class; full of rage and calling for large-scale social change. It continued with Virchow's writings on typhus, where he found the social seeds of disease and prescribed the overthrow of the capitalist social system. However, over time, positivist methods grew in dominance – this signaled an important shift in the research agenda; much of the scholarly literature on the social determinants of health today, whilst firmly interested in inequities, does little to examine the sources of social power. It draws attention to the health effects of material deprivation and social inequality – but shies away from calling for changes in the power structure; it seeks to alleviate, but not eliminate, poverty (Himmelstein, 2002).

We can examine the question of "why has it been so difficult to 'prove' or 'disprove' the Wilkinson hypothesis?" by reflecting on the limitations of the dominant epistemological framework of this area of research: positivism. Forbes and Wainwright suggest that one major limitation of this field has been its reliance on survey data. They argue that "the data used to support these psycho-social theories are dangerously over-stretched...as a result they are somewhat under developed" (2001: 802). They argue that this field has been heavily constrained by its commitment to positivist methods and suggest that positivists (they place Wilkinson firmly within this tradition) have confused description with explanation: the relationships under study may exist "in the mathematical world of survey statistics... [but] not in the social world" (2001: 811). That is, we find common characteristics of people in poor health (description) and argue that these characteristics are "determinants" of poor health (explanation).

Forbes and Wainwright are perfectly correct to highlight the positivist inclinations of much of this field of research – however, as I discuss below, I think that they are unjustified in their assessment of its implications.

Interestingly, a similar critique has been put forth by Scambler (who as we saw in Chapter 1, has lamented the theoretical impoverishment of medical sociology):

> The research literature on the sociology of health inequalities is disappointing, perhaps most conspicuously so when the focus is on social class. Published papers too often betray a poverty of sociological imagination and ambition of a kind roundly and forcibly condemned by C. Wright Mills a generation ago. The reason for this state of affairs are several ... [including] a continuing medical sociological commitment to (neo-) positivist methodologies and "variable analysis", underpinned by empiricist philosophy in general ... and a failure on the part of medical sociologists to distinguish between explanatory and predictive power, resulting in a stultifying lack of interest in generative mechanisms.
>
> (2001: 35)

I disagree with both criticisms. Overall, this (admittedly) predominantly quantitative field has done much to bring into focus personal troubles, public issues, and the interconnections between them. In my view, this field of research has been largely successful in avoiding both abstracted empiricism and grand theory – tendencies which Mills, as noted earlier in this book, derided as "withdrawals from the tasks of the social sciences" (1959: 50).

A better understanding of the Wilkinson hypothesis may be generated in the future if the positivist-inclined analyses are complemented by more wide-ranging theoretical perspectives inspired, perhaps, by critical realism (see Benton and Craib, 2001). This has been introduced by Coburn (2004), in his call to expand the focus of the income inequality–health field of research. He suggests that we need an alternative approach, one that investigates the causes and not just the effects of income inequality (this approach has considerable sympathy with the neo-material explanation of health inequalities). For Coburn, this represents "a broader, more contextualized and more sociologically meaningful causal model" (2004: 43). One implication of this approach is that our analyses will likely have a more global perspective than they currently do – they will no longer be bounded by the nation-state as much of this literature has been.

The importance of a global approach is echoed in Farmer's recent book describing his experiences of treating HIV and tuberculosis patients in rural Haiti:

> [t]he cost of modern inequality is even greater than that calculated by Wilkinson and others who define "societies" as nation-states. When he writes that "it is clear that the main problems of poverty (at least within the developed world) are problems of relative poverty", Wilkinson misses the worst of it. ... The sick of rural Haiti, urban Peru, and sub-Saharan Africa may be invisible to those tallying the victims of modern inequality, but they are, in many senses, casualties

of the very same processes that have led to crime and decreased social cohesion "at home".

(1999: 281)

This field of research, which at times has been dominated by epidemiology, statistics, and economics, may hesitate to answer Coburn's and Farmer's suggestions. Sociologists may be best positioned to do so – perhaps by linking with other areas of sociological research such as globalization and human rights. This implies a continued effort to investigate the health effects of income inequality – but the scale and character of the enterprise must be expanded: we must look not just at the effects, but also the causes of income inequality, and, indeed, we must also investigate other types of inequalities – not just that based on income. To take on this challenge, medical sociologists will need to continue to draw from its rich tradition of quantitative research – which is uniquely capable of identifying patterns and relationships – but will also need to embrace insight based on interpretivism and critical realism. A flexible theoretical and methodological approach is clearly needed.

Interpretivist Approaches in Health Inequities Research

Quantitative health inequalities research gives us detailed knowledge on the social patterning of ill health and enables us to identify and theorize about the social forces underlying those effects. Parallel to this tradition, medical sociologists have employed interpretivist approaches to study the lived experience of health issues and health inequality. This approach to research reads quite differently than quantitative reports on health inequities – yet they also contain powerful analyses often based on Mills' conceptualization of sociology. However and unfortunately, medical sociology – like sociology in general – has been characterized by a distinct quantitative–qualitative divide (Mechanic, 1989) that has inhibited meaningful dialogue amongst researchers using different methodological tools and working with different epistemologies and ontologies.

In their analysis of the epistemological divisions in the health inequalities literature, Wainwright and Forbes develop a scathing attack not only on positivist research but also on interpretivist research. They argue that "too often the obsession with 'lived experience' blinds interpretivist researchers to the broader social context in which those experiences are played out" (2000: 267). Whilst they argue that interpretivist approaches can be useful as an "antidote to the atomistic and superficiality of the survey method" (Wainwright and Forbes, 2000: 265), they ultimately reject this tradition for its ontological and epistemological constraints. They argue at the core of the problem is the tendency [within interpretivism] to lock the theory within a uni-dimensional perspective. Uni-dimensional in the sense that the setting is defined by the views of the participants rather than in relation to any broader social forces which many be beyond the consciousness of those participants. Indeed the approach ignores the possibility of "false consciousness" propagated by the forces necessary for maintaining the prevailing social order, presently capitalism.

(2000: 265)

Their analysis is clearly provocative and is intended to encourage thinking of the philosophical and theoretical problems with research on health inequities. However, as was the case with their critique of the positivist tradition of health inequity research, I believe their rejection of interpretivist approaches in this area is premature. The following section will highlight the work of two authors, Laurie Abraham and Paul Farmer, who have certainly avoided the pitfalls identified by Wainwright and Forbes. Abraham's *Mama Might Be Better Off Dead* (1993) provides readers with a personal account of what it means to live under the dual pressures of poverty and ill health. Working with an interpretivist epistemology and a qualitative methodology, her ethnographic study of the failure of health care in Chicago is a classic in this field.

"Mama Might Be Better Off Dead"

The book is essentially the personal story of the Banes family as told to and experienced by Abraham during the year May 1989–April 1990. She witnessed their poverty first-hand, documenting their daily struggles for security, income, and health. She also witnessed their interactions with health care providers, often sitting in on clinical consultations and hospital visits; her book is record of the pathogenic effects of poverty and racism. Her book is fundamentally a story about inequity: "Just as doctors use CAT-scans and other instruments to uncover disease, this book exposes glaring inequities in health care access and quality that exist between the moneyed and the poor, inequities that existed long before the middle class began to feel the pinch" (Abraham, 1993: 3).

It is a story that could only be told in the style of an ethnographer; a thick description that allows the reader to immerse herself in the social world described in the text. Like other ethnographies of life below the poverty line, Abraham's book, whilst conveying *information*, does more: it facilitates *understanding* of a reality far removed from that experienced by most of its readers. She tells the story of a woman whose doctor became angry when, after she had presented with hives caused by an allergic reaction to her cat, she refused to get rid of the animal. The doctor eventually understood: "she told me that if she got rid of the cat, there was nothing to protect her against rats" (1993: 19). Abraham summarizes a key part of her interview with the doctor: "Another woman brought her two-year-old to the clinic with frostbite, so Dr. Jones dispatched his nurse practitioner to visit her home a block away ... The nurse discovered icicles in the woman's apartment because the landlord had stopped providing heat" (1993: 19). Abraham's rich text is filled with such experiences.

Her central argument is that the US health care system *fails* the poor, and particularly, poor African–Americans who fight against poverty and racism:

> For the most part, the diseases that Jackie [Banes] and her family live with are not characterized by sudden outbreaks but long, slow burns. As deadly infectious diseases have largely been eliminated or are easily cured – with the glaring exceptions of AIDS and now drug-resistant tuberculosis – chronic diseases have stepped into their wake, accounting for much of the death and disability among both rich and poor. The difference is that for affluent whites, diabetes, high blood pressure, heart disease, and the like are diseases of aging, while among poor blacks, they are more accurately called diseases of *middle-aging*.... Nation-wide, the incidence of kidney failure among blacks is four times that among whites. Much of that racial difference results from kidney failure caused by hypertension, a disease that usually can be controlled by medication. In other words, a significant portion of the kidney failure among blacks is largely preventable with regular care ... The casualties that high blood pressure inflicts on blacks are enormous; they suffer strokes at twice the rate of whites, and there are sixty thousand excess deaths a year among blacks from hypertension-related diseases.
>
> (Abraham, 1993: 19, 28–29)

Her analysis is a powerful mix of epidemiology, sociology, anthropology, and historical analysis. Readers of her book will surely agree that she shares the same passion and outrage that characterized the works of Engels and Virchow. Consider the following passage:

> Whose fault is it that Robert did not have health insurance, and that at least thirty-five million Americans are without it today? What about doctors' inability to communicate to patients in a way that makes them understand their illnesses – whose fault is that? Who is responsible for the many poor minorities who are so socially and economically isolated that they cannot take advantage of the medical system in the same way that many whites can?
>
> (Abraham, 1993: 34)

And like Engels and Virchow, she concludes that "[t]he poor need more than medical insurance" (Abraham, 1993: 258). Like many researchers who work with or utilize aspects of conflict theory, she is at once awed by the power of medicine, distressed about its unequal distribution in society, *and* worried about its expansionist tendency (implicitly, an argument against medicalization). Abraham writes: "There will always be a 'ragged edge,' a new disease to conquer, and unless we set explicit restraints, we'll consume all the country's resources chasing immortality, while starving the other institutions that can make life worth living" (1993: 259). Her analysis ultimately leads us away from the health care system itself and towards the social determinants of health.

Her work also signifies the complexity of the social determinants of health. Whilst much of the literature surrounding the Wilkinson hypothesis has focused on income and income inequality, Abraham's analysis brings to the foreground issues of gender and race/racism. At the same time, her work signals how lessons emerging from feminist, post-colonial, and critical race theories may be applied in health research. These have all formed an integral part of the recent literature on health inequities. For example, awareness of the differences between sex as a biological characteristic and gender as a social construction is increasingly displayed in epidemiological research (Doyal, 2003), and calls for "gender-based analysis" are influencing the design, implementation, and evaluation of health policies, particularly in countries like Canada (Hankivsky, 2006). In an important extension of the Wilkinson hypothesis, empirical studies have also begun to examine the pathogenic effects of gender inequality (Kawachi et al., 1999b).

Abraham's ethnography speaks to the health effects of racism and discrimination. These are known to be particularly pronounced in the United States; consider, for example, McCord and Freeman's classic study of excess mortality in Harlem, New York. Their analysis of census data and death certificates showed that black men in Harlem were less likely to reach the age of 65 than men in Bangladesh – a country with a far lower level of economic development and poorer health services. They concluded that "Harlem and probably other inner-city areas with largely black populations have extremely high mortality rates that justify special consideration analogous to that given to natural-disaster areas" (1990: 173). To be clear, McCord and Freeman do not posit biological grounds for these inequities. The pathogen in question here is racism.

This is supported by my own work on the health transitions of immigrants to Canada. From empirical research using large-scale survey data, we know that the health of immigrants is better than that of the Canadian-born population at the time of arrival (Beiser, 2005; Pérez, 2002), due partly to a self-selection process and Canadian immigration policies (Hyman, 2004; Laroche, 2000; Oxman-Martinez et al., 2000). However, after settling in Canada, the health status of immigrants deteriorates. Studies have shown that immigration to Canada is associated with unhealthy levels of weight gain (McDonald and Kennedy, 2005), increased likelihood of developing some chronic conditions (Pérez, 2002), and increased rates of depression (Ali et al., 2004). Analysis of the Longitudinal Survey of Immigrants points towards "visible minority" status and the experience of discrimination as important drivers of the health transitions of immigrants (De Maio and Kemp, 2009). Along these lines, research in the United States points towards discrimination as an important pathway through which the health of immigrants and their descendants erodes in that country (Viruell-Fuentes, 2007). These findings signal the importance of racism as a social determinant of health – a notion with clear echoes of conflict theory that at the same time opens our theoretical gaze to new possibilities emerging from anti-racist and post-colonial bodies of literature.

Recent years have seen impressive advancements in an area of scholarship referred to as intersectionality (Schulz and Mullings, 2006). This has given impetus to research that examines how race and class intersect with gender to produce health whilst at the same time emphasizes that race, class, and gender should not simply be seen as characteristics of individuals, but should be understood as social relations. For Mullins and Schulz, race should be conceptualized "as relations between groups rather than as something that people of color 'have' and whites do not. Similarly, gender is considered to be a set of social relations rather than an attribute of individuals" (2006: 6). They go on to argue that traditional epidemiological methods (based on a positivist epistemology and quantitative methodology) will have difficulty incorporating these conceptualizations; that by their very nature and assumptions, these models call for discrete variables that exert independent effects on a dependent variable and are therefore ill-suited to disentangling the complex interactions between race, class, and gender. This is very much an ongoing debate in the literature; my own position is that quantitative studies have an important role to play in this venture, particularly studies utilizing new techniques of multi-level analysis that enable analysis of compositional factors (i.e., qualities of individuals) and contextual factors (i.e., qualities of areas or groups) (Diez-Roux, 2002). Mullings and Schulz disagree, and instead call for ethnographic or case study research designs which "contribute to an understanding not only of relationships between concepts, but of the processes and the meanings that those processes and relationships hold" (2006: 7). It is to this kind of research that I now turn our attention to.

"Where are the Virchows of Global Public Health?"

Paul Farmer, author of *AIDS & Accusation* (1992), *Infections and Inequalities: The Modern Plagues* (1999), *Pathologies of Power: Health, Human Rights, and the New War on the Poor* (2003), and numerous other books and journal articles, offers one of the most inspiring examples of social research on health inequities in recent years. He is perhaps uniquely qualified to do so, given his training as an anthropologist and as a medical doctor (specializing in infectious disease). He describes his work as *historically deep and geographically broad* ethnography; an approach that is both steeped in the lived experience of his patients, particularly those in rural Haiti, and in global political economy.

The quality of Farmer's writing at times far surpasses the rest of the field; it is a powerful blend of anger, understanding, and empathy, drawing with considerable skill from anthropological theory (particularly literature on folk beliefs and cultural practices), history (particularly of Haiti, where he has conducted most of his work), epidemiology, and sociology. It is a clear testament to the value of overcoming disciplinary boundaries and the quantitative–qualitative divide. Quite simply, if we are to appropriately study health inequities – and if, following Farmer, we are to actually do something about the inequities we study – we must engage with insights from a range of empirical and theoretical bodies of literature from a diverse set of research fields.

In many ways, Farmer's work illustrates the continuing legacy of Engels and Virchow. He has poignantly questioned: "where are the Virchows of global public health?" (1999: 267) and argues that "throughout the world, but particularly in what is termed the 'Third World,' much of human suffering is caused or aggravated by social forces, and social forces should be studied by medical anthropologists" (1992: 259). He has called his work a "protest" against the social forces that pattern inequities in health and a call for recognizing the primacy of the right to health.

His research is based on the concept of *structural violence*, which he defines as "a host of offensives against human dignity: extreme and relative poverty, social inequalities ranging from racism to gender inequality, and the more spectacular forms of violence that are un-contestedly human rights abuses, some of them punishment for efforts to escape structural violence" (2003: 8). This concept is inherently sociological in nature, drawing a direct relation between personal troubles and public issues, or human suffering and the social forces that underlie it. Farmer's work is also rich in terms of social theory. It has clear connections to world-systems theory, and in particular the work of Immanuel Wallerstein (1974).[3]

Interestingly, much of Farmer's recent work, particularly *Infections and Inequalities*, can be seen as a dialogue with Wilkinson. Farmer offers an ethnographic perspective on the relationship between inequality and health outcomes (particularly HIV/AIDS, tuberculosis, and multi-drug resistant tuberculosis (MDRTB)), and advances our understanding of the issue in important ways. He calls for empirical research on the relationship between social inequality and the development of MDRTB, noting that in settings of shared wealth or poverty, MDRTB is unlikely to develop. In the first setting, access to efficacious treatment will control tuberculosis. In the second setting, few have access to drugs and therefore resistance to the drugs is unlikely to develop. However, Farmer argues, in settings of inequality – where poor and rich coexist – forces leading to MDRTB may actually be strengthened. This is because of the unequal access to treatment that is characteristic of such areas; some people will receive treatment, others will not, and some will receive treatment on a sporadic basis – and it is this third situation (sporadic treatment) that leads to drug-resistant strains of tuberculosis. In other words, Farmer agrees with Wilkinson that inequality is pathogenic; indeed, Farmer calls inequality itself the fundamental cause of illness.

However, his work is also a critique of the Wilkinson-inspired literature. As we have already noted, he criticizes the common practice among health researchers of basing their studies on nation-state boundaries. This is surely a reflection of the influence of world-systems theory on his thinking; it is also a reflection of the reality of Farmer's daily life, for he holds a clinical appointment at one of the finest hospitals in the United States (the Brigham and Women's Hospital in Boston, Massachusetts) as well as a teaching appointment at Harvard University, but spends most of his time in one of Haiti's most impoverished areas (and most recently, Rwanda). He knows from his empirical work of the ties that bind societies, of how decisions made at the World Bank or International Monetary Fund headquarters in Washington DC or the WHO headquarters in Geneva influence the lives of *billions* of people. And his work is a reflection of the tension created by living a life that spans the worlds of the rich (he argues that any first-world university qualifies as such) and the poor (and he appropriately cites Haiti and Rwanda as extreme examples). Farmer continues to work as a practicing physician and is one of the founders of Partners In Health, an international charity which brings free health care services (particularly for HIV/AIDS and tuberculosis) to poor people in Haiti, Peru, Rwanda, Lesotho, Malawi, and other countries.

Conclusion

From the preceding pages, I hope the following lessons can be discerned: (1) Inequities in health are reflections of social divisions, or as Farmer argues "social circumstances account for biomedical outcomes" (1999: 240). (2) Analysis of health inequities requires a multi-faceted methodological and theoretical toolkit. Wilkinson's quantitative approach is to link inequality to psychosocial effects of relative deprivation. In contrast, Abraham's ethnographic research points us towards structural violence that is interwoven with racism and class divisions; together, these forces produce unnecessary illness and premature death – a situation that Engels and Virchow lamented over 150 years ago. (3) Understanding patterns of inequitable illness – and more importantly, doing something about them – requires analyses of both individuals and populations.

Furthermore, it calls for an ontology of disease that is informed by the construct of embodiment. Diseases have biologic physio-anatomic characteristics; as such, engagement with the biomedical sciences is an important element of any serious attempt to improve population health. At the same time, social researchers are particularly well-positioned to provide a counterbalance to individualistic accounts of illness and their ensuing health promotion messages. Farmer notes

> Exaggeration of patient agency is particularly marked in the biomedical literature, in part because of medicine's celebrated focus on individual patients, which inevitably desocializes. Strong behaviourist trends mar much of the psychological literature on tuberculosis. Similar critiques of modern epidemiology have also been advanced. But it is social science that has underlined the importance of contextualization, and so our failure to complement clinicians' views with more robustly contextualized ones is all the more significant. Who better than social scientists to find sad irony in the fact that a rhetoric of patient "agency" is applied only after populations have been subjected to a series of external attacks, of which contagious disease is only one? The poor have no option but to be at risk for tuberculosis; thus tuberculosis is merely one factor in an environment of structural violence. For most populations . . . the chances of acquiring infection, developing disease, and lacking access to care are structured by a series of systematic forces.
>
> (1999: 259)

Farmer, like Abraham and other researchers working on health inequities, is awed yet distressed by modern medicine:

> The vast, if still largely potential, power of modern medicine stems in great measure from its focus on the biological sciences. No one who has access to the vast array of drugs and diagnostic tools of a modern hospital could fail to appreciate the century's remarkable return on investments in bench science. No one who confidently prescribes a new medication could fail to appreciate the double-blinded controlled trial. But the narrow or uncritical use of these tools is one reason for physicians' blindess to the large-scale forces that generate sickness. . . . Physicians again need to think hard about poverty and inequality, which influence *any* population's morbidity and mortality patterns and determine, especially in a fee-for-service system, who will have access to care.
>
> (1999: 10–11)

It is this very concern over access to health care and the power of medicine that I will examine in the next two chapters. Chapter 5 examines health care systems, contrasting public and private approaches whilst at the same time analysing the power of the profession of medicine. Chapter 6 examines the ever-expanding medical sphere itself – are more and more of life's problems being "medicalized"? If so, what is driving this process and what are its consequences?

5

Health Care Systems

Engels and Virchow taught us that underlying social and political structures are the most important drivers of a population's health, a lesson that is overwhelmingly supported by contemporary research on health inequities. Now classic studies have also questioned the role of medicine as producer of health, with social theorists like Illich arguing that modern medicine is iatrogenic and actually produces illness. Alongside that work, McKeown's (1976) and McKinlay and McKinlay's (1977) empirical analyses have demonstrated that dramatic declines in death rates from infectious diseases in England and the United States in the twentieth century were not associated with the development and use of medical measures for those conditions; for example, death rates for scarlet fever declined before knowledge of penicillin, and death rates for tuberculosis declined before the development of izoniazid. Most recently, Wilkinson (1996) has shown that, among industrialized countries, life expectancy is not at all associated with the percentage of national income that a country spends on its health care. These works indicate that for most populations, the formal health care system – whilst important – is not the key determinant of health; what influences health status are the social conditions in which we live.

However, can this argument be taken *too far*? Can it be twisted, so that it no longer serves its original intent of improving population health? That is the concern raised by Poland et al., in their political economy-based critique of the population health perspective. Poland et al. write: "We are concerned that the rhetoric of the determinants of health, framed in terms that health care does not produce population health, provides convenient cover for those who wish to dismantle the welfare state in the name of deficit reduction" (1998: 786). In other words, if health care systems do not produce health, why should governments fund them? Why should we as a society care about equitable access to health care services if what truly matters are downstream social determinants?[1] Indeed, if Illich is right and health care is iatrogenic, shouldn't we seek to dismantle bureaucratic health care systems to the fullest extent possible? In this light, the argument that the health care system does not itself produce a healthy population is co-opted and used for purposes that Engels, Virchow, and contemporary writers such as Wilkinson and Abraham would disagree with.

Poland et al. also take issue with the apparent neglect of the health care system as a determinant of health by medical sociologists. Their argument calls for a more nuanced appreciation of the health care system:

> While the contribution of health care to reductions in overall morbidity and mortality rates at the population level may be unclear, this is not to say that it makes no difference to case fatality rates for specific illnesses. Furthermore, a sizeable proportion of medical procedures are aimed not at increasing survival, but at improving quality of life: not only procedures such as cataract, hernia, and hip operations, but also palliative care for the mentally ill, and the management of chronic ailments (diabetes, for example) for which cures do not exist...
>
> (1998: 787)

They explicitly acknowledge and appreciate the contributions of McKeown and more contemporary writers such as Wilkinson, but at the same time, urge us to redefine our research gaze so that it does not only focus on the social determinants of health but also on issues within the formal health care system. This raises critical questions: How have medical sociologists studied health care systems? Have parts of sociology's theoretical literature contributed to these analyses? Is integration between the social determinants of health literature and work on health care system reform possible? This chapter examines these questions primarily through the lens of the Marxist-influenced political economy perspective, the area of medical sociology that has been most consistently engaged by questions of health care system structure and reform.

Health Care Systems as Outcomes of Political Struggle

Health care systems are acts of political philosophy (Cockerham, 1999). They reflect dominant values in a country's political system, values which determine the role of medical care as a *commodity* or as a *public good*; something to be purchased under market mechanisms or an entitlement of citizenship or human rights. Reflective of this position, Wiktorowicz (2006) argues that discussion of health care reform is a highly politicized arena, with values and traditions shaping how we may see the role of government in health care. An important first lesson from this literature is that health care systems are outcomes of political struggle; they reflect the end result of competition between complex forces. Importantly, these forces need not necessarily be concerned with achieving optimal health outcomes (leaving aside the difficulty in defining what optimal health is at the population level and how it would be measured).[2] Indeed, the health care system in any given country is not necessarily the best system for that population in terms of day-to-day medical care. In the section below, I examine two ideal type models of health care to enable a comparative analysis of different systems.

Comparing Health Care Systems

Social researchers have made important contributions to this field by developing models of health care systems; ideal types that enable a comparative analysis of the structure of health care systems and their key components. In this section, I want to discuss two such models. The first originates in the writing of Wiktorowicz (2006) and the second is from Busfield (2000). Both models will help us to understand the salient characteristics of health care systems, and at the same time, allow us to understand how they differ from country to country. In discussing their models, I analyze important issues facing the US health care system, before moving on to two case studies of health care systems and their reform through conflict: Canada in 1962 and present-day Venezuela.

Wiktorowicz's (2006) analysis begins with an acknowledgement that most countries, regardless of the actual design of their health care systems, have three goals in common regarding health care: social protection, redistribution, and efficiency. Social protection reflects the notion that all health care systems involve some mechanism to enable those with few material resources to access health care. Of course, some health care systems place a far higher priority on this goal than others, and some systems are by design better equipped to realize it. Redistribution describes the function that any health care system necessarily involves some rebalancing or redistribution of costs between individuals, employers, and the state. In the absence of some sort of redistributive or cost-sharing mechanism, all health care expenditures would be out-of-pocket expenditures, a situation that would result in economic inefficiencies and hardship across the socio-economic spectrum, but particularly among the poor and middle class. In practice, different systems vary dramatically in their implementation of strategies for redistribution and in the importance they give to the goal of diminishing the burden of health care for the poor. This is clearly the case if we contrast the situation in a country with a universal health care system with the United States, where medical expenditures are the leading cause of personal bankruptcy (Angel et al., 2006; Kovner and Knickman, 2005). The final shared goal (efficiency) is fundamental to any health care system, and refers to efficiency in the delivery and consumption of services. This has been a significant component of contemporary debates on health care in countries across the globe, with all countries attempting to balance the goal of economic efficiency, or cost-effectiveness, with the principle of equity and social justice.

Although all health care systems may have these three goals in common, their strategies for achieving them vary widely. To analyze these differences, Wiktorowicz proposes a two-by-two model which contrasts how the system is financed (public versus private) and how services are delivered (public versus private). This typology is illustrated in Figure 5.1.

In terms of financing health care services, Wiktorowicz suggests that a public system is one where all citizens contribute to and pay for the system through their personal income and other taxes or contributions (for example, through direct deductions from gross income). The result is a system that spreads the cost of illness across the entire population. In other words, the cost of illness is not borne only by those in need of actual medical care and the system can achieve universal coverage – in principle, if not in practice. This type of financing arrangement places particular emphasis on the goals of social protection and redistribution. Wiktorowicz explains: "in publicly insured systems, healthy individuals who do not require extensive health care services subsidize those who become ill and require treatment" (2006: 248). A publicly financed health care system is therefore by definition a social contract, one where costs of services are shared across the population and where health care is accepted as a public good.

Wiktorowicz's (2006) analysis also points to an important consideration with respect to efficiency: publicly financed systems may be particularly

Delivery	Financing	
	Public	**Private**
Public	Britain, Sweden (National health services)	–
Private	Canada, France (Public insurance systems)	US (Private insurance)

Figure 5.1 Wiktorowicz's typology of health care systems

Notes: Countries like Germany and Switzerland also incorporate private financing and private delivery; yet their systems are best seen as a mixture of private insurance (through employment), government subsidies, and mutual aid societies.

Source: Wiktorowicz, M. E. (2006). Health care systems in evolution. In D. Raphael, T. Bryant and M. Rioux (Eds), *Staying Alive: Critical Perspectives on Health, Illness, and Health Care* (pp. 241–262). Reprinted by permission of Canadian Scholars' Press Inc.

cost-effective, since the government acts a single purchaser of services and products (pharmaceutical drugs, for example). Economists label this a *monopsony*, akin to a monopoly, which describes a situation of a seller that has control of the market; in this case, it is the buyer that has that unified power. This is particularly important given the rising burden of expenditure on pharmaceutical products in health care systems around the world (Blech, 2006; Moynihan and Cassels, 2005). For example in Canada, expenditure on drugs surpassed total expenditures on physicians in 2000 and has increased as a percentage of total health care expenditure ever since (Marchildon, 2006). The result is that every year Canadians now spend more on pharmaceutical drugs than they do in doctors' services. If states (or in the case of Canada, provinces) can harness monopsony power, they gain an important edge in negotiations with pharmaceutical companies over the price of drugs.

Wiktorowicz's (2006) model indicates that health care systems can also be based on the principle of private financing. The clearest example of this is the United States, which relies heavily on individually contracted health insurance as a mechanism for financing the costs of health care.[3] The US health care system is based on the philosophy of the free market, where private provision of medical services dominates (Gordon, 2003; Ruggie, 1999). As a result, the United States is widely cited as the only advanced industrial country without a national health care system based on universal access, over 45 million Americans are without health insurance, and millions more only have limited coverage, through which a serious illness would mean financial devastation (Angel et al., 2006). It is important to note, however, that the extent of the population covered by health insurance differs substantially from state to state, with several claiming nearly universal health coverage (Ruggie, 1999). Only about 20 per cent of Americans are covered by the two major federal public health programs (Medicare, a program which aims to cover the elderly or disabled, or Medicaid, a program which aims to cover the indigent) (Angel et al., 2006). These programs – whilst incredibly important to millions of Americans – are best seen as government efforts to address market failures in the wider health care system. The dominance of the principle of private financing is not challenged by these public programs.

Social researchers have generated much-needed insight into issues of health care in the United States, as was evident in the ethnographic writing of Abraham (1993) discussed in Chapter 4. Another notable study on the challenges facing the US health care system was recently published by Angel et al. (2006). They make a compelling case for the need to radically change the American system of health insurance, focusing on the challenges faced by poor Americans in obtaining *and maintaining* health insurance coverage. That is, rather than framing the issue as a distinction between having insurance and not having health insurance, Angel et al. note that for many people, the battle is one to maintain continuous coverage for both themselves and their dependent children. The task for the empirical social researcher in this case is one of witnessing. For many researchers, this translates into direct engagement in policy debates, a sort of applied sociology that explicitly sees social action as part of its mandate.

Angel et al.'s project entailed an ambitious mixed methods study in three major cities of the United States – Chicago, Boston, and San Antonio. Their study collected a combination of quantitative survey and qualitative interview data. This mixed methods design was particularly important for the researchers, who explain that

> ... the national statistics on the number of Americans without health insurance are disturbing in and of themselves, but they cannot convey the complexity and urgency of the real-life situations that poor and working-class families face as a result of the instability of their medical care coverage and the resulting variability in their access to health care.
>
> (2006: 111–112)

The authors are successful in their attempts to convey this complexity by presenting narratives rich in ethnographic detail interwoven with descriptive findings from their structured surveys in Chicago, Boston, and San Antonio.

The challenge of fulfilling bureaucratic requirements for eligibility for Medicaid is central to their book. The ethnographic narratives emphasize the fact that Medicaid does not provide block family coverage; each member of the family has to be certified and re-certified independently of others. For the families in the study, this often meant having to miss work, since many of the families relied on public transportation, and often had to spend an entire day traveling across the city to attend their appointments. For workers in low-wage/low-security service sector jobs, this sometimes resulted in having to choose between keeping a job or being able to meet the bureaucratic requirements of Medicaid. In other cases, workers had to choose between a low-paid job without health insurance but that would nevertheless negate their claims to Medicaid, or deciding to remain unemployed.

Studies like these shed light on the political philosophy that underlies the US health care system, reminding readers from outside of the United States of the perspective many Americans hold with respect to the state. Angel et al. note that "unlike the citizens of Europe, Americans do not receive, and for the most part do not expect, free higher education, state-mandated vacations, family allowances, or guaranteed health care as basic citizenship rights" (2006: 37). This philosophy can be seen in many of the experiences analyzed in their study; for the poor, the experience of having to constantly apply for certification under Medicaid was a reminder that they were asking for too much. Angel et al. reflect on their findings

> reliance on public programs is stigmatizing. Rather than receiving health care as a citizenship right or as an employment benefit, those families that rely on Medicaid must reaffirm their pauper status on a regular basis in order to continue to receive services. As our interviews revealed, the recipients of publicly funded social services, including health services, live with that daily reality of sanctions, rejection, and humiliation.
>
> (2006: 98)

This constant reminder of deprivation and social exclusion is a significant barrier to achieving optimal levels of health. Indeed, although Angel et al. do not explicitly engage with the research on the Wilkinson hypothesis or the literature on the pathogenic effects of chronic low-level stress or the lack of social capital discussed in Chapter 4, their study reaffirms much of that literature, and highlights how these determinants of health may be compounded by features of a health care system.

The situation of health insurance in the United States is framed as a "crisis" partly because of the expanding reach of the problem. Angel et al. note that

> ... a growing fraction of the working poor and even members of the middle class find it difficult to obtain and afford adequate and continuous family coverage. What we illustrate with detailed survey and ethnographic data is that for the working poor the nature of work and the nature of health care contribute in an interactive manner to economic instability and to frequent cycling in and out of poverty.
>
> (2006: 21)

Importantly, they suggest that this may lead to a solution: "Increasingly, instability in health care coverage, like instability in employment, is moving up the job hierarchy and affecting more working and middle-class families. If there is any hope for change in the system, it arises from the fact that the poor are no longer the only victims" (2006: 126). In other words, the public issue underlying health care in the United States begins to be recognized. Wiktorowicz, in describing the distinction between public and private financing, explicitly states a preference for the public model. The empirical work presented here supports that assertion, yet their analysis also highlights the powerful vested interests that impede efforts to reform the US health care system in that direction.

The acceptance of the principle of private financing for health care is an important signal of a country's political and social attributes, or the characteristics of its welfare system. Here, medical sociology overlaps with political science, with both fields investigating issues of welfare regimes.

One of the most important theorists in this area, Esping-Andersen (1990), suggests there are three types of welfare state regimes: the liberal, the social-democratic, and the corporatist. His analysis suggests that the US model of welfare provision is characteristic of the liberal welfare regime grounded in *laissez-faire* principles, where benefits of welfare are limited and seen as emergency solutions for market failures. Under this model, entitlement rules are very strict and "often associated with stigma; benefits are typically modest" (Esping-Andersen, 1990: 26–27). This is clearly the experience documented in Angel et al.'s empirical study of health care in the United States. A key difference between these ideal types lies within the concept of *de-commodification*, or the extent to which access to social resources, including health care, is not completely determined by market criteria. In this light, a country's primary mechanism for dealing with health care expenditures tells us something about the characteristics of its dominant political values.

Wiktorowicz's (2006) second analytical dimension concerns the delivery of services. In a public delivery system, health care providers are employees of the state. This is the case, for example, in Britain and Sweden. Interestingly, Wiktorowicz argues that this has resulted in "less than optimal health care" (2006: 250); however, she makes this claim without further elaboration or empirical data for verification. In contrast, France and Canada have systems based on private delivery; in these countries, health professionals are independently employed and bill the state for their services. However, care must be taken to differentiate for-profit and not-for-profit private delivery. The former is characteristic of the US system and the latter describes the French and Canadian systems.[4] Notably, the United States is the only industrialized country to blend private financing and for-profit private delivery. Wiktorowicz (2006) argues the optimal scenario is a publicly financed system based on not-for-profit private delivery. She argues that such a system can take advantage of its monopsony power to more effectively control costs and provide universal coverage, while taking advantage of the responsiveness typically associated with private delivery.

Wiktorowicz's (2006) model is theoretically useful in highlighting differences based on public or private mechanisms. However, it does not cover many of the finer details of a health care system, including the ownership and management of resources, the status of doctors, and the entitlement principles which dictate who can access services. Busfield's (2000) theoretical model for comparing health care systems (see Figure 5.2) does just that and is considered below.[5]

This model identifies three general ideal types of health care provision (public, private, and voluntary) and compares them in relation to five dimensions. In this model, the ideal type of a public (or state) health care system is one where services are owned and managed by the state and users are entitled to services based on citizenship (or permanent residency

	Public	Private	Voluntary
Ownership and management	State	Independent practitioner	Charity
Entitlement	Citizenship	Ability to pay	Medical/social need
Cost to user	Free	Fee for service	Free
Doctor's status	Salaried	Self-employed	Honorary
Funding	Taxation	Charges	Donations

Figure 5.2 Busfield's typology of medical care models

Source: Busfield, J. (2000). *Health and Health Care in Modern Britain* (pp. 88). By permission of Oxford University Press.

in the country). Additionally, under the ideal type public system, services are provided free at the point of service, doctors are salaried public servants, and the system's funding comes primarily from general taxation. An ideal type private system differs in substantial ways. It works under the principles of a self-regulating market, with entrepreneurs (doctors) providing services based on user's ability to pay. Services under this ideal type are funded by direct fee-for-service arrangements. Notably, universal coverage is not necessarily achieved; access to health care services is regulated by users' ability to pay. The third ideal type in Busfield's typology is a voluntary system or charitable system; a system funded by donations, where the status of doctors is an honorary (non-paid) one and where entitlement is based on need, not on ability to pay. As ideal types, the value of these models does not rest on their ability to describe a particular country's health care system. Instead, they serve as templates for the purposes of comparison.

Busfield suggests that the private health care model can be further broken down into private practitioner, providential, and commercial models (see Figure 5.3).

These models reflect the complexity that underlies private systems of health care. The private practitioner model describes a classic situation where providers are self-employed, own their practices, and provide services based on users' ability to pay. In contrast, providential (not-for-profit) or commercial (for-profit) systems describe situations where companies may own and manage equipment and practices, and where doctors may be independent or salaried employees.

All of these scenarios exist within the US health care system. Indeed, the role of doctors is particularly important in contemporary discussions of reform in the US health care system. Caplan's (1989) analysis of this issue uses the concept of *commodification* from an explicitly Marxist

	Private practitioner	Providential	Commercial
Ownership and management	Individual practitioner	Providential group (non-profit-making)	Commercial company (profit making)
Entitlement	Ability to pay	Ability to pay/insurance	Ability to pay/insurance
Cost to user	Fee for service	Fee/insurance premium	Fee/insurance premium
Doctor's status	Independent	Independent	Salaried
Funding	Charges	Charges/insurance	Charges/insurance

Figure 5.3   Busfield's typology of private care models

Source: Busfield, J. (2000). *Health and Health Care in Modern Britain* (pp. 89). By permission of Oxford University Press.

perspective. His innovative use of Marxist concepts of class, contradiction, and crisis enables an understanding of the multi-dimensionality behind current problems with health care in the United States. He criticizes the view that the commodification of health care is a recent phenomenon in the United States and, instead, traces the historical trajectories of physicians from entrepreneurs to wage labourers.

The use of Marxist theory allows us to unpack the notion of commodification; for Caplan, it does not only apply to patients using market mechanisms to finance health care services (as Esping-Andersen's model implies), but also applies to the very means of producing health care services. His analysis identifies an important characteristic of the US health care system – the corporatized physician, which he argues is analogous to a wage labourer, the central actor in Marxist theorizing.

From this perspective, social researchers have investigated the so-called *proletariatization* of physicians. For Caplan, such physicians are "limited in their diagnosis and treatment of patients by the dictates of private profitability" (1989: 1146). The much-valued professional autonomy of medical doctors is here challenged by capitalist and bureaucratic forces. Caplan argues that this is one of the several crises that co-exist (perhaps in a reinforcing manner) within a wider crisis in American health care, concluding that

> ...the current health care crisis is at least three crises: (1) a crisis for capitalists in securing the adequate health of their workers at the lowest possible cost to profit; (2) a crisis for physicians who are unable to be ancient producers of medical care and are becoming wage laborers with less authority and control

over the medial process; and (3) a crisis for all wage laborers who are receiving corporatized medical care increasingly limited by profit constraints. While all three crises are closely related, their collapse into a single undifferentiated crisis mystifies the existing class struggles in American health care.

(1989: 1146)

The first and third of Caplan's crises are issues to which social epidemiologists and medical sociologists have paid close attention; once again, work on health inequities comes to the forefront. The proletariatization of physicians has also concerned social researchers (Coburn, 1988; Haug, 1988; Navarro, 1988). Indeed, Busfield's model explicitly incorporates the status of the medical profession, something of substantial importance to medical sociologists since the work of not only of Parsons but also of Freidson.

As noted, in the *Profession of Medicine*, Freidson (1970a) offered one of the first major works of medical sociology. Parts of the book, as explained in Chapter 3, examine the social construction of disease and refined Parsons' conceptualization of the sick role. Other parts of the book investigate the nature of professions, how they establish and protect their power, and their relationship with ideology. Freidson's analysis begins with Parsons and it would be useful for us to briefly trace this connection, as it is an excellent example of how our core concepts in medical sociology have been refined over time as a result of debates between major theoretical frameworks, in this case, structural functionalism and symbolic interactionism.

Researchers in the 1950s had begun to examine professions as a particular type of occupation, one that entailed prolonged and expensive training in a specialized field of study and also involved a sense of duty or service to the community (see Clarke, 2004). Parsons' (1951) analysis of the professions was an important component of that literature, and suggested that professions have four salient characteristics: (1) universalism; (2) functional specificity; (3) affective neutrality; and (4) a collectivity orientation. Applied to medicine, these characteristics imply that doctors work with universalistic norms; they apply the same knowledge to all patients. Doctors also restrict their work to health-related matters (functional specificity), refrain from emotional involvement, thus providing impartial judgement over treatment decisions, and exhibit an altruistic desire to help other people (a collectivity orientation). Parsons' work on the professions has been criticized for uncritically accepting the on-the-surface appearance of the medical profession; indeed, there is clearly very little scope for critical reflection in Parsons' analysis – his image of the medical profession, like his image of society, is one based on consensus.

This is something that social researchers have subsequently tried to address. Recent work emphasizes that as a profession, doctors have worked hard to establish and then maintain their collective power (Clarke,

2004). Medical doctors have sought to subordinate competitors (nursing is a classic example of this), and/or limit competition through legal or other restrictions, as is the case with pharmacists (who cannot prescribe medicines; their role is limited to distribution). This was clearly the case in Willis' (1983) empirical study of the medical profession in Australia, which suggests that along with these mechanisms, the profession of medicine also sought to exclude competitors. For example, one might think of chiropractors and practitioners of alternative or indigenous healing techniques being called "quacks", medical doctors effectively denying their claims to legitimacy.

For Freidson, the profession of medicine is best understood as intertwined with the ideology of medicine. That is, the profession refers to both doctors as an occupational group but also to ideas about the role of medicine in society. Central to this is the notion of autonomy – what Freidson refers to as "freedom from the control of outsiders" (1970a: 137). The profession of medicine, from this perspective, is particularly concerned with securing and protecting its autonomy in relation to the state. Freidson's analysis suggests that medicine's claim for autonomy and for professional status rests on three assertions: First, medical knowledge is complex, requiring many years of dedicated education and training. Secondly, medical work is based on objective, scientific modes of operation; and finally, medical professionals work with a sense of communal duty. They put the public's welfare at the forefront of their activities (a rephrasing of Parsons' collectivity orientation). Clarke points out that

> this view is ideological – and it has served the medical profession very well. Through the perpetuation of such a view the public has come to believe that doctors are "morally superior" individuals who deserve to be trusted, to dominate the practice of medicine, to hold a monopoly in the construction, maintenance, and spread of what is taken to be official "medical knowledge", to control standards for their training, and to discipline their errant members themselves.
> (2004: 272)

The power of the medical profession is therefore a critical element not only as a characteristic of the health care system, but also because it shapes the very way we think about health and illness in the first place. As a powerful, autonomous collective, the medical profession holds extraordinary power to shape the frame that governs discourse about health and the role of medicine in society.

Thus far, we have seen that the structural functionalism of Parsons focused on the components which make up medicine's claim to professional status (universalism, functional specificity, affective neutrality, and a collective orientation). The symbolic interactionism of Freidson refined Parsons' thinking, and brought to our attention not only the traits or characteristics of the medical profession, but also its ideology – the ideas that underlie its autonomy claims. We can also examine the role of doctors and the medical profession from a conflict/Marxist theory perspective. Here, the focus is on how medical professions assert and maintain power and how they react when governments enact legislation which disturbs their autonomy. Below I examine two examples where medical professionals have played controversial roles by *opposing* reforms that would bring about universal access to health care services.

Case Study I: Canada's Health Care System

Canada has a predominantly publicly financed and privately delivered health care system (Mhatre and Deber, 1992). It is a decentralized system, complex in its organization, yet succinctly clear in its underlying principles. It centres around a piece of federal legislation: the 1984 Canada Health Act (CHA), which in turn, is built from the 1957 Hospital Insurance and Diagnostic Service Act and the 1968 Medicare Act (Colvin, 1994). Under the CHA, the provision of health insurance is the responsibility of the provinces and territories, which must meet the five central principles outlined in Figure 5.4.[6] Funding comes primarily via transfer from the federal to provincial governments (Health Canada, 2001; Williams et al., 2001).

Principle	Description
Universality	All residents of a province/territory must be entitled to insured health services on uniform terms and conditions.
Comprehensiveness	Provincial/territorial insurance plans must cover hospital, physician, and dental–surgical services.
Accessibility	Provincial/territorial insurance plans must provide reasonable access on uniform terms and conditions, unimpeded by extra charges or other financial barriers.
Portability	Residents moving from one province to another must still be covered by their original province for a period of at most 3 months, after which time the new home province assumes responsibility for health coverage.
Public administration	Health insurance plans must be administered and operated on a non-profit basis by a public authority. These authorities are in turn responsible to the provincial or territorial governments.

Figure 5.4 Principles of the Canadian health care system

	Canada	**US**[a]	**UK**
Ownership and management	Private	Private	State
Entitlement	Citizenship	Ability to pay	Citizenship
Cost to user	Free at the point of service for patient	Fee for service/insurance premium	Free at the point of service
Doctor's status	Self-employed	Self-employed/Salaried in some HMOs	Salaried
Funding	Taxation/Employment contributions	Charges	Taxation

Figure 5.5   A comparison of the Canadian, US, and UK systems

Source: [a] To facilitate comparison, US commentary excludes mention of Medicare/Medicaid systems. These programs, while being key components of the American system, are perhaps best seen as government interventions to address market failures in the wider health care system, which is increasingly based on the "managed care" model.

All three of Wiktorowicz's goals – social protection, redistribution, and efficiency – are embedded within these principles. For example, the goal of social protection is reflected in the principle of accessibility and universalism, and the goal of redistribution is linked to the principle of accessibility. Figure 5.5 applies Busfield's typology to Canada and, for comparison, the United States and Britain.

Canada's health care system shares the following two features of Busfield's public model: entitlement based on citizenship and funding (primarily through public revenues, in this case employment contributions and to a lesser extent taxation). However, it also incorporates key features of her private model: the status of doctors as self-employed rather than salaried employees of the state, and ownership/management of services in private, rather than state, control.

The system described above did not come into existence without significant conflict. Canada, like the United States, did not follow the post-World War I pattern seen in many European countries which enacted legislation for government-administered health insurance. Opposition to such systems was evident in Canada as early as 1912, with an entry in the *Canadian Medical Association Journal* warning "that government insurance plans would undermine the spirit of charity in medicine [and] turn physicians into civil servants" (Feldberg and Vipond, 2006: 226). Coburn et al., in their analysis of the history of the *Canadian Medical Association* (CMA), note

CMA concern with the health insurance issue was initially muted. The development of national health insurance in Britain in 1921 raised questions, but the main response seemed to be that "it couldn't happen here"; the idea of lay intervention in the medical field seemed remote. Canadian doctors were preeminently independent entrepreneurs dealing with unorganized patients, and the idea of organized third parties intervening in the payment system was an alien one.

(1983: 416)

A serious attempt by the Canadian Prime Minister William Lyon Mackenzie King to introduce national health insurance following World War II failed due to opposition from the provinces, who saw the federal government's proposal as an encroachment on their jurisdiction (Feldberg and Vipond, 2006). A similar plan by US President Harry S. Truman failed due to fears of socialist medicine in that country (Gordon, 2003).

Powerful forces were against the development of Canada's health care system. The history of this conflict can yield rich sociological insights and is worth reviewing. Historians of the current Canadian health care system trace its origins to Tommy Douglas, the Premier of Saskatchewan in the early 1960s. Douglas' social democratic government passed legislation for the first comprehensive medical insurance plan in the country (until the 1962 Saskatchewan Medical Care Insurance Act became law, the province's health care system was a mixture of Busfield's public, private, and voluntary models).

Douglas' plan was based on compromise; he sought to create a system that was "acceptable both to those providing the service and those receiving it" (Naylor, 1986: 182). A key feature of this plan was the status of doctors, an important dimension in Busfield's typology. Douglas rejected European models that paid doctors a salary or by capitation (that is, based on the number of patients they saw), and instead, retained physicians' preferred system, a fee-for-service model of payment. The status of doctors was unchanged; they remained independent practitioners, but instead of billing patients, they billed the province (i.e., a single-payer system). This was particularly important to Douglas, who wanted a system where patients would not see a doctor's bill when in need of medical services. This is a situation of public financing and private delivery described by Wiktorowicz (2006). Most importantly, Douglas' plan incorporated universality; his plan "promised all citizens, regardless of financial circumstances, a comprehensive system of medical services that was financed through taxes and administered publicly" (Feldberg and Vipond, 2006: 277–228). Douglas' Saskatchewan plan (Medicare) was an inspiration for Canadians and incorporated into federal legislation a few years later.

However, Saskatchewan's physicians vehemently opposed Douglas' proposal and launched a historic 23-day strike when the legislation came into effect in 1962 (Badgley and Wolfe, 1965; Thompson and Salmon, 2006). According to Ostry, physicians believed it was an illegitimate infringement by the government on their financial and professional relationships with their patients. Their resistance was also based on the success of private medicare plans which, if legislated out of existence, would result in direct financial losses for the physician owners and shareholders. Thus, Saskatchewan physicians' opposition to the provincial medicare plan was based on fears for their autonomy and income.

(2006: 43)

The Saskatchewan government brought in doctors from Britain's NHS to keep up medical services in the province, over the opposition of Saskatchewan doctors.

One of the most authoritative histories of the strike was written by Robin Badgley, a sociologist and Samuel Wolfe, a physician, both at the University of Saskatchewan. Their framing of the event is quite striking:

The medical profession, accustomed to exercising its prerogatives without external constraint, opposed legislation by a government elected by the people. As the struggle continued the issues at stake became secondary to a test of strength between the profession and its powerful allies and the government... By withholding vital services to the population the medical profession tried to overthrow the government.

(1965: 463–464)

In this light, we can see that the history of Canada's health care system is in many ways a history of political, perhaps even class, struggle. And at the centre of that struggle was the medical profession.

Also at the heart of the conflict was the mechanism for financing health care expenditures. Prior to the 1962 legislation, physicians held a position of monopoly; they determined their fees and largely shaped their relationships with private insurance agencies, whose reach had grown throughout the 1950s (Clarke, 2004). The Douglas legislation radically altered that situation and created a monopsony. Badgley and Wolfe point out that "a fundamental tenet of its ideology was the organization of tax-financed health services, including a system for paying doctors' bills. It placed great reliance on collective and co-operative action for the public's good" (1965: 468). Underneath the issue of payment mechanism, however, were issues of politics and professional dominance. For doctors, government involvement in the financing of clinical visits meant: (a) a loss of autonomy and (b) the specter of greater public scrutiny over its accounting. Both outcomes were completely unsatisfactory to a profession that had until then experienced unparalleled control of its affairs.

Physicians tell the history of the 1962 strike in a slightly different way. Badgley and Wolfe quote a doctor's article in a local Saskatchewan newspaper in 1962, where he questions "Is there any hope of immediate relief from this arrogant government dictatorship?" (1965: 470). More recent accounts use similar frames; for example, a letter in the *Canadian Medical Association Journal* describes the strike as a protest against "an abrogation of doctors' democratic right to negotiate their working conditions" (Baltzan, 2002: 987). In his letter recounting the strike of 1962, Baltzan questions the labeling of the event as a strike, and the editors of the journal entitled his letter "The Lockout of '62". He recalls: "...we closed our offices but continued to operate hospitals and emergency departments. True, our services were for emergency cases only, but the definition of 'emergency' was broad..." (2002: 988). Baltzan notes that the province was on the brink of violence during this period, and links this to what he calls "fascist" clauses in the original wording of the 1962 legislation.

The strike of 1962 had a significant effect on the standing of the medical profession in Canada. Badgley and Wolfe note

> It is doubtful if organized medicine elsewhere in Canada will again seek to test the power of a democratically elected government. Not only was the attempt unsuccessful but it tainted the reputation of a great profession in the eyes of the public and forced it to reassess both its ideals and its role in society.
>
> (1965: 465)

On this prediction Badgley and Wolfe turned out to be incorrect. Although strikes by physicians have been relatively rare events in labour history (Thompson and Salmon, 2006), particularly when compared with other industries, they have taken place since 1962, perhaps most famously in the province of Ontario in 1986 when the 17,000 member Ontario Medical Association authorized physician strike that lasted 25 days. In this case, the medical profession opposed government legislation which had made extra-billing illegal (extra-billing referring to a practice of adding fees payable by patients, on top of the costs paid by the government-funded insurance plan). The strike failed, with public opinion decidedly against the striking doctors (Clarke, 2004).

For some analysts, the Ontario strike marks a period of declining dominance from which the medical profession in Canada has never recovered (Coburn et al. 1983).The recognition of the medical profession's self-interests has arguably led to a decline in the status enjoyed by medical doctors, with the image of a healer being replaced in the minds of many with that of *homo economicus*.

Case Study II: Venezuelan Health Care Reforms

The discussion above focused on the example given by Canada's health care system. We have seen that it is a publicly financed but privately delivered system based on the principle of universalism. Political and professional conflicts influenced the system, from its origins in the efforts of the Douglas government of Saskatchewan in 1960s and the ensuing strike by doctors in that province to block legislation enacting a public heath care system. These types of conflicts are not just in the past, however.

Another important example of political conflict and health care reform is given to us by present-day Venezuela. The country is currently in the midst of a revolution (Guevara, 2005; Harnecker, 2005; Ramiréz, 2006; Syliva and Danopoulos, 2003) headed by the democratically elected government of Hugo Chávez (Gott, 2005). Chávez's "Bolívarian" revolution (named after Simón Bolívar (1783–1830), one of Latin American's most important heroes of its independence battles with the Spanish Crown) has received a great deal of attention in the popular press and in the field of political science (Castro, 2005; Ellner, 2001; Maya and Lander, 2005; Ramiréz, 2005). It has been a very divisive topic, drawing out deeply entrenched political biases and long-standing schisms between the left and the right. This literature has been particularly concerned with debates on the democratic versus authoritarian values of the Bolívarian revolution, the role of petroleum (Venezuela is a leading exporter of crude oil), and the implications of Venezuela's revolution on Latin America's "left turns" (see Hershberg and Rosen, 2006). However, the implication of the Bolívarian revolution on health care in Venezuela has, until very recently, received less attention. This is unfortunate, because an analysis of how the Venezuelan health care system has changed under the Bolívarian revolution – and how the established Venezuelan medical profession has fought against these changes – tells us much about the nature of the profession of medicine and signals the political nature underlying arrangements for the delivery and financing of health care systems.

Like many other countries in Latin America, Venezuela's health care system has long-espoused the principle of universalism and public financing. But in practice, inequities in access to health care services (and in health outcomes) have been quite substantial, and the presence of private schemes for delivery and financing have resulted in multi-tiered systems – private systems for the wealthy and under-funded public systems for the poor. In this way, Latin America's standing as the most unequal region in the world in terms of income (Berry, 1998; Hoffman and Centeno, 2003) is reflected in its health care systems.

According to the Pan American Health Organization (PAHO) (2006), chronic under-funding of public services and growing rates of poverty in the region meant that the principle of universal access was never actually reflected in the day-to-day lives of Venezuelans. They report:

> As in many other countries of Latin America, at the beginning of the 1980s the health services system in Venezuela was characterized by acute underfunding,

direct and indirect privatization (based on fees-for-services or requests for donations from users), cutbacks in the maintenance of infrastructure, and fragmentation and lack of articulation between multiple participants responsible for regulation, financing, insurance, [and] service delivery.

(2006: 7)

Venezuela launched wide-ranging reforms of its health care system in the 1990s. These reforms were pushed by international financial organizations such as the International Monetary Fund and the World Bank and were broadly consistent across the region[7] – they entailed a shift towards greater private-sector involvement in the delivery, financing, and ownership of the health care system and a dismantling of pre-existing public systems (Abel and Lloyd-Sherlock, 2000; Muntaner et al., 2006b).[8] The principles of this process were documented in the 1993 World Bank *World Development Report: Investing in Health*. The report called for the limitation of state investment in health care and for the facilitation of private-sector involvement. Some researchers have called this process the "exportation of US-style managed care" (Iriart et al., 2001; Stocker et al., 1999; Waitzkin and Iriart, 2001).

In practice, this meant that multinational corporations became central to the delivery and ownership of health care resources. In the case of Venezuela, this resulted in a dramatic rise in private health care facilities; by 1997, fully 73 per cent of health care expenditures in the country were private and the introduction of user fees made the public health system inaccessible to many poor Venezuelans (who actually comprised a majority of the population at the time) (Muntaner et al., 2006a). PAHO notes that, in effect, this

...ruled out any aspirations for universal delivery of public health services, and social programs ceased to be proposed in terms of achieving broad social reforms (or the reduction of inequalities). Instead, objectives were trimmed to more limited targets as a partial response to the funding crisis and the negative impact of economic adjustment programs. The more transcendent aspirations, such as equity and the redistribution of income, were postponed. Public investment in health, which had been 13.3 per cent in the national budget in 1970, fell to 9.3 per cent in 1990 and 7.89 per cent in 1996, representing only 1.73 per cent of gross domestic product.

(2006: 8–9)

The surprise election of Chávez in 1998 brought widespread changes to Venezuelan government and society as a whole. In 1999, the Venezuelan people enacted a new constitution and, among other principles, re-affirmed that health is a fundamental right to be "guaranteed by the Venezuelan State, based on co-responsibility on the part of all citizens" (PAHO, 2006: 21). Three articles of Venezuelan's constitution are particularly important for its health care system, beginning with Article 83, which explicitly recognizes that health is a fundamental right of all citizens and the responsibility of the State to guarantee, as part of the right to life. Article 84 calls on the state to develop a universal, intersectoral, and decentralized public health system which gives primacy to health promotion and disease prevention. An important element of this article is that it also explicitly states that the community has the right and duty to participate in the decision-making process of the health care system, including matters of policy planning, implementation, and control of public health institutions. Article 84 also enshrines the health care system's principles: gratuity (i.e., it is free at the point of service), universality, completeness, fairness, social integration, and solidarity. Lastly, Article 85 of the Bolívarian constitution states that the financing of the public health system is the responsibility of the State. It does not rule out the presence of a private health care system, but it does proclaim the State's role as regulator of both public and private systems.

Soon after enactment of the constitution in 1999, Venezuela's health care system faced a dramatic test: torrential rains caused widespread and extensive flooding in the state of Vargas, one of the most marginalized regions of the country. The rains and ensuing floods were by all definitions a public health disaster; a dangerous situation, that if not controlled, could have led to outbreaks of waterborne diseases and threatened the lives of tens of thousands of people. At the same time, devastated *barrio* residents needed access to primary health care services.[9] As part of its long-standing tradition of international medical aid, Cuba sent over 400 health care workers to help the Venezuelan authorities to deal with the disaster. The Venezuelan government also requested the help from the Venezuelan Medical Association – a request that was denied. Muntaner et al. note that the government

> requested the help of Venezuelan physicians, asking them to go into the *barrios* to attend to the acute needs of the under-serviced populace. However, the majority of Venezuelan physicians refused, citing security concerns and a lack of infrastructure as their primary reasons. Behind these explicit objections lay an organized opposition by the Venezuelan medical establishment to the health care reform efforts sparked by the Bolívarian government.
>
> (2006b: 119–124)

The Venezuelan government, seeing the successful Cuban programs in Vargas, expanded the program nationwide and dubbed it *Misión Barrio Adentro*.[10] President Chávez created a presidential commission and charged it with the task of re-creating the Venezuelan health care system so that it lived up to the principles of the new constitution. The result is as follows: over 20,000 Cuban medical professionals are currently in Venezuela, providing free, comprehensive treatment. The government has also established new medical schools throughout the country in an effort to eventually wean itself off reliance on Cuban doctors.

Barrio Adentro has revolutionized Venezuela's health care system. It relies on community organization, a central principle of the program. Community-level Health Committees are a mechanism whereby Venezuelans participate in the day-to-day administration of their health care services. It is also a mechanism that enables *Barrio Adentro* medical personnel to enact a holistic and comprehensive model of health care services; when patients visit the clinic, not only are symptoms treated, but appropriate connections are made with other issues, including food security, sanitation, employment, and other social determinants of health. Only with ongoing community participation in the decision-making process of the health care service can these issues be adequately connected with the day-to-day medical encounter.

PAHO data suggest that *Barrio Adentro* has already had positive effects in terms of population health. For example, child mortality from diarrhoea and pneumonia has declined. Diabetes – a chronic disease that is widely underreported and undiagnosed, particularly in poor areas – is being treated more effectively. PAHO data indicate that over 300,000 new cases of diabetes were diagnosed in 2004 and 2005. This is not a sign of an increasing prevalence of diabetes; instead, it signals a new-found strength in the health care system for diagnosis and treatment. PAHO notes: "This rate has been rising as the clinics' diagnostic capacity increases with the creation of more comprehensive diagnostic centers. It is expected to achieve an optimum level of case-finding in the future, especially among groups for which this opportunity has been largely unavailable" (2006: 97). *Barrio Adentro* has not only changed the way diabetes is diagnosed in the country, it has also changed how it is treated: "even though insulin has been in use since 1921 . . . access to its use for diabetic patients continues to be a problem in Latin America and the Caribbean. In Venezuela, it has been distributed at no cost [through *Barrio Adentro*]" (PAHO, 2006: 98).

As already noted, opposition from Venezuela doctors to *Barrio Adentro* has been fierce. In 2002, the Venezuelan Medical Association conducted a national work stoppage which shut down the majority of outpatient clinics and public hospitals in the country. In 2003, they filed a lawsuit arguing that Cuban doctors were not qualified to practice medicine in Venezuela; they also enacted media campaigns to raise concerns about the quality of care provided by Cuban doctors (PAHO, 2006). PAHO (2006) also reports cases where Venezuelan pharmacists refused to fill prescriptions written by Cuban doctors and where hospitals refused to receive patients who had been sent by *Barrio Adentro* doctors.[11]

Barrio Adentro has brought long-standing divisions to the forefront. On the one hand, we have the principle of health as a fundamental human right. On the other, we have a medical profession that is often at odds with principles of public financing, delivery, and administration of health care services. We have seen that physicians in Canada have gone on strike in opposition to the CHA and its principles of universality, comprehensiveness, accessibility, and public administration. In contemporary Venezuela, doctors have gone even further in their opposition to the presence of Cuban doctors who would treat the poor without requiring that they pay for services.

Conclusion

The examples of Canada and Venezuela, and the ongoing debates in the United States over health insurance – signal the political nature of health care systems. All of the examples discussed in this chapter illustrate not only the important differences that exist between different health care systems but also the challenges that they face in common. All health care systems, regardless of their specific design, address the goals of social protection, redistribution, and efficiency. Ideal typologies developed by Busfield and Wiktorowicz enable comparative analysis of different health care systems around the world, and how they negotiate public and private approaches for financing and delivery of services.

Analysis of health care systems has also benefited from a close connection to the sociology of the professions; taking a political–historical approach, this tradition centres its theoretical gaze on medicine as a profession. This approach – with important links to the pioneering work of Parsons and Freidson – brings to the forefront the role of medical professionals as active agents which shape the health care system.

At times, as was the case in the Canadian strike of 1962 and present-day conflict in Venezuela, the medical profession can be seen to be at odds with principles of equity and universalism. From the perspective of conflict theory, this is not a surprise. Sociologists working in the tradition of sociology-of-medicine have generated valuable insight into these situations; such research is well-positioned to make important contributions to public debates on the nature of our health care systems. At the same time, sociologists have brought attention to the power of the pharmaceutical industry as a force which shapes how we deliver health care services. It is to this work, focused on the concept of medicalization, to which we now turn our attention to.

6
Medicalization

In Chapter 4, we encountered the ethnographic work of Laurie Abraham, the author of *Mama Might Be Better Off Dead*. We considered several passages from her book, one of which I would like to repeat here: "There will always be a 'ragged edge,' a new disease to conquer, and unless we set explicit restraints, we'll consume all the country's resources chasing immortality, while starving the other institutions that can make life worth living" (1993: 259). What Abraham describes as a "ragged edge" refers to the concept of medicalization – perhaps medical sociology's most important contribution to sociology's theoretical stock.

Medicalization has been defined by Irving Zola as the "the process whereby more and more of everyday life has come under medical dominion, influence and supervision" (1983: 295) and by Peter Conrad as "defining behavior as a medical problem or illness mandating or licensing the medical profession to provide some type of treatment for it" (1975: 12). It literally means "to make things medical" – but this very broad definition hides the nuanced ways in which the concept has been used theoretically and empirically in medical sociology. The concept is now understood to refer to a variety of different social mechanisms, some of which operate at a conceptual level (how we *think* about disease), at the institutional level (as a society, how we *treat* or *manage* disease), or through our interaction with physicians and health care professionals (how we *communicate* information on disease) (Conrad and Schneider, 1980). This multi-dimensionality has required medical sociologists seeking to understand medicalization to use a wide range of empirical methodologies and theoretical perspectives.

This chapter begins with an overview of the concept of medicalization, identifying its early manifestations in relation to research on social control. As we will see, the concept has recently received a great deal of attention with respect to the role of the pharmaceutical industry in defining, as well as treating, a growing number of "medical conditions". This will raise important links between research on medicalization and the contemporary phenomena of "condition branding" and "astro-turfing";

the former describing the creation of new disease concepts as markets for pharmaceutical products, and the latter referring to the creation of "fake" grass-roots movements/patient groups funded by pharmaceutical companies which aim to raise "awareness" about particular conditions (Moynihan and Cassels, 2005).

This chapter also explores the important connections between medicalization research and sociological theorizing – returning once again to the structural functionalism of Parsons and the sick role before moving on to the social constructionism of Becker's labeling theory, Foucauldian notions of surveillance, and finally, more recent work by theorists such as Giddens on "late modernity" and Beck on "risk society". These connections will allow us to further explore a key theme of this book; the dynamic interplay between theoretical and empirical realms of medical sociological research.

Theories of medicalization have changed substantially over the past few decades (Busfield, 2006a). Indeed, recent medical sociological research has examined a crucial tension inherent in the concept: on the one hand it describes an uncritical and gullible population, which is under the control of imperialistic medicine and the profit-seeking pharmaceutical industry; but on the other hand, empirical research on medicalization has linked with notions of the powerful "informed patient" and has suggested that medicalization may oftentimes be driven by patients themselves, rather than the medical profession or medical institutions (Ballard and Elston, 2005). In practice, it is often very difficult to actually distinguish these positions. These issues have important implications for wider debates in sociology, including questions of personal agency and social structure. To what extent is the development of disease constructs for hyperactivity, social anxiety, shyness, and aging driven by the medical profession, the pharmaceutical industry, or individuals? When individuals form groups such as "Children and Adults with Attention-Deficit/Hyperactivity Disorder" (CHADD), do they compose a genuine grass-roots social movement, whose goal it is to change the way society sees and deals with certain diseases? Or are these groups a reflection of the vested interests of what has recently been termed the "medical–industrial complex"? How should we understand the complex interests involved in decisions over the creation of disease categories?

Development of the Concept

The concept was probably first used in the English language in a 1970 *New England Journal of Medicine* article on the topic of sexually active teenage girls (Aronson, 2002; Busfield, 2006a), which noted: "Sexually active teenage-girls have a physical examination by a pediatrician, a pelvic examination by a gynecologist, a blood count, urinalysis, tine test and dental survey, followed by home visits by a public-health nurse ... [This] represents a 'medicalization' of sex that is probably self-defeating" (Gordis, 1970: 709). This early use of the concept hinted at the possible negative effects of incorporating more and more of life's activities and issues within the medical sphere; however, this notion was not developed until the concept entered sociological discourse.

The concept itself was then really explored in detail by Irving Zola, an American sociologist, at the 1971 meeting of the British Sociological Association Medical Sociology Group. He published his analysis in 1972 in an influential paper which argued that medicine itself was becoming an institution of social control; a "new repository of truth, the place where absolute and often final judgements are made by supposedly morally neutral and objective experts" (1972: 487). Zola's analysis is built upon the 1950s and 1960s writings of Parsons as well as Freidson's social constructionist refinements of Parson's work. Examination of these early connections and the links subsequently made by medicalization researchers with political economy and feminism (see Chapter 3) highlights the usefulness of this concept for the development of social theory.

Through the concept of the sick role (see Chapter 3), Parsons noted how medicine acted as a legitimatizing institution. In other words, the sick role offers a way for illness to be socially regulated, and thus sanctioned, work towards societal equilibrium. What qualifies as illness – which conditions are medicalized – is therefore a very important question, because it gives a person access to the benefits of the sick role. This would include, for example, leave from the expected duties and obligations of a position of paid employment and perhaps respite from duties and obligations in the home. The notion of the sick role truly underlies the development of the concept of medicalization.

However, this was not something that particularly concerned or interested Parsons. It was Freidson who, in discussing the sick role and the profession of medicine, highlighted the notion that medicine could determine and define the very meaning of illness; that is, medicine did not simply adjudicate claims for sick role benefits, it defined the basis of what conditions would be accepted as illness. For Freidson, medicalization reflected a profession concerned with expanding its territory and dominance:

[Medicine] is active in seeking out illness ... One of the greatest ambitions of the physician is to discover and describe a "new" disease or syndrome and to be immortalized by having his name used to identify the disease. Medicine, then, is oriented to seeking out and finding illness, which is to say that it seeks to create social meanings of illness where that meaning or interpretation was lacking before. And insofar as illness is defined as something bad – to be eradicated or contained – medicine plays the role of what Becker called "the moral entrepreneur".

(1970a: 252)

From this perspective, medicalization is a product of vested self-interests; it is not necessarily a conspiracy by the medical profession, but a result of professional values which value discovery and innovation highly and which rest on the notions of knowledge accumulation and progress.

Interestingly, a similar link to Becker's work was made by Conrad (1975) in his analysis of the medicalization of hyperkinesis (today labeled ADHD or attention-deficit hyperactivity disorder). For Conrad, the central "moral entrepreneurs" behind the medicalization of hyperkinesis were pharmaceutical companies (who identified an important market for Ritalin and similar products) and the Association for Children with Learning Disabilities, who sought acceptance for medical treatment of hyperactive behaviour amongst school children. This raised the notion that medicalization, whilst perhaps primarily a result of territorial expansion, may also be driven by actors other than medical doctors.

Freidson recognized that "the medical profession has first claim to jurisdiction over the label of illness and *anything* to which it may be attached, irrespective of its capacity to deal with it effectively" (1970a: 251, emphasis mine). This implicitly suggests a process of territorial (for some, imperialistic) expansion, wherein an increasing proportion of life is brought under the medical domain and, as Freidson recognized, this was not dependent on the existence of efficacious treatment options. It also represents a significant break with the Parsonian model of medical sociology; indeed Lupton (1997b) convincingly argues that the concept of medicalization can be seen as a repudiation of the structural functionalism espoused by Parsons in the 1950s. From this perspective, disease categories are social and political constructs, rather than "objective" scientific/medical categories. The notion of medical imperialism was more fully developed by later medicalization researchers, most notably by Ivan Illich in his influential book *Limits to Medicine* (1976); Zola himself, although a critic of the *process* of medicalization, did not believe that it was a result of professional imperialism by doctors and medical professionals. Instead, in Zola's view "the explanation of medicalization lay outside the motives and actions of doctors" (Busfield, 2006a: 101).

Zola was primarily interested in the social control properties of medicalization. In other words, by defining the parameters of the sick role, medicine had ultimate control over what was deviant behaviour. This notion has been subsequently developed by Conrad, who noted that "medicine, as opposed to the church, the family or the state (through its criminal justice systems) was becoming the dominant institution of social control, as certain categories of deviant behaviour were redefined as medical rather than moral problems" (Ballard and Elston, 2005: 230). For some medicalization researchers, this reflects the changing nature of society described by contemporary theorists such as Giddens and Beck; indeed, for Williams and Calnan, "doctors have become the secular priests of late modernity and a fixed point of reference in an increasingly uncertain world" (1996: 1618). Importantly, engagement with the theoretical work of Giddens and Beck has led to a substantial refinement of medicalization as a construct; it has not only been useful for examining the role of medicine and medical doctors in "risk" society, but it has also been helpful to integrate theorizing on medicalization with Giddens' and Beck's analyses of social reflexivity. The result, as we will see in this chapter, is that a stronger, more nuanced, conceptualization of medicalization is now in use.

Medicalization as social control describes a transition, wherein conditions or behaviours shift along a continuum: from *sin to crime to sickness* (Conrad, 1992). The clearest example of this transition is "deviant behaviour" such as alcoholism (Schneider, 1978). In an historical analysis of the development of the disease concept of alcoholism, Schneider's work highlights the advantages offered by the medical frame of seeing alcoholism as a disease: if alcoholism is a disease, its sufferers can access the sick role; their condition is no longer a product of their free-will but the symptoms of an underlying pathology over which they have no control.

Schneider's review of the origins of the disease concept of alcoholism in the United States suggests that alcoholism was first seen as a sign of moral degeneration; that a person, who regularly – and opposed to their real self-interests – drank to excess, held the blame for their behaviour. This conceptualization of the problem drinker was based on the acceptance of the philosophy of free will; in this view, people *chose* to drink to excess and could therefore be held culpable for their behaviour. According to Schneider, "the 'ownership' of the problem of drunkenness during this period fell to leading clergy and civil authorities, joined occasionally by prominent citizens concerned about the use of spirituous liquors among workers, farmhands, and other persons of lesser station" (1978: 362).

The notion that what we now perceive of as alcoholism might be a result of underlying pathology, rather than free will, was first articulated by Benjamin Rush, a US physician. In his 1784 book *An Inquiry of the Effects of Ardent Spirits Upon the Human Body and Mind*, Rush developed a mental "addiction" model to account for the effects of alcohol on the body, and believed that inebriety developed progressively over time, ultimately generating a loss of control over one's drinking habits. Importantly, Rush did not posit physiological mechanisms through which the "addiction" operated; yet his work generated an alternative approach to the then-dominant view of the church that repetitive, harmful drunkenness was a reflection of one's free will and therefore an individual's responsibility. According to Schneider, physicians of the time began to use phrases such as "craving" and "insatiable desire" to characterize problematic drinking habits. These phrases began to hint at a diminished role for "free will" explanations and an expanded role for treatment and therapeutic options to what bordered on a mental illness.

The 1935 founding of *Alcoholics Anonymous* (AA) in the United States brought new-found prominence to the notion of alcoholism as a medical condition. Their position is clear: "Alcoholism is a disease and the alcoholic a sick person. The alcoholic can be helped and is worth helping. This is a public health problem and therefore a public responsibility" (Chafetz and Demone, 1962: 142). Coinciding with this proclamation, researchers of the time began to modify the disease concept of alcoholism, so that it was no longer seen as a vaguely defined mental illness, but that it had a physiological basis.

This view gained strong support among AA, an organization whose famous 12-step program has a strong resemblance to Parsons' sick role. Many analysts of the AA program interpret the first and third steps of the program, which call for the alcoholic to (a) admit their powerlessness over alcohol, and (b) make the decision to turn their will and their lives over to the care of God (as they understand Him), along Parsonian sick role lines (Schneider, 1978). According to Norris, "this turning over of self direction is akin perhaps to the acceptance of a regimen prescribed by a physician for a disease" (Norris, 1976, quoted by Schneider, 1978: 366). As such, not only is alcoholism a disease, but its sufferers are to be seen *as patients* entitled to the benefits of the sick role. The highly lauded work of AA was a key factor in the medicalization of alcoholism. Such was the perceived (if not measured) effectiveness of the AA program, that US physicians by the early 1970s began to see the referral of patients to the program as the best professional strategy for dealing with alcoholism in their practices (Jones and Herlich, 1972).

The disease concept of alcoholism then received a substantial boost with the research conducted by E.M. Jellinek (a physiologist) at the Yale Center for Alcohol Studies during the 1940s–1960s. Using data collected via a questionnaire in an issue of the *Alcoholic Anonymous* newsletter, Jellinek constructed a new model of alcoholism; one that clarified the definition of alcoholism as a disease by distinguishing two subtypes ("alcohol addicts" and "habitual symptomatic excessive drinkers") and four categories of alcohol addiction. According to Jellinek, only the version of alcoholism experienced by "alcohol addicts" qualified as a medical illness; only they experienced a sustained and entrenched loss of control over their drinking.

In elaborating the notion of loss of control, which he saw as the crux of the distinction between disease- and non-disease forms of alcoholism, Jellinek identified four categories of alcohol addiction: Alpha, Beta, Gamma, and Delta. Jellinek described the first two categories as non-disease forms of alcoholism: Alpha alcoholics experienced drinking problems that interfered with their lives – but they did not suffer from an underlying medical pathology. Beta alcoholics differed only in that their alcohol intake could be seen to have negative bodily effects (e.g., cirrhosis of the liver). In contrast, Gamma and Delta alcoholics experienced a progression from psychological to physiological forms of addiction – this was defined by "1) acquired increased tissue tolerance to alcohol, 2) adaptive cell metabolism, and 3) withdrawal symptoms" (Schneider, 1978: 368).

According to Jellinek, Gamma alcoholism was the most typical form of the disease in the United States, whilst Delta alcoholism (which was not characterized by a loss of control over quantity of consumption but rather a lack of ability to abstain for prolonged periods of time) was more common in European countries such as France (Schneider, 1978). Critically for Jellinek, problem drinking and living problems arising from frequent intoxication were distinct from manifestations of alcoholism as a medical pathology. This distinction set limits on what could, or should, be treated medically (Schneider, 1978); some forms of drinking were deviant acts to be managed by law enforcement – interestingly, Jellinek described this as a problem for "applied sociology". Other disease-forms of drinking were medical in origin and, according to Jellinek, were to be treated by the medical profession. Notably, this overlaps with two phases of the *sin to crime to sickness* transition.

Physiological addiction was central to Jellinek's model of alcoholism as disease; he drew similarities between the effects of alcohol on the body and the effects of narcotics on the body. This further legitimated a medical frame for the disease of alcoholism; from this perspective, alcohol addiction, like drug addiction, was medically based and should be treated with medical intervention. Partly based on Jellinek's research, the American Medical Association issued a statement in 1956 officially recognizing alcoholism as an illness: "The Council on Mental Health, its Committee on Alcoholism, and the profession in general recognizes this syndrome of alcoholism as illness which justifiably should have the attention of physicians" (quoted in Schneider, 1978: 368). For Jellinek, the acceptance by the medical profession of the disease concept *was proof* that the disease existed: "Physicians know what belongs in their realm. . . . [A] disease is what the medical profession recognizes as such. . . . [T]he medical profession has officially accepted alcoholism as an illness; whether a part of the public likes it or not, and even if a minority of the medical profession is disinclined to accept the idea" (1960: 12). This is clearly a reflection of Becker's (1963) labeling theory; just as a deviance is not a fixed property or characteristic of a particular act/behaviour, but the application of a label, a disease is only a disease once it has been labeled as such by the medical profession.

Consistent with the social constructionist basis of the concept of medicalization, Schneider suggests that an historical perspective on the disease concept of alcoholism teaches us that "whether or not a given condition constitutes a disease involves issues of politics and ideology – questions of definitions, not fact" (1978: 370). This influential analysis also introduces an issue that has been the focus of subsequent analysis by medicalization researchers: the causes, or "engines" (Conrad, 2005), behind medicalization. For Schneider:

> that certain forms of deviant drinking are now or have been for more than one hundred and fifty years medicalized is not due to a medical "hegemony," but reflects the interests of the several groups and organizations assuming, or being given, responsibility for behaviors associated with chronic drunkenness... The disease concept owes its life to these variously interested parties, rather than to substantive scientific findings. As such, the disease concept of alcoholism is primarily a social rather than a scientific or medical accomplishment.
>
> (1978: 370)

This is a particularly important point in the development of the concept of medicalization – does the concept, at its foundation, describe a process of professional expansion (medical "hegemony", or imperialism) or does it reflect other, wider, social processes?

Overall, the medicalization of deviant behaviour such as alcoholism had three important implications. First, it shifted "responsibility" of the deviant act; it was no longer an act of *free will* but a consequence of medical condition. Additionally, it fostered the development of "therapeutic" rather than "punitive" interventions, and lastly, it strengthened the role of medicine as an institution (Ballard and Elston, 2005; Conrad and Schneider, 1980; Lowenberg and Davis, 1994). These implications reflect the *sin to crime to sickness* transition that was at the crux of the early work of writers such as Zola, Conrad, and Schneider.

We can see clearly a tension developing in the conceptualization of medicalization – does the concept describe, along the lines of Freidson's analysis of the medical profession, a process of professional expansion? Is it a foundational element of social control mechanisms, as suggested by Zola? Or, if Schneider's historical analysis of the disease concept of alcoholism is indicative of the process of medicalization, then is the creation of a disease category a reflection of societal attitudes and beliefs, rather than a product of a territorial profession? Are disease concepts generated from the "bottom up"?

The notion that medicalization describes the imperialistic properties of the medical profession (it is always wanting to control new territory) leads us to a concern about medical authority. This perspective is most clearly seen in the writings of Ivan Illich, an Austrian-born philosopher and anarchist. Illich, author of numerous books, including *De-Schooling Society* (1971), was critical of a system "that claims authority over people who are not yet ill, people who cannot reasonably expect to get well, and those for whom doctors have no more effective treatment than that which could be offered by their uncles or aunts" (1976: 120–121). Illich saw some merit in Parsons' formulation of the sick role, but noted that in modern society, it demands a certain level of self-delusion, with doctors needing to believe that their treatments are effective and patients needing to abide with the doctor's instructions and support their view. In Illich's analysis, the position is fundamentally flawed. Instead, he saw considerably more value in the work of Michel Foucault, particularly his work in *The Birth of the Clinic* (1994 [1973]). Illich argued that the medicalization of life fundamentally changed the very experience of being human; as we internalize medical definitions and medical solutions, we come to be ever more tightly bound within regimes of surveillance. The very definition of what it means to be human shifts from religious/philosophical/artistic consideration and comes to be under the domain of medicine. The outcome is a diminishing sense of autonomy and self-determination. Illich notes:

[d]uring the last generations the medical monopoly over health care has expanded without checks and has encroached on our liberty with regard to our own bodies. Society has transferred to physicians the exclusive right to determine what constitutes sickness, who is or might become sick, and what shall be done to such people.

(1976: 6)

For Illich, this is above all, an issue of power and personal autonomy.

From Illich's perspective, the medical profession, together with underlying processes of industrialization and bureaucratization, "has not only 'duped' the public into believing that they have an effective and valuable body of knowledge and skills, but have also created a dependence through the medicalization of life which has now undermined and taken away the public's right to self determination" (Williams and Calnan, 1996: 1610).

More generally, Illich was concerned with the effects that medicalization had on people's development, writing:

... [c]onsciously lived frailty, individuality and socialization of the human being make experiences of pain, illness and death an essential part of life. The ability to cope with these three things autonomously is the basis of human health. If human beings become dependent on the bureaucratic administration of their intimate realm, they renounce their autonomy. In truth, the miracle of medicine is a devilish illusion. It consists in getting, not only individuals, but whole sections of the population to survive on an inhumanly low level of personal health ... [Medicine] set out to improve and equalize the opportunity for each man to cope in autonomy and ended up destroying it.

(1976: 274–275)

How we view health and illness, for Illich, is an all-important reflection of the state of personal freedom and autonomy. From this perspective, medicalization is a powerful force which rests on beliefs of scientific progress and our ability to conquer disease. Illich's analysis is a warning against this hubris. Whilst not eschewing medicine altogether, he is deeply sceptical of its true potential to improve health status (indeed, his argument rests on the notion that industrialized medicine actually makes us sick).

More generally, the concept of medicalization gives us a unique perspective on the fundamental sociological question: How is order maintained in society? To what extent is society based on consensus versus conflict? With links to the structural functionalism of Parsons, medicalization can be used to describe a process of consensus building or system maintenance. From this perspective, medical conditions are conditions which society accepts as requiring access to the sick role; otherwise, deviancy occurs and social control mechanisms are activated to deal with the problem. Shared beliefs about what constitutes illness therefore serve as a Durkheimian boundary maintaining system, and whilst disease definitions may change from time to time (influenced, in part, by advances in medical research), their definitions nevertheless reflect societal values about what should be treated within the medical sphere.

However, viewed as a social control issue, medicalization brings to light issues of *power*. The influential philosopher Michel Foucault is relevant here; his theories serve as both an anchor to the concept of medicalization and as a critique of its development in the literature (Lupton, 1997b). As an anchor, a Foucauldian notion of surveillance medicine supports the concept of medicalization by describing the ever-growing reach of the medical gaze (Armstrong, 1995). This is implicit in the writings of Zola, Conrad, and Illich. However, a Foucauldian take on medicalization also brings to light important contradictions – and it is here that Foucault's conceptualization of power comes into play. Specifically, Foucauldian theory can be used as a critique of the medicalization thesis because of his conceptualization of power as productive, rather than merely repressive. Foucault notes:

> What makes power hold good, what makes it accepted, is simply the fact that it doesn't only weigh on us as a force that says no, but that it traverses and produces things, it induces pleasure, forms knowledge, produces discourse. It needs to be considered as a productive network which runs through the whole social body, much more than as a negative instance whose function is repression.
>
> (1984: 61)

From this perspective, medicalization should not merely be seen as a strategy of a powerful vested interest (the medical profession); that would be merely a repressive power (Lupton, 1997b). Foucault's notion that power produces rather than merely represses suggests that a strategy of shifting power from the medical profession to patients would not necessarily solve the problem identified by Zola, Conrad, and Illich. In other words, it is not a question of *which group* (the medical profession or patients) holds power – as noted in Chapter 3, Foucault saw the limits to analyses centred on "who is or is not free in relation to the power system" (1977: 27). Instead, he argued for analysis of the underlying discourse, and how power flows through categorizations.

Applying a Foucauldian perspective, Lupton argues that "power is not a possession of particular social groups, *but is relational, a strategy which is invested in and transmitted through all social groups*" (1997b: 99, emphasis mine). The result is that strategies of "de-medicalization" that involve shifting decision-making power from the medical profession to lay people are doomed to fail because whilst such strategies may indeed limit the power of one group, they paradoxically encourage a greater medicalization by ultimately resting such health-related decisions on the shoulders of individuals. For example, this could take the form of internalising notions of "risk factors" for disease and re-shaping our lives around the prevention of future illness.

Alternatively, a class perspective on medicalization suggests that the increased use of a medical frame serves the interest of the ruling capitalist class. From this perspective, medicalization strengthens individualization (increasingly through pharmacological treatment); the social roots of problems are obscured, and social determinants of health such as income inequality (Kawachi and Kennedy, 2002; Wilkinson, 2005), which call for changes at the macro-level of society, are ignored. Indeed, a central message coming from the pharmaceutical industry is that chemical solutions are possible to an ever-growing range of illnesses – the ultimate cause of these illnesses are thereby also reduced to chemical imbalances within the individual, thus bringing us back to the medical atomism that is one of Virchow's legacies. Moynihan and Cassels express the political economy implications of medicalization as follows: "while the boundaries defining disease are pushed out as widely as they can be, by contrast, the causes of these supposed epidemics are portrayed as narrowly as possible" (2005: xvi). This supports the atomistic tendency of modern Western biomedicine, and we begin to see health solely as personal troubles and lose their connections with public issues (Mills, 1959; also see Chapter 1).

At the same time, medicalization supports the basic profit drives of the capitalist economy; illness in this case becomes a market and pharmaceutical innovation a product for sale. A consequence of this is that the vast majority of expenditures for health research is devoted to illnesses that affect primarily the highly industrialized world (Neufeld et al., 2001). For Moynihan and Cassels, this is fundamentally an issue of social justice:

[i]n this age of globalization, is it conceivable that we in the wealthy developed world will continue to spend billions every year diagnosing and medicating

children whose symptoms include *often fidgets with hands or feet* and prescribing lifelong speed to adults who *drum their fingers*, when each year millions of children and adults just across our borders will die early from preventable and treatable life-threatening diseases? Surely this is one obscenity too many.

(2005: 81, emphasis in original)

The concept of medicalization also offers us an important perspective on more recent theorizing by Giddens on "late modernity" and Beck on "risk society" (Tomes, 2007). Williams and Calnan, critical of the early formulations of medicalization developed by Freidson, Illich, and even Foucault, worry that "there is a danger of exaggerating the hold which modern medicine has over contemporary experience" (1996: 1611) and suggest that perhaps a process of de-medicalization may also be occurring in late modern societies. Their theoretical argument is that the lay populace is evermore sceptical of modern biomedical approaches – and that to further our understanding of the role of medicine in society, we need to turn to new approaches from Giddens and Beck, noting that "...whilst medicalization theorists may have been inaccurate in assuming 'blanket dependence' in the past, this is even more so now in light of these newer theoretical perspectives" (1996: 1609).

What do Giddens and Beck offer medicalization theory? For Williams and Calnan, these theorists fundamentally change the "contours" and "existential parameters" of life; their notions of modernity as a "reflexive" order and "risk" change how we may perceive of the power of medicine. From this perspective, "...all beliefs and practices are subject to systematic examination, critical scrutiny and revision in light of changing social circumstances. Reflexivity, therefore, become [sic] a *chronic* and defining feature of 'late' modernity, involving a never ending cycle of re-appraisals, re-assessments and revisions which span all aspects of modern social life" (1996: 1612, emphasis in original). Williams and Calnan argue that if we adopt Giddens' argument that life in "late" modern society is characterized by constant "revision in the light of new information and knowledge" (1996: 1612), the notion of medicalization as an all-powerful force that "dupes" lay people is misguided. Instead, they see an increasingly pluralised medical marketplace, with competing authoritative voices: "...the clinical gaze has shifted, particularly in general practice, to more biographical forms of medicine which emphasize patient subjectivity and the psycho-social context of disease. As a consequence, the boundaries between medicine and sociology have become increasingly blurred" (1996: 1612). The merit of this position is questionable, however, when we consider alternative ways of conceptualizing the ever-growing power of the pharmaceutical industry as an "engine" behind medicalization.

Williams and Calnan's use of Giddens and Beck with respect to "risk" is particularly interesting. They note that "modern risks are increasingly the product of human interventions of many different sorts – what Giddens refers to as the 'manufactured' risks and uncertainties of modern social life" (1996: 1613). Importantly, they argue that risks of these kinds "cannot simply be understood in class terms. Rather, in 'risk' society we are all ultimately confronted with a similar fate from which it is difficult if not impossible to escape" (1996: 1614). Yet whilst they seek to diminish the explanatory power of early medicalization theorists like Illich (indeed, at times calling his approach simplistic), their analysis overlooks the very issue that was at the crux of Illich's critique against medicine – iatrogenic effects. Their approach to class – that it cannot be used to understand risk in contemporary society – also overlooks a clearly important issue in contemporary discussions of medicalization: side-effects from psychotropic medications, including anti-depressants. Analysis informed by notions of class would examine, for example, the social patterning of mental illness, psychotropic medication prescriptions, and how side- effects are treated according to class location. Along these lines, Busfield notes how the use of psychotropic medications does not feature in Giddens' writing on anxiety and risk, "even though the widespread use of psychotropics could be regarded as a marker of that anxiety" (2006b: 299). The absence of this line of analysis in the risk literature is striking and clearly signals an area of needed research.

Williams and Calnan argue that the "mediation" of contemporary experience which is a defining feature of Giddens' and Beck's theorizing should also be considered with respect to our conceptualization of medicalization. They note that the media plays a "mysticficatory" and "de-mystificatory" role in relation to modern medicine and controversially conclude that "[t]he media add yet another powerful challenge to the medical citadel and increasingly come to put medicine on 'trial' with the lay populace as its 'jury' " (1996: 1616). They argue that this generates a "re-skilling" of the lay populace and eventually supports what Giddens labeled the emergence of "life political agendas".

It is difficult – if not impossible – to reconcile the accounts provided by Zola, Freidson, Illich, and most recently, Moynihan and Cassels on the one hand and Williams and Calnan on the other. Clearly, they hold complex and contradictory views on the concept of medicalization and its relevance in the contemporary world. However, much can be gained by unpacking the concept of medicalization; doing so may open up a theoretical or empirical perspective through which to further our understanding of this complex concept.

On the Causes of Medicalization

An important part of the medical sociological literature in this area has attempted to examine the social forces behind medicalization. For Conrad

(2005), these social forces – or "engines" – have changed over time. He argues that until the 1990s, the main social forces behind medicalization were the medical profession, social movements and interest groups, and inter-professional or organizational conflicts of the kind we saw in Chapter 5. Notably, Conrad (2005) argues that the pharmaceutical industry was not a central actor in the early work on medicalization. However, he goes to argue that the "engines" behind medicalization have changed, particularly since the 1990s – and that now, the main social forces behind medicalization are biotechnological and pharmaceutical companies, consumers, and the managed care industry. For Conrad, by the end of the 1990s, "changes in the organization of health care, medical knowledge, and marketing had created a different world of medicine" (2005: 5). In effect, Conrad argues that "medicalization is now more driven by commercial and market interests than by professional claims-makers" (2005: 3). This is a fundamental shift in theorizing about medicalization; a shift which places the pharmaceutical industry at the centre of the analysis.

Indeed, recent research on the power of the pharmaceutical industry has re-vitalised the concept of medicalization. In *Selling Sickness: How the World's Biggest Pharmaceutical Companies are Turning Us All Into Patients*, Moynihan and Cassels (2005) provide a clear example of this trend. Their book examines how markets for pharmaceutical products are created, shaped, and expanded by an evermore aggressive industry. In this process, the distinction between marketing and science becomes increasingly blurred. At the centre of their work is the observation that "the marketing strategies of the world's biggest drug companies now aggressively target the healthy and the well. The ups and downs of daily life have become mental disorders, common complaints are transformed into frightening conditions, and more and more ordinary people are turned into patients" (Moynihan and Cassels, 2005: xi). Tellingly, their book begins with the authors recounting a story wherein the chief executive of Merck – one of the world's biggest pharmaceutical companies and maker of the antidepressant Zoloft (sertraline) – told *Fortune* magazine that he found it distressing that the company had limited its potential market to only sick people. Instead, the Merck executive wanted to model his company on Wrigley's – the maker of bubble gum, because then, his company could *sell to everyone*.

Moynihan and Cassels examine the notion of *condition branding* – the use of marketing principles to "create" diseases. They describe the process as follows: "sometimes a little-known condition is given renewed attention, sometimes an old disease is redefined and renamed, and sometimes a whole new dysfunction is created" (2005: xiii). For example, their analysis examines the marketing strategies used by pharmaceutical companies to frame high cholesterol as a disease construct, when it is perhaps more appropriately seen as one risk factor among many that can shape your chances of heart disease or stroke. They argue that our objective should be to reduce heart disease, stroke, and premature death from these causes, and not just lower cholesterol levels in populations. They worry that "[a]s with many other medical conditions, the definition of what constitutes 'high cholesterol' is regularly revised, and like other conditions the definition has been broadened in ways that redefine more and more healthy people as sick" (2005: 3). It is this very tendency for expansion that is symptomatic of medicalization. The result is that, currently, cholesterol-lowering drugs generate revenues of more than $25 billion a year for the pharmaceutical industry (which has enjoyed remarkable success in shaping discourse surrounding what are acceptable and non-acceptable levels of cholesterol) (Moynihan and Cassels, 2005). Another notable example of condition branding includes the development of "pre-menstrual dysphoric disorder" (PMDD), for which the US Federal Drug Administration has recently approved Prozac. The maker of Prozac has gone on to market the drug as Sarafem after market research with doctors and potential patients indicated that a too-close association with the Prozac "brand" would limit potential appeal of PMDD (Moynihan and Cassels, 2005). The marketing campaign behind the development of "social anxiety disorder" to open up a marketing niche for Paxil is a third example.

Payer (1992) previously described this phenomenon as "disease-mongering"; and whilst we may debate the name of the process, its implications clearly signal a heightened medicalization of everyday life. Conrad (2005) has called the practice of marketing a disease first and selling drugs to treat those diseases second a common feature of the "post-Prozac" era. Similar analyses are presented in a large number of recent books, including *Super Pills* (Manners, 2006), *Inventing Disease and Pushing Pills* (Blech, 2006), *Overtreated* (Brownlee, 2007), and *Overdo$ed America* (Abramson, 2004).

Along with condition branding, a number of alternative channels through which the pharmaceutical industry advances the process of medicalization is illustrated in the literature. Some of these channels involve their interaction with individual doctors or with the medical profession as a whole or with the general public (see Figure 6.1).

The most important channel through which the pharmaceutical industry influences processes of medicalization is through research funding. Quite simply, it is industry that funds the vast majority of clinical trials around the world; that gives them tremendous power in deciding which compounds are investigated and which diseases are targeted. Much of the funding that comes through pharmaceutical companies is described as "independent research grants" and presented as being at "arms length". However, systematic reviews have shown that the industry's influence via research funding has a substantial effect on results (Blech, 2006). For example, an analysis of 159 clinical trials published in the prestigious *British Medical Journal* from 1997 to 2001 revealed a pronounced

Interacting with individual doctors	Interacting with the medical profession	Interacting with the public
– Research funding	– Sponsoring of conferences and symposia	– Astro-turfing
– Sales force visits to doctors	– Influence on government regulators	– Direct-to-consumer advertising
	– Advertising in professional journals	

Figure 6.1 Industry channels for promoting products

relationship between researchers' financial ties to sponsoring companies and the likelihood that their paper reported positive results for the treatment intervention (Kjaergard and Als-Nielsen, 2002); a relationship supported by subsequent studies by Lexchin et al. (2003) and Healy (2003). Industry-sponsored clinical trials also make up the substantial bulk of evidence that is examined by regulatory bodies in North America and Europe at the time of drug approval, and whilst alarm has been raised about conflicts-of-interests, the situation has not improved in recent years (Moynihan, 2003b; Moynihan and Cassels, 2005).

A second channel through which the pharmaceutical industry can encourage processes of medicalization is through its sales force visits to doctors. Consider that just between 1996 and 2001, the number of sales representatives employed by pharmaceutical companies in the United States rose from 42,000 to 88,000 – an increase of 110 per cent (Blech, 2006). The results is that studies from several countries indicate that 80–95 per cent of doctors regularly meet with drug company sales representatives, "despite evidence that their information is overly positive and prescribing habits are less appropriate as a result" (Moynihan, 2003c: 1189). It is during these visits that pharmaceutical company representatives pass along published articles that they want doctors to read (these articles often having been written under the sponsorship of the company itself and/or "ghost-written" by public relations companies yet credited to academic researchers) and discuss new products or indications for new products.

Along with strategies that target individual doctors, the pharmaceutical industry can shape discourse around disease constructs by sponsoring conferences and symposia dedicated to particular themes. For example, Blech (2006) has written about industry condition branding related to "male menopause" by sponsoring scientific events (where industry-sponsored research was presented). Similarly, Moynihan (2003a) documents efforts to create a market for "female sexual dysfunction" (given the commercial success of Viagra and newer treatments for male sexual dysfunction, one can clearly see how lucrative this market could be). Additionally, industry efforts to shape the development and content of "clinical practice guidelines" has been profound (Choudhry et al., 2002). This is a very important channel through which medical practice is shaped, particularly because it is congruent with growing trends in many countries towards so-called "evidence-based" medicine. Perhaps most importantly, the pharmaceutical industry shapes regulations on medications through direct interaction with the US Food and Drugs Administration (FDA) and other regulatory agencies (Abraham, 2005). This influence is highly significant, considering that more than half of the FDA's drug review work is funded directly by companies with vested interests in the products being reviewed (see Healy, 2003).

Industry interactions with the public are dominated by two important strategies: *astro-turfing* and, in the countries where it is legal, direct-to-consumer (DTC) advertising. "Astro-turfing" – the creation of fake grass-roots movements – has been particularly effective in recent years. For example, the pharmaceutical industry has funded CHADD (Children and Adults with Attention-Deficit/Hyperactivity Disorder), a community organization that has been playing an important role in shaping discourse surrounding these disease constructs, which whilst still debated (Rafalovich, 2005) are nevertheless now an important market for the industry. Conrad's analysis of this group is reflective of its effectiveness: "spokespeople from such groups often take strong stances supporting pharmaceutical research and treatment, raising the question of where consumer advocates begin and pharmaceutical promotion ends. This reflects the power of corporations in shaping and sometimes co-opting advocacy groups" (1992: 9).

The most studied channel through which the pharmaceutical industry influences societal thinking about medications is through DTC advertising. Indeed, such activities make up a significant proportion of industry's overall activity; it often surprises people to learn that brand-name pharmaceutical companies spend *more on advertising than on research and development* (Blech, 2006). This is despite that DTC advertising is only legal in the United States and New Zealand (however, advertising in professional journals and magazines is allowed throughout the world). Insight into the significance of DTC is offered by Mintzes et al. (2002), who carried out a questionnaire study of patients and primary care doctors in the United States and Canada. They note that brand-name pharmaceutical companies spent almost US$2.5 billion dollars in DTC advertising in 2000, with this figure growing rapidly throughout the 1990s. Their study indicates that patients who went into a medical consultation and *requested* a medication were 8.7 times more likely than patients who did not request a medication to receive a prescription for it. Mintzes et al. concluded that "[p]atients' requests for medicines are a powerful driver of prescribing decisions" (2002: 279). This reflects the profound effect advertising of pharmaceutical products can have on the process of medicalization. Companies know that advertising of particular medications – or when that is not permitted by law, that advertising of particular diseases – can lead to increases in market share for their product. This follows the basic premise of condition branding – create markets for diseases and sales of product will follow.

Medicalization as a Multi-Dimensional Concept

But is this perspective too simplistic? Recent discussions in the medical sociological literature have highlighted an implicit tension in the concept of medicalization; a tension between: "a docile lay populace, in thrall to expansionist medicine" (Ballard and Elston, 2005: 229); and an "expert patient", empowered with knowledge and awareness of risks to their health. According to Ballard and Elston, "...there is now a significant body of literature that suggests that medical dominance and medicalization are not synonymous and that lay persons are not necessarily passively dependent in the process of medicalization or disadvantaged by it" (2005: 233). In other words, does the concept of medicalization lead us to examine the imperialistic properties of the medical profession? Does the concept lead us to examine something more complex? For example, what if we examine the basic questions of (1) How do things get "medicalized"?; and (2) What are the *social forces* or *social mechanisms* underlying the process of medicalization? For Ballard and Elston, the early writings on medicalization paint a one-sided picture; they argue that the concept also needs to be seen as a bottom-up process: "...people are becoming both more skeptical about and more dependent on medical and technological developments, and are both active and passive within the medical encounter" (2005: 237). In other words, Ballard and Elston argue that medical dominance and medicalization are not synonymous; that medicalization can – and is sometimes – driven by patients themselves (a notion that is problematized if we consider the results of the Mintzes et al. questionnaire study discussed above).

Why would this be the case? Perhaps because a medical diagnosis serves important functions; above all, it legitimizes a condition and grants individuals access to the benefits of the sick role (Broom and Woodward, 1996). This will be examined in greater depth in Chapter 7, when we discuss the dynamics that underlie the medical encounter.

Can we also observe patterns of de-medicalization, or situations in which the medical frame has lost authority? A classic example of this effect is homosexuality, which until 1974 was officially considered in the DSM as a disease. For Williams and Calnan, writing in the mid-1990s, "far from modern society being characterized by an extension of medical control, current trends suggest that a process of 'de-medicalization' may in fact be taking place" (1996: 1611). It is at first difficult to reconcile this notion with the processes described by Moynihan and Cassels; indeed, given dramatic increases in utilization rates for prescription medications such as antidepressants, anti-psychotics, and tranquilizers (Beck et al., 2005; Busfield, 2004; Healy, 2003), it is tempting to conclude that the medicalization of everyday life is indeed occurring. Indeed, at the same time that more and more people are taking prescription medications, empirical and theoretical research in medical sociology has explored the counter trend of de-medicalization. This is congruent with Ballard and Elston's observation: "at the turn of the 21st century, far from there being an inexorable trends towards medicalization, there seems to be oscillation between medicalization and de-medicalization of many aspects of everyday life" (2005: 238). In the following section, I discuss an important qualitative study that aimed to tease apart the complex and contradictory forces embedded within the concept of medicalization.

Empirical Research on Medicalization

A large number of empirical studies have been published utilizing and developing the concept of medicalization – they serve us as excellent examples of how theoretically informed empirical research may indeed be carried out. For example, Lowenberg and Davis (1994), in a qualitative study of holistic health practices, developed three distinct analytical dimensions behind the concept of medicalization:

(1) Locus of causality – the extent to which the sources of illness are identified as being within the self or are believed to be external to the self;
(2) Status relationships between practitioners (e.g., doctors) and "patients" – the extent to which marked status differentials are created and reinforced in the medical setting; and
(3) The pathogenic sphere – the range of issues that are thought to influence one's health status (e.g., highly focused on symptomatology or expanded to included "lifestyle" factors such as spiritual well-being).

Lowenberg and Davis use these analytical dimensions to tease out contradictory simultaneous movements towards greater medicalization *and* de-medicalization within holistic health. They note that holistic health practices are seen as different from traditional Western biomedical (allopathic) medicine; the concerns of holistic health practitioners often encompass spiritual well-being, nutritional balance, stress reduction through lifestyle changes, and improving the quality of interpersonal relationships. In other words, holistic health practitioners and clients would not reduce health issues to imbalances in neurotransmitters or to levels of lipids in the bloodstream. On the surface, holistic health practice therefore seems to indicate a process of de-medicalization. Lowenberg and Davis take this as the starting point for their study and note that holistic health practice "is so widely taken to be an augury of society's evolution toward some future de-medicalized state. But in terms of what goes on in the actual everyday practice, to what extent does holistic health fulfill this promise...?" (1994: 586). To explore this question, empirical research was needed.

Their research took place over four years in the mid 1980s. Their empirical data were generated through participant observation in a holistic dental office and further field-based research in a holistic family practice clinic which included licensed physicians, nurses, psychologists, and nutritionists. They also analyzed "cultural materials" and documents associated with the clinics and holistic health in general. For instance, they joined the Association for Holistic Health, and attended conferences and workshops for health professionals. They also conducted interviews with holistic health practitioners, leaders of the holistic health movement, and patients who sought care in the clinics. Their analysis was informed by the qualitative, interpretive tradition of grounded theory (see Text Box 6.1) (Corbin and Strauss, 1990; Lofland and Lofland, 1995; Pidgeon, 1996).

Text Box 6.1: Grounded Theory Analysis

Grounded theory is a general strategy for the analysis of qualitative data. First developed in Glaser and Strauss' (1967) *The Discovery of Grounded Theory*, it has been very influential within medical sociology (see, for example, Wilson et al., 2002). Under this approach, data collection, analysis, and theory are closely woven together. Grounded theory analysis is iterative, in that it involves a constant back and forth between data collection, analysis, and theory development. It incorporates notions of theoretical saturation (data collection ceases once new data do not meaningfully alter the emerging theory) and coding (wherein transcripts from interviews are analyzed through a variety of flexible coding strategies – but this is unlike more traditional forms of structured content analysis as the aim of the coding is to generate concepts that lead to substantive or formal theory; the coding does not aim to produce statistical summaries of the data). This is in stark contrast to more traditional, deductive approaches to research which may begin with a theoretical assertion and develop by formulating hypotheses and testing those hypotheses with empirical data.

For Lowenberg and Davis, the analytical dimensions of locus of causality, status relationships, and the pathogenic sphere are helpful because they can be used to further refine the general concept of medicalization.[1] Their first dimension refers to a defining characteristic of medicalization – the placing of the locus of causality for any given illness or condition outside of the self (but not the body); that is, disease states are brought about by "impersonal and morally extrinsic agents and processes" (Lowenberg and Davis, 1994: 583). For example, from this perspective, sources of illness will often be seen as having a biological and/or neurochemical basis. This is of course also a defining characteristic of the Parsonian sick role, wherein the sick person is not responsible for his or her condition – the locus of causality is external to the self. In contrast to this external locus of causality, a de-medicalized perspective holds that the self is responsible (and by extension culpable) for their condition. In the extreme, this has historically been reflected in the view that alcoholism is a product of free will and that alcoholics can control their behaviour. But this is also reflected in the more contemporary view that holds "lifestyle factors" as the cause of illness – this perspective holds that it is up to individuals to exercise, eat nutritious food, and take care of their bodies.

For Lowenberg and Davis, "... holistic health moves the locus of causality back towards the self, in direct opposition to causality conceptions within the allopathic medical model. ... In that sense holistic health definitely represents the process of de-medicalization..." (1994: 587). This has very important implications – this aspect of de-medicalization reverses the *sin to crime to sickness* transition. For Lowenberg and Davis, this leads to an (unintended) antihumanistic consequence of the holistic model of health: "the shift in responsibility can be used as a rationale to reduce medical services to the poor, withdraw a variety of resources from the sick and disabled, and stigmatize those who are ill" (1994: 587). Furthermore, "in the more radical forms of holistic health, individuals are seen as 'choosing' to be ill; recovery is similarly seen as a volitional choice" (1994: 588). In their empirical research, Lowenberg and Davis observed clear cases were patients displayed stigmatization, blame, and guilt because of their failure to enact necessary lifestyle changes: "Diet and nutritional change evoked the greatest amount of self-condemnation observed in the clinic. As one patient lamented, 'the diet changes are really hard. I've been guilty of throwing so much junk into my body over the years!'" (1994: 589). This is clearly a reversal of the medicalized locus of causality; the source of illness – and the responsibility for treatment – rest once again on the individual. According to Lowenberg and Davis, this represents a "return shift in the direction of imputation of sin and moral failure in relation to not only illness, but lifestyle lapses" (1994: 589).

For Lowenberg and Davis, the second analytical dimension behind the concept of medicalization focuses on status relationships between practitioners and "patients". Within a medicalized frame, authority rests within medical professionals (see Chapter 7 for a more detailed discussion of authority and power within the medical encounter). Once again, holistic health practice represents a step towards de-medicalization within this dimension. For Lowenberg and Davis, "the relationship between the physician and patient in the holistic settings studied had definitely shifted towards a more egalitarian stance" (1994: 590). Empirical observations and interviews played a critical role in their analysis; they cite patient comments which contrasted metaphors of biomedical doctors as "Gods" in white jackets with the more egalitarian stance of holistic physicians, in terms of their more casual attire, their use of lay vocabulary, and willingness to use first names rather than titles and last names. Notably, the egalitarian relationship encouraged in the holistic health clinics extended to the sharing of information; for example, Lowenberg and Davis report patients being able to view their medical charts. Diminished status differentials were also noted at the interactional and socio-linguistic level; "patients observed in the setting more frequently initiated, questioned, expressed feelings, and contradicted physicians during interactions than one would expect in a traditional allopathic medical setting" (1994: 591). Notably, holistic health physicians also displayed a more affective stance towards their patients, thus violating Parsons' affective neutrality. Lowenberg and Davis reported observing staff–patient interaction which they characterized as "warm"; including hugging and conversational exchanges on personal and social issues – leading to their conclusion that in terms of status relationships, holistic health practice can be described as de-medicalizing.

The pathogenic sphere is the third of Lowenberg and Davis' analytical dimensions, and represents the key contribution that their empirical research makes to the refinement of the concept of medicalization. In contrast to the first two analytical dimensions, an examination of the pathogenic sphere indicates that holistic health represents contradictory simultaneous movements towards medicalization and de-medicalization. According to Lowenberg and Davis,

> holistic health definitely represents a drastic increase in medicalisation. . . . the holistic model puts increasing areas of everyday life under medical scrutiny because of the emphasis on lifestyle modification, along with the beliefs in body-mind continuity. . . . [under this model] people come to think of concepts such as stress, grief, and friendship in terms of a direct causal relationship with health and illness. This expansion of the legitimate medical or health arena is so marked that the shift could appropriately be called the "medicalisation of lifestyle".
>
> (1994: 592)

In Foucauldian terms, this represents a significant growth in the "medical gaze", and most importantly, an internalization of that gaze. It is the richness of their empirical data that allows Lowenberg and Davis to conclude

> The paradox of holistic health with respect to the "medicalisation of society" thesis, therefore, is that while one of its major injunctions violates the thesis, the other more than supports it. The denial to patients of the privilege to be absolved from responsibility for their illness smacks strongly of demedicalisation, while the application of a health–illness paradigm to nearly every domain of life represents, if anything, a massive thrust in the direction of medicalisation.
>
> (1994: 584)

Their empirical research, based on years of participant observation, document analysis, and interviews, has contributed to the refinement of the concept of medicalization in important ways. It allows us to see an increased level of complexity behind the concept; it is no longer a vaguely defined term for "making things medical" but a multi-dimensional concept with complex and sometimes contradictory tendencies.

Conclusion

Medicalization is one of medical sociology's most important concepts. It is at the heart of some of the most important theoretical works in this field, including Freidson's refinement of Parsons' seminal ideas on medicine and society. It is also at the heart of Illich's critique of bureaucratic health care and modern life. Recent theoretical (Ballard and Elston, 2005) and empirical (Lowenberg and Davis, 1994) work has pushed the boundaries of what we know about this concept. A nuanced understanding of the concept allows us to see the links between a macro-level political economy of health care and the pharmaceutical industry (as developed in Chapter 5 and 6) with micro-level investigations of physician–patient interactions, discussed in the next chapter.

7

The Medical Encounter

Erving Goffman (1983) taught us that it is in the everyday interactions between people where much of "society" takes place. It is where roles are defined, enacted, and perhaps contested, where power is asserted and negotiated, and where discrimination is experienced. It is where emotions come to the foreground of experience. This "micro" focus to sociology has been immensely important in the development of medical sociology, and continues to offer health-related social research important insights into health and illness (Ainsworth-Vaughn, 1995).

We find an important example of what Goffman called "interaction order" in the medical encounter, or the face-to-face meeting of doctors and patients during a health care visit. It is a rich area of research, full of methodological complexity and nuanced theorizing. At its core, research in this area analyzes power, how it is established and maintained by medical professionals and how it is challenged by patients. Also central are human needs, pain, anxiety, and the desire to help. Insight into these issues is offered by Lupton, who notes that

> it should be taken into account that doctors and patients have different, and often conflicting, interests: doctors, to perform their duties of the professional in the medical workplace, seeking to earn a living and progress in their career; patients, to alleviate the physical pain or discomfort that is disrupting their lives.
>
> (2003: 8)

Social researchers, particularly those identifying with the model of sociology *in* medicine, work with the hope that understanding the nature of these conflicting interests and how they play out in daily medical interactions may ultimately lead to knowledge that helps to generate good health outcomes. For example, this could involve new ways of communicating ideas regarding treatment options or perhaps improved mechanisms for informing patients about the possible side-effects of medications.

	Stage	Description
Medical history	Chief complaint	Identification of the patient's primary concern
	Present illness	Elaboration of the chief complaint, its characteristics, when symptoms began
	Past history *	Background information not necessarily pertinent to the present illness
	Family history *	Information on illnesses and deaths in the patient's immediate family; may not be pertinent to the present illness
	Social history *	Other demographics
	Systems review *	Identification of additional information about the present illness that may have been left out
Physical examination		Laying on of hands
Other investigations		Initiation of one or more additional tests (e.g., laboratory tests)
Diagnosis		With results from previous stages, the doctor reaches a decision regarding the nature of the chief complaint
Plan		Therapeutic strategy for dealing with the chief complaint

Figure 7.1   A traditional medical encounter

Notes: * These components are frequently dropped from a typical medical encounter.
Adapted from: Waitzkin (1991).

Most medical encounters are resolved to the satisfaction of all those involved. What is at issue for social research – and note that this follows Berger's definition of a sociological problem quite closely – is not so much when encounters are problematic, but how they are structured in the first place. It is the regular, everyday, taken-for-granted structure of the medical encounter that has drawn sociological interest in the past 50 years. This structure is relatively well-defined for Western medicine and is depicted in Figure 7.1.

Under this model, a medical encounter begins with a medical history, before proceeding to physical and other investigations (as needed), a diagnosis, and a treatment plan. Waitzkin (1991) notes that this structure appears in most textbooks on clinical methods for medical students. Empirical research on doctor–patient communication has also confirmed the use of this structure as an organizing framework, although there are always exceptions and encounters that follow a different format, depending on a range of factors, including the nature of the ailment being discussed.

However, it is not this on-the-surface structure of the medical encounter that has drawn the interest of social researchers. They have placed far more importance on the *deeper* structure of the encounter and on the social roles that are embedded within it. As may be expected, social researchers have been particularly interested in questions of power differentials as experienced in medical talk. To investigate these themes, they have used a rich mix of empirical techniques, including in-depth interviewing (Lupton, 1997a; Werner and Malterud, 2003), questionnaires (Waitzkin, 1991), conversation analysis (Campion and Langdon, 2004), and even secondary analysis (May et al., 2004). Importantly, this area of research has included positivist (Waitzkin, 1991), interpretivist (Werner and Malterud, 2003), and critical realist (Porter, 1993) epistemologies. The integration of these different methodological and epistemological approaches offers many lessons; above all, a comparison of these works reminds us of the different ways in which researchers have approached the generation of knowledge and will encourage us to develop a reflexive attitude towards our own positions on research strategies.

The chapter begins with an overview of Szasz and Hollender's (1956) classic typology of doctor–patient interaction. Their typology – with clear links to Parsons' sick role – describes varying interaction styles, with correspondingly different dynamics of power between doctors and patients. Contemporary empirical studies which have used Szasz and Hollender's model in interesting ways will be highlighted. The chapter then examines the literature on the medical encounter with respect to medically unexplained symptoms, gender, and the reflexive self. Researchers with an explicit connection to feminist theory have investigated these issues and have made notable contributions. For example, researchers have examined conflicts that arise during the medical encounter when a patient suffers from "non-diseases", or conditions that the biomedical community has resisted accepting as legitimate illnesses (Nettleton, 2006; Wileman et al., 2002). Studies have also been conducted that examine the nature of the "work" done by female patients in order to be believed and taken seriously by male doctors (Werner and Malterud, 2003) – what dramaturgical sociologists like Goffman would call "impression management". Overall, these studies tell us a great deal about the power dynamics that underlie the medical encounter and also feedback to wider debates on medicalization, gender roles, and interpersonal communication.

This chapter returns our attention once again to the concept of the sick role, an important element of research on the medical encounter (Gerhardt, 1979, 1989). As we saw in Chapter 3, the Parsonian sick role has been refined over time, partly as a result of empirical findings and partly as a result of theoretical critiques. Its use in the literature on the medical encounter has been particularly nuanced, and as we will see, draws extensively from his links with psychoanalytic theory (Lupton, 1997c). Research on the medical encounter has also explored innovative links to the influential theories of Anthony Giddens and Ulrich Beck; these links – which actually take the form of critique – are explored in the second half of this chapter.

The chapter concludes with a reflection on the need for research strategies to synthesize insights from analyses of the micro-politics of the medical encounter with the macro-politics of health inequities and healthcare reform. This is very much an area of ongoing work in medical sociology, and much remains to be done.

Models of the Medical Encounter

Early in the development of medical sociology, Szasz and Hollender (1956) introduced a theoretical typology of the medical encounter. They suggested that typical doctor–patient interaction fits one of the following three scenarios: activity–passivity, guidance–cooperation, or mutual participation (see Figure 7.2).

As described below, these models allow for varying dynamics within the medical encounter and perhaps differ in their usefulness in relation to the severity of the patient's symptoms (Cockerham, 2004). Their typology has been widely tested using empirical techniques and remains in use today.

Activity–Passivity

Szasz and Hollender's first model – activity–passivity – is an ideal type wherein the physician becomes a so-called "perfect agent" (Gafni et al., 1998). This describes a knowledgeable physician who assumes authority

Model	Description
Activity–Passivity	Physicians as perfect agents with (near) total control over agenda-setting and decision-making
Guidance–Cooperation	Elements of dominance and submission are present in the encounter, but the patient takes a somewhat more active role in agenda-setting and decision-making
Mutual Participation	"Informed" patient is a full participant in agenda-setting and decision-making

Figure 7.2   Szasz and Hollender's typology of medical encounters

Source: Szasz, J., and Hollender, M. (1956). The basic models of the doctor–patient relationship. *Archives of Internal Medicine*, 97, 585–592.

over the patient to make decisions, and justifies this imbalance by the asymmetry of information experienced by the two parties (physicians in this case holding professional expertise on which they can base treatment decisions). Gafni et al. describe this ideal type: "the doctor possesses the knowledge needed for making a treatment decision regarding the patient's illness and for assessing the expected effectiveness of health care interventions in improving the patient's health status" (1998: 347). The position is described as that of a perfect agent because it assumes that the doctor's decision-making process is informed by knowledge of the patient's wants and needs. Cockerham suggests that this model applies in emergencies or serious life-threatening situations; here "...the situation is desperate as the physician works in a state of high activity to stabilize the patient's condition. Decision making and power in the relationship are all on the side of the doctor, as the patient is passive and contributes little or nothing to the interaction" (2004: 186). Communication in this model is very much a one-way process; to the extent that the patient communicates, it is simply to convey information regarding symptoms and preferences. Decision-making power is clearly monopolized by the physician or health care worker.

The activity–passivity model is by definition a scenario based on a power asymmetry. Analysis of this differential has involved conversation analysis – one of the most important methodological tools for researchers interested in the medical encounter (Waitzkin, 1991). By analysing the text of conversations that take place between doctors and patients in the practice of medicine, researchers have been able to examine the extent to which the activity–passivity model is seen in daily practice, and – perhaps most importantly – they have been able to identify discursive techniques used by medical professionals to establish and maintain conversational dominance. Such techniques include the asking of direct closed-ended questions, the use of first names for patients but titles (e.g., Dr. Smith) for doctors, and the interruption of patients' narratives if they deviate from the normative medical script (Weitz, 2007).

A classic example of this type of interaction is given by Fox (1993) in his study of communication strategies used by surgeons with their patients. Fox's study is one of the major contributions of post-modern social theory to medical sociology and is therefore worth exploring in some detail. It is also a fascinating use of ethnographic research methods within a theory-focused piece of research. His study examines the discourse that takes places between surgeons and their patients shortly after an operation has taken place, a scenario that clearly fits Szasz and Hollender's activity–passivity model. Fox notes that oftentimes, post-surgical ward "rounds" (wherein the surgeon will check up on patients and consult with nurses and other health care professionals involved in the care of the patient) involve "communication" between surgeons and patients "with the latter as silent – sleeping or heavily doped – individuals, unable to offer their version of what is happening to them as they undergo the experience of surgery. Under these circumstances, surgeons have it mostly their way ..." (1993: 17). These meetings are almost always brief; the surgeon moves quickly from patient to patient, and the patient is often drowsy from the residual effects of surgical anaesthesia or the actual effects of analgesics (to ease post-operation pain). All this on top of the anxiety and strain that is experienced by the patient severely limits the type of interaction that may occur between surgeons and patients in the post-surgical round.

However, as Fox observed, post-surgical ward rounds, particularly once the patient has begun to recover from the trauma of surgery, do involve significant communication between surgeons and patients – and it is that very communication that he analyzes with the aid of post-structuralist social theory. Fox notes: "... patients as conscious human agents have the potential to affect the content and the course of these interactions, and consequently the possibility also to influence the discourse within which these interactions occur" (1993: 17). Furthermore,

> from a postmodern perspective, the 'ward round' is an attempt to organise inter-actions between surgeons and patients ... [researchers ought to examine] the fine detail of the techniques used by surgeons to sustain hegemonic discourse, the continual threats to this discourse from patients, and the strategies they adopt to cope with these challenges.
>
> (1993: 20)

His analysis, following Foucault, is therefore particularly concerned with the discursive structures which dominate interaction between surgeons and patients.

His research is based on the post-structuralist technique of "decon-struction", which for Fox, makes present what is denied in the explicit discourse: "the ambiguity of surgery itself" (1993: 20), which he notes is derived from its nature as both a healing and harming act. His analysis – whilst clearly ethnographic and implicitly sharing features with grounded theory techniques commonly used by qualitative researchers – is particu-larly shaped by its connection to social theory. Fox notes: "the postmodern perspective on power as constituted by 'knowledge', by the discursive strategies by which the powerful can claim to speak the truth about some-thing, places language at the centre of the analytical stage" (1993: 38). Taking issue with Derrida's focus on absence, or "gaps" in texts, Fox argues for a post-structuralist approach to "deconstruction", wherein "the ideological claims of text are exposed, the very things which the author of discourse would deny come to be seen as the bedrock without which the discourse would founder" (1993: 38). The results of his "deconstruction" are presented in Figure 7.3.

Position	Surgery has healed the sickness of the patient
Negation	Surgery has led to injury of the patient
Negation of negation	Patient physiology, wound condition, and prognosis all indicate that healing has occurred, the surgery is successful, and the surgeon is a healer
Deconstruction	The surgeon has organised post-operative interactions so as to sustain silence over the injurious nature of surgery, and its threatening relations of meaning for surgical authority

Figure 7.3 Fox's deconstruction of post-operative discourse

Source: Fox, N. J. (1993). Discourse, organization and the surgical ward round. *Sociology of Health & Illness*, *15*(1), 16–42. By permission of Blackwell Publishing.

Fox's analysis indicates that surgeons shape and control post-operative discourse in such a way that their claim to be healers is privileged. Fox refers to this as a hegemonic discourse, one that denies attention to the notion that surgery has led to the injury of the patient or that it has involved unacceptable risk to their health. Above all, this "hegemonic discourse" ensures that post-operative interaction moves towards acknowledgement of a surgery's "success" and upholds the surgeon's status as a healer.

Fox identifies three general themes, or what he calls a "loose categorization of surgical discourse": (1) the discourse on patient physiology, (2) the discourse on wound conditions, and (3) discourse on recovery and discharge. He points out that the themes are hierarchical; patients undergoing recovery from surgery will typically pass through discourse 1 before moving on to 2 and 3. All three of the themes are also surgeon-centred; they revolve around technical knowledge. Fox uses ethnographic data comprising of case reports and conversation excerpts to illustrate each type of discourse:

> during interactions with patients, surgeons seek to constitute two foci in their discourse. The first is the operative procedure itself (or its marker – the wound). The second is the status of being healed. The discourse on recovery/discharge is the most forward-looking, focusing on the new status of the patient as a success of surgical healing. Where patients have not progressed to a stage where this is possible, their progress is assessed in terms of physiological condition (the removal of sickness) and wound condition . . .
>
> (1993: 36)

Indeed, there is a notable progression in Fox's surgical discourse model, with the focus of conversation initially centred on the patient's physiology (a typical example of this being the results of a test) before moving on to discussion of the wound (which Fox notes is a marker that the surgery has been carried out) and, eventually, recovery/discharge. The three themes can be invoked at different times by surgeons, depending on the severity of the patient's condition and their stage of treatment. All, however, signal the "success" of a surgery. For example, discussion of the wound healing is "used discursively to suggest the 'success' of surgery, before the latter can be assured" (1993: 32).

Fox reports that patients frequently attempted to assert control of the discourse by switching the theme from physiology to recovery/discharge ("When can I go home?"); often this resulted in the surgeon implementing discursive techniques to assert control. Indeed, his observations and conversation texts reveal repeated attempts by patients to challenge the structure of the discourse. This may simply involve the patients asking direct questions of the surgeon regarding specifics of the surgery or of their recovery. Fox notes:

> These challenges are rarely successful in upsetting the surgical discourse ... [surgeons use discursive techniques] to counteract and disempower patients who try to set the agenda. Surgeons organize these interactions in many ways which serve to rhetorically mark their power: they walk or process around the ward while the patient is confined, undressed, separated from fellows with whom s/he might form a counter-culture of patient-centred discourse. They use various props: screens, white coats, notes which patients cannot see. Yet the necessity of linguistic interaction can still threaten this whole edifice ...
>
> (1993: 22)

These techniques protect the surgeon's choice of discourse and help them to maintain control over the agenda, thus falling nicely within the activity–passivity model.

In many ways, Fox's study blurs medical sociology and the sociology of organizations. His conclusion is that

> the surgical ward round is a strategy adopted to organize a set of social practices which require interactions between surgeons and patients post-operatively. ... [the] organization of ward rounds ensures that a very highly controlled discourse is sustained, with few opportunities for patients to intervene or to introduce their own agenda for interaction ... Virtually every element of organization which constitutes these interactions within the framework of the "ward round" seeks to ensure that the surgeon's discourse remains unchallenged.
>
> (1993: 39)

In this light, we can see that power, knowledge, and the medical encounter are inextricably intertwined.

Reflecting on the theoretical links between Fox's "deconstructionist" analysis and Parsons' structural functionalist account of the sick role, we can see connections that are not explicit in Fox's article. Both Fox and Parsons are interested in the behaviour of medical professionals and patients, and both theorize about the forces that underlie their behaviour. However, they give attention to radically different aspects of the medical encounter. Parsons, as I have already noted, focused primarily on the normative behaviour by which society sanctions illness behaviour and on the sociology of the professions, particularly norms of conduct for doctors. In contrast, Fox focuses on the discourse by which the actions of surgeons and patients are shaped and controlled. This is firmly in line with his post-modern approach to social research. Fox writes

> The "ward round" is a discursive strategy entered upon by particular agents for their own reasons. The concern of the postmodern social analyst is not primarily with the minutiae of the outward manifestations of activities which are carried out during this discursive strategy, but how these activities – the fictive "ward round" – serves discourse, and what is driving that discourse.
>
> (1993: 19)

In this example, theoretical concerns have explicitly shaped the nature of the medical sociological study, including the type of evidence that is sought, and how that evidence is interpreted. Fox's study differs from Parsons' work due to his use of post-modern theory and post-structuralist techniques of deconstruction.

Guidance–Cooperation

Szasz and Hollender's second model – guidance–cooperation – describes a situation where the patient begins to take a more active role in the medical encounter, but where notable elements of dominance and submission nevertheless remain present. The physician continues to make the decisions, and the patient is expected to comply with the physician's instructions. However, the power asymmetry that is characteristic of the activity–passivity model is diminished. This ideal type of medical encounter has a clear relationship to the norms described in Parsons' sick role, particularly its fourth component, which calls for the patient to seek technically competent help and *cooperate* with the physician.

Lagerløv et al.'s (1998) study of the doctor–patient relationship and the management of asthma illustrates the contemporary relevance of this aspect of Szasz and Hollender's model. Their study is also a clear example of sociology *in* medicine, for they work with the objective of improving the way doctors treat asthma in general practice. Their work begins with a medically defined problem: the development of national and international guidelines for the treatment of asthma has not improved care for asthmatics in general practice. This is a problem that has also been noted in other countries, including Britain (Roghmann and Sexton, 1999), Canada (Dean,

2000), and the United States (Kuschner, 2000). A consequence of this problem is that asthma – usually a condition that can be controlled with a combination of preventive medications (inhaled corticosteroids, which reduce inflammation in the bronchial tubes) and emergency rescue medications (short-acting bronchodilators, which quickly open up the airways) – remains uncontrolled for many people, resulting in avoidable healthcare costs, unnecessary morbidity, and even deaths (Brown et al., 2003; Krahn et al., 1996; Suissa et al., 2000).

Lagerløv et al. argue that through a better understanding of how doctors communicate with patients regarding asthma care, it will be possible to design better disease management strategies, meaning that more patients will be prescribed appropriate medication and will know how and when to use them. In this case, identifying the underlying dynamics of the medical encounter may yield benefits in terms of patient care via improved educational interventions with doctors.

Their study involved qualitative interviews with 20 general practitioners in Oslo. The data were analyzed by the three authors, with each researcher reading and coding the interview transcripts on their own. The analysis then continued with a comparison of each researcher's coding system leading to a consensus. Their article deals with a variety of themes, including how doctors conceptualize asthma as a disease construct and their views on effective mechanisms for knowledge acquisition. However, it is Lagerløv et al.'s findings on the doctor–patient relationship that are most relevant here. They note that whilst "the doctor–patient relationship has changed dramatically during recent years, the doctor becoming less authoritative and the patient more autonomous..." (1998: 88), their data indicate a continued strong presence of both activity–passivity and guidance–cooperation models of interaction. Consider the following interview excerpts they report:

I tell the patients that it is dangerous to skip their medications, their lungs will be destroyed, and that they will enjoy a better life when taking their medication as prescribed (...) If I think a certain patient needs a medication, I try to play down the side effects (...) So it becomes the way I want it to be...

(1998: 86)

I do at least try to inform them about the principles concerning the whole concept; about different drugs and the rationale behind their use (...), you could explain this a hundred times, but after a while they do not understand the difference between one drug and another...it is frustrating, as you at least have hoped they would have understood the fundamentals of medications. But actually, there are many patients who don't...

(1998: 86)

Lagerløv et al. interpret these two quotes as symbolic of a particular approach to asthma care and the medical encounter that is congruent with the activity–passivity model. For them, within this model, "the doctor behaves like a parent towards a child" (1998: 88). It is important to note that the doctors were interviewed by a fellow doctor, which perhaps explains the candour exhibited in the first quote. If interviewed by an outsider, perhaps the doctor would not have freely admitted to such (seemingly unethical) tactics.

Interestingly, other doctors in their study indicated different approaches to interacting with patients, with one admitting: "I do not know what it may feel like having problems in breathing . . . I do not have asthma" (1998: 86) and another stating

> I profoundly believe in the importance of patients understanding why they need treatment; then they will also know how to go about it. I tell them to be responsible for their own treatment. I write the prescription (. . .). The patients are the ones to implement the treatment. If they don't give a damn, they will get worse, not the doctor . . .
>
> (1998: 86–87)

These last two quotes are more indicative of the guidance–cooperation model of interaction. Here, the doctor remains a source of knowledge, a source of technical expertise. However, the patient is acknowledged as a source of expertise in their own right; they are the ones who experience the debilitating symptoms of asthma and they are the "ones to implement the treatment".

Mutual Participation

Szasz and Hollender's third model – mutual participation – describes an ideal type wherein the patient is a *full participant* in the decision-making process. One manifestation of this model has the patient emerge as an "informed patient" (Gafni et al., 1998), one who aides in the decision-making process by reading and consulting medical literature and thus is able to voice preferences. Under this model, the patient becomes a sort of consumer, a buyer with the choice of supplier. This potentially gives the patient a remarkable position of power, particularly if we adopt Weber's position that power refers to the probability that persons within a social relationship will be able to carry out their will despite resistance (see Lupton, 1995). In the context of the medical encounter, power for a patient may involve being able to obtain a diagnosis that they feel they need or perhaps the medication they believe will help them. In the discussion below,

I examine how this model of medical interaction plays out in a particularly difficult clinical situation.

The Medical Encounter and Unexplained Symptoms

An important branch of the literature on the medical encounter examines *medically unexplained symptoms* (the most famous examples of this being chronic fatigue syndrome and chronic muscular pain, or fibromyalgia). These cases – where the experience of the patient may clash with the medical training of the physician – offer important clues to the underlying structure of the medical encounter. For Werner and Malterud, "these disorders challenge medical care and knowledge, because effective methods for diagnostic procedures, treatment, and prevention are lacking" (2003: 1410). Studies in this area have explored the notion of medically unexplained symptoms from the perspective of both physicians (Reid et al., 2001; Wileman et al., 2002) and patients (Johansson et al., 1996; Ware, 1992; Werner and Malterud, 2003). These studies offer unique viewpoints on what can be frustrating, tension-filled meetings characterized by unresolved credibility claims (patients wanting to be "credible") and contested knowledge claims (physicians seeking to maintain authority in situations where they may not be able to alleviate painful symptoms or provide effective curative treatment). Ultimately, research on contested medical encounters reveals much about the negotiation that ultimately leads to the creation of new disease constructs – an important aspect of medicalization.

What is the perspective of health care professionals with respect to medically unexplained symptoms? This was the question underlying Reid et al.'s (2001) study of general practitioners. They used a postal questionnaire to collect data from a random sample of 400 GPs in the South-West Thames region of England. Notably, they achieved a satisfactory response rate of 75 per cent, an important methodological detail in postal questionnaires (without a good response range, it is difficult to draw much meaning from these types of studies). More specifically, Reid et al. used a series of Likert scales to measure attitudes and beliefs related to the management of patients with medically unexplained symptoms. Their results are fascinating: a very high percentage (93 per cent) of the respondents agreed that these patients are "difficult to manage", fully 84 per cent agreed that these patients have "personality problems", and 64 per cent agreed that they had an underlying (although undiagnosed) psychiatric illness. Table 7.1 presents results on GPs' attitudes towards their role in the management of patients with medically unexplained symptoms.

These data display important patterns. For example, fully 46 per cent of GPs agreed or strongly agreed that they would prescribe psychotropic

Table 7.1   Examining GP's attitudes towards medically unexplained symptoms

	Agree or strongly agree *n* (per cent)	Disagree or strongly disagree *n* (per cent)
Provide reassurance	279 (98.9)	3 (1.1)
Not to get involved	74 (26.2)	208 (73.8)
No involvement at all	3 (1.1)	279 (98.9)
Refer for further physical investigations	177 (63.9)	100 (36.1)
Prescribe psychotropic drugs	127 (46.4)	147 (53.6)
Act as a gatekeeper to prevent inappropriate investigation	262 (93.6)	18 (6.4)
Provide counseling and psychological management	236 (83.7)	46 (16.3)

Source: Reid, S., Whooley, D., Crayford, T., and Hotopf, M. (2001). Medically unexplained symptoms – GPs' attitudes towards their cause and management. *Family Practice, 18* (5), 519–523. By permission of Oxford University Press.

drugs in circumstances of medically unexplained symptoms. That is, *psychotropic drugs would be prescribed in the absence of a clear diagnostic of mental illness.* Over 90 per cent agreed or strongly agreed that their role was to act as a gatekeeper to prevent *inappropriate* investigation; they perceived that patients with such conditions were likely to make inappropriate requests for specialist health care services. Additional comments from GPs on the questionnaires display a high level of frustration; one doctor lamented the questioning of doctors' ability and skill that they saw as characteristic of an age of "increased patient expectation", and other GPs noted: "Most of MUS [medically unexplained symptoms] are related to not wanting to go back to work...", and "I would like to have enough courage to tell the MUS persons that nothing is wrong; you are wasting your time and my time. You must try to learn to live with your symptoms" (Reid et al., 2001: 521). These data not only reflect a considerable level of frustration, but from a patient's point of view, illustrate formidable barriers that often keep patients with medically unexplained symptoms from receiving the benefits of the sick role.

The situation, as may be expected, is quite different from a patient's point of view. Consider Johansson et al.'s (1996) study of women's experiences of medical encounters in the context of medically unexplained musculoskeletal disorders. Reflective of an interpretivist epistemology, their study relied on qualitative in-depth interviews with a sample of 20 women in Sweden. They carried out their study under the framework of grounded theory (Charmaz, 1983; Corbin and Strauss, 1990); an appropriate choice, given the broad nature of their research question and the fact that the study did not aim to test any specific hypotheses or theoretical assertions. One of the particularly interesting features of this study is that three of the four co-authors are family physicians; their self-described sense of failure and frustration in relation to medical encounters with women with medically unexplained pain was the basis of the study. Faithful to interpretivism, they wanted to know how patients themselves experienced these encounters.

The women in their study reported patterns of distrust and described strategies aimed at improving their chances of experiencing a good encounter – this being defined as an encounter in which their condition was acknowledged, understood, and treated. The women emphasized their experiences of not being taken seriously, of not being treated as credible patients. An interview excerpt illustrates this clearly:

> When the doctor arrived, he had a ready-made diagnosis and *didn't listen to what I said*. I talked to him about my back pain and how I perceive that the trouble in my feet and legs is connected with the spine. *He said that was pure rubbish*. I found him brusque and unkind. And I was frightened and worried. He wanted to give me psychic drugs, anti-depressants. I said I didn't want that. He sat down to write a prescription *without further explanation. I asked for sleeping pills, but he refused*. He prescribed vitamin B and something else *he didn't explain*, then he left. I felt that *I'm not welcome* in the health care system ....
> (Johansson et al., 1996: 499, emphasis in original)

Comments such as this one document the participants' experience of being ignored, disregarded, and rejected in the medical encounter. Of course, retrospective accounts may not give us an *accurate* account of exactly what happened in any particular medical encounter; this is one person's account. Viewed from an interpretivist epistemology, however, comments like this one hold truth in the sense that they allow us to understand reality from the point of view of the person expressing these comments. As such, they give us a valuable perspective on the nature of the medical encounter.

The analysis reported by Johansson et al. implicitly makes use of Parsons' sick role. They write: "the ultimate position in the search for medical attention was 'to be under a doctor'. Delegating the responsibility to the doctor has its advantages. It implied shelter under a doctor, whose task was to 'keep hold of the patient', her body and her recovery" (1996: 500). In other words, women in this study sought admittance to the sick role, something which doctors had power over but were hesitant to invoke in light of the diagnostic and therapeutic uncertainty characteristic of medically unexplained symptoms.

Johansson et al.'s findings offer insight into the negotiation that underlies Szasz and Hollender's typology of medical encounters. Whilst clearly experts in their conditions, and therefore perhaps best suited to the mutual participation model, it appears that the women in this study *wanted* to fit into *any* of the models, even activity–passivity (as long as it meant that the doctor acknowledged their condition and was therefore willing to do something about it). What was truly important to them was entry into the sick role. Johansson et al. conclude by noting the asymmetrical relationship that exists between doctors and patients:

> there is a normative pattern whereby the doctor's role is characterized by high status and control; the doctor leads and the patient follows. All participants described situations where their attempts to question and discuss assumptions were met by correcting, mastering comments such as "that is pure rubbish". Doctors find it problematic to handle distrust and to demonstrate their own weakness.
>
> (1996: 501)

This asymmetrical relationship, previously seen in the ideal type of physician as *perfect agent* (Gafni et al., 1998) becomes particularly contested in a situation of medically unexplained symptoms.

The Medical Encounter and "Doing Gender"

From a patient's perspective, the presentation of medically unexplained symptoms or contested diseases in the medical encounter holds particular problems, the most important of which is the issue of credibility. Werner and Malterud use this issue to examine the notion of "doing gender", which they explain as follows: "In sociological and feminist research, gender and illness have been viewed as not merely something we 'are' or 'get', but also as social practices that we 'do' or 'express' in social encounters" (2003: 1410). This suggests that gender is not only a social construction but also a social performance; an act based on interaction. Given this existing theoretical framework, Werner and Malterud problematize femininity as performed in the medical encounter. Feminist theorizing, then, takes a central role in their study of the "work" done by women to be treated as credible patients by male doctors in the medical encounter.

Their data originate from a series of ten in-depth semi-structured interviews with women with chronic muscular pain – one of the most commonly reported medically unexplained symptoms. As was the case with Johansson et al.'s study, Werner and Malterud did not actually record and analyze conversations between doctors and patients; the data in this study are retrospective accounts provided by the women patients. These accounts were not compared with the doctor's recollection of the encounter; a methodological feature consistent with interpretivist research strategies. Werner and Malterud explain: "We will never know exactly what happened; only what the patient perceived in their encounters with the doctors..." (2003: 1416).

Their findings reveal much about the medical encounter and push the boundaries of Szasz and Hollender's model of medical interaction. The women in this study struggled to enact a mutual participation model of interaction, only to find their efforts rejected by doctors. They report remarkable struggles to be believed and to receive effective treatment, which would either cure their condition or at least alleviate its most pressing symptom, pain. One woman in the study remarked: "On my third visit, I just stood up – because I was so angry – and said to the doctor 'I expect you to write a referral to the hospital now, because I want a second opinion – as my whole leg ached' " (2003: 1412).

The following excerpt provided by Werner and Malterud is illustrative of an informed patient attempting to develop a mutual participation model of interaction:

> Muscle pain is not merely caused by tension, mental disturbances, stress, and how one tackles life – or that one is a woman. There is more to it than that: it often has an organic cause, so I tend to feed people with research results and emphasize how real it is.
>
> (2003: 1412)

The interviewee has clearly taken on the role of an informed patient (Fox et al., 2005; Shaw and Baker, 2004); she knows about the aetiology of her condition and rejects the common misconceptions surrounding it. Interestingly, two of the women noted that they sent a letter to their doctor *before* the appointment with information on their condition; for these women, this was a way of setting limits for the upcoming encounter and taking charge of the nature of the discourse. Of course, there are drawbacks to this type of action: first, it requires a great deal of effort from the patients at a time when they are perhaps not well positioned to do so (given that they may be in substantial pain, as was the case with this sample). Secondly, the strategy may backfire, and doctors may react negatively to their attempts to take control of the encounter (indeed, this seems quite likely, particularly if we consider the results published by Reid et al. (2001)). One woman in the Werner and Malterud study reflects: "You have to tread rather softly, because once you antagonize them it's not certain that you are any better off. So there are in fact some comments and events that you just have to accept" (2003: 1413).

Their data also point to the remarkable efforts some of the women in the study took to *look appropriately* in a medical encounter, highlighting the notion of gender as a performance. The experience of one of the women in the study is reflective of this notion:

Before [the consultation] – though I actually rather regret this now – I had been to a solarium. I hadn't actually remembered that I was going to visit the doctor the following day. I had put on some make-up, and I was wearing a pair of jeans and a completely normal, long-sleeved pullover. The weather had been quite sunny. I had slept well that night, and I actually did look pretty healthy. And when I arrived, he [the doctor] remembered the letter I had sent him about my pain, and said: "You're not ill!" I didn't answer – because what could I say? After a while he said: "You certainly don't look ill!" And I remember I was thinking, goodness, am I the only healthy-looking person with this disease?

(2003: 1413–1414)

Other women in the study, in another clear sign of the performance aspects of gender, reported that they felt that they should also not look healthy at a consultation; that if they looked *strong*, they would not be accepted as patients with chronic pain. This was part of an intricate balance: the women could not look healthy, but they could also not look like they were not coping, for fear of being labeled mentally ill and treated with psychotropic drugs.

According to Werner and Malterud, the women "struggled to be perceived as somatically ill, whilst simultaneously avoiding appearing mentally unbalanced... women with chronic fatigue syndrome and fibromyalgia repeatedly find themselves being questioned, particularly by doctors, and judged to be either not sick or suffering from an imaginary illness" (2003: 1414). Interestingly, this finding is congruent with the results of Reid et al.'s (2001) study of general practitioners' attitudes towards patients with medically unexplained symptoms, where almost half of the doctors surveyed indicated that they are willing to prescribe psychotropic drugs for patients with these symptoms, despite the absence of a clear diagnosis of mental illness.

In their recollections, the women in Werner and Malterud's study describe the hidden *rules* of the medical encounter. These rules may be referred to as "credibility work"; that is, the work done by patients in order to be treated as credible. For the women in this study, credibility work involved finding a balance between acting as a passive/active patient and also involved finding an "acceptable" gender role. For Werner and Malterud, active patients, in this case women who had their own thoughts regarding examination methods and treatment, risked "being perceived as quarrelsome, whining, or mentally disturbed, getting no further help" (2003: 1415). This closed the possibilities of enacting a mutual participation model of interaction. At the same time, the very nature of their condition (as medically unexplained) closed opportunities for more traditional modes of interaction, the activity–passivity or guidance–cooperation model, since the doctors were unwilling/incapable of accepting their role in such models. For the women in this study, this resulted in frustrating medical encounters that did little to alleviate their pain.

Feminist theory, and the concept of patriarchy in particular, plays an important role in the interpretation of Werner and Malterud's research. Their data are focused on a particular interaction, the medical encounter, and tell the story of "credibility work". In one interpretation, this is therefore a story of relational power, of micro-politics, and of strategies used by women to influence their interaction with the health care sector. However, as the authors point out: "At a micro-level, efforts to be perceived as a credible patient in medical encounters may be interpreted as enacting relational power. However, in a macro-perspective, the same strategies can be regarded as adjustments to a normative, biomedical template of disease, which appears to be gendered" (2003: 1411). The study therefore enables a better understanding of gender as performance within the medical encounter, but it leaves the underlying problem – a largely patriarchal medical system – untouched. Addressing this limitation and bringing into focus the nexus between the micro-politics of the medical encounter and the macro-politics of health care reform remain a critical challenge for social researchers.

The Medical Encounter and the Reflexive Self: A Critique of Giddens and Beck

As noted above, Szasz and Hollender's third model of medical interaction – that of mutual participation – describes an ideal type wherein the patient is a full participant in the decision-making process. Lupton connects this model to an increasing sense of consumerism in Western societies, which in the case of the medical encounter, frames "doctors simply as suppliers of services, competing amongst themselves and seeking to maximize their income by selling professional expertise" (1997a: 373). Within this model, Lupton argues that "patients *qua* consumers are urged to refuse to accept paternalism or 'medical dominance' on the part of the doctor, to 'shop around', to actively evaluate doctors' services and to go elsewhere should the 'commodity' be found unsatisfactory" (1997a: 373). This clearly represents a fundamental shift in relations in comparison to the activity–passivity or guidance–cooperation models; it radically alters the distribution of power within the medical encounter and diminishes the standing of the medical profession. As identified earlier in this chapter, such a stance was criticized by doctors in Reid et al.'s study – with one doctor in particular lamenting the questioning of doctors' ability and skill, something they saw as a defining characteristic of an age of increased patient expectations.

To better understand this sense of consumerism within the medical encounter, Lupton draws insight from two of the most important social theorists of the past few decades: Anthony Giddens and Ulrich Beck.

More specifically, she connects a consumerist approach to health care with Giddens' notion of the "reflexive project of the self", which she notes "draws upon the assumption that in late modern Western societies individuals constantly seek to reflect upon the practices constituting the self and the body and to maximize, in an entrepreneurial fashion, the benefits for the self" (1997a: 374). Lupton goes on to write: "There is, therefore, a congruence between the notions of the 'consumerist' patient and the 'reflexive' actor. Both are understood as actively calculating, assessing and, if necessary, countering expert knowledge and autonomy with the objective of maximizing the value of services such as health care" (1997a: 374). She calls into question, however, how this concept applies to the lived experience of patients in the medical encounter.

Beck's notion of risk is also central to Lupton's argument. For example, she writes: "One of the major sociologists of reflexivity, Ulrich Beck, claims that doubt and uncertainty in relation to expert knowledges, or what he claims a 'new modesty' in relation to their claims, may be beneficial, engendering greater curiosity, [and] openness..." (1997a: 380). However, she is also critical of this concept, and how it applies to patients' experiences in the medical encounter, writing that "in the context of medical knowledge, ... such doubt is untenable for most people who are faced with chronic pain, a failing body, severe disability, or possible death" (1997a: 380). She therefore questions the extent to which Giddens' and Beck's notions of reflexivity and risk contribute in a meaningful way to understanding doctor–patient interaction. Or conversely, does the medical encounter shed light on a possible limitation to their theorizing?

Lupton's approach to examining these questions involved in-depth qualitative interviews with 60 lay people living in Sydney, Australia. The interviews focused on respondents' experiences with medical practitioners over their lifetime; that is, the interviews were not focused on any one particular medical encounter or specific doctor, but on the individuals' lifetime of experience interacting with medical professionals. Lupton's description of the interview data is reflective of an interpretivist epistemology:

> The interview data were treated as texts, in which narratives were recounted by the participants. Such data are treated not as "*the* truth" of people's thoughts and experiences but as "a situated truth" that inevitably is shaped through the particular context in which it is elicited. That is, it was assumed that as in any account of behaviour, experiences, thoughts and opinions, the nature of the interview context itself influences the data in ways that are impossible to eliminate from the research process.
>
> (1997a: 375, emphasis in original)

Like other studies of the medical encounter discussed above, Lupton's research places primary emphasis on the interviewee's perspective as a *lived experience*. As such, primacy is given to how respondents have made sense of their encounters with healthcare professionals; the analysis does not rest on any sort of "objective" record of conversation in a doctor's office.

According to Lupton, the respondents in the study held a general view that the status of the medical profession had diminished in recent times, that "doctors as a group are no longer necessarily viewed or unproblematically accepted as 'heroes in white coats' " (1997a: 379). Importantly, her analysis also points to areas of heterogeneity in terms of expectations of medical interaction. Some respondents were far more willing than others to declare support for a consumerist attitude towards health care. Lupton notes that older people were more deferential to the medical profession than younger people, and that university-educated professionals were likeliest to challenge the doctor's authority by seeking detailed information on their conditions.

This implies an important social patterning to patients' preferences with respect to medical encounters. Consider one of her respondent's comments (a 59-year-old male lawyer):

> You know, I am a professional too and I know how much better a job I can do for my client if I have a client who will challenge me and ask me questions and tell me what outcome the client is looking for, how the client likes to go about it and so on and so forth. And I can see the right 'patient/doctor', if you like, can produce a much better result and be more satisfying on both sides.
>
> (Lupton, 1997a: 379)

This respondent's preference for a mutual-participation model of medical encounter is clear; and interestingly, he supports this preference by comparing the doctor–patient relationship (notice that he refers to the patient–doctor relationship, the order perhaps implicitly reflecting the distribution of power) to that of the client–solicitor relationship.

Lupton notes that "people with lower levels of education were also somewhat more reverent when discussing doctors, often because of their respect for the years of education and arcane knowledge that doctors had acquired to become medical professionals" (1997a: 378). One respondent compares the decision-making power of doctors to that of umpires, suggesting that a clinical decision regarding treatment is their "call". The comments from another interview, this time with a 28-year-old salesman, are reflective of this position: "...they've done all their studies. Like if you've studied for so many years you're going to know a lot more than I'd know if I went to a doctor. Yes, I respect them" (1997a: 378). For Lupton, these differences are very important, for they reflect fundamentally different expectations of patients with respect to their health care. If we interpret her findings from the perspective of sociology *in* medicine, the fact that some groups may be more likely than others to adopt consumerist attitudes and *prefer* mutual-participation modes of interaction is something that an efficient health care system ought to accommodate. However, many respondents voiced a preference for a more traditional passive patient role. She concludes that in fact, people may pursue both consumerist and "passive patient" positions, depending on the situation. Efforts to improve doctor–patient communication need to consider ways of acknowledging this variability of preferences.

Lupton's findings are perhaps most important when interpreted from the perspective of sociology *of* medicine. From this perspective, findings from a health-related study feedback to the larger discipline; the focus is on the sociological implications of the results. Lupton uses the findings from her empirical study as a way of critiquing Giddens' notion of the reflexive project of the self and Beck's conceptualization of risk. Lupton notes that not all of her respondents preferred the mutual-participation model; that many actually accepted and called for a more traditional mode of interaction with their doctors. She writes

> ...the late modern notion of reflexivity presented by writers such as Giddens...tends to privilege, above all, a conscious and rational state, involving continual monitoring and criticism based on a challenging approach that is itself reliant on knowledge. The privileged representation of the patient as the reflexive, autonomous consumer simply fails to recognize the often unconscious, unarticulated dependence that patients have on doctors.
>
> (1997a: 380)

Furthermore,

> it may be difficult to adopt the ideal-type consumer subject position, if one is suffering from pain, distress and illness and the attendant emotions of fear and anxiety. Some people may respond to such situations in which loss of control seems imminent by adopting the consumerist position; others prefer to allow an authoritative figure to "take over". Both subject positions may be viewed as "rational" responses to a distressing and frightening situation.
>
> (1997a: 380)

A patient's experience, which as Lupton correctly points out may indeed be defined by pain, distress, fear, and anxiety, may therefore represent a failure of modernist notions of reflexivity.

Instead, Lupton suggests that the power dynamics embedded within the medical encounter (and such dynamics exist in all three of Szasz and Hollender's models) may be best interpreted from the perspective of Foucauldian social theory. Such an approach sees power as a strategy, and not as a property of one group over another. As we saw in Chapter 6, from a Foucauldian perspective, power does not merely *repress*, it *produces*. Lupton argues that a Foucauldian perspective on power relations within the medical encounter suggests that the current vogue in urging patients to behave consumeristically and doctors to relinquish their 'power' over patients and behave instead as patient advocates is somewhat ill-theorized. If power relations are central, and irreducible, to the construction of both doctor and patient, then it is senseless to call for a negation or absence of power in the medical encounter.

(1995: 159)

Lupton argues that her empirical findings support this interpretation, with many of her respondents calling for a professional yet detached, author-itative doctor. For Lupton, this represents a nuanced engagement with Foucault. She concludes

... calls to "democratize" professional/patient relations in the medical encounter ignore the ways in which power differentials and apparent "dehumanizing" may benefit both health care professional and patient. To behave in the professional role in the context of the medical workplace, it is incumbent upon both doctors and nurses to "objectify" the patient at some level. Patients will often accept this and even expect it in their quest to receive appropriate medical care.

(1995: 162)

In this light, our understanding of the medical encounter is dramatically deepened through an engagement with social theory.

A (Re)Turn to Parsons?

Lupton's use of the medical encounter as a way of critiquing Giddens and Beck reveals an important theoretical tension. As we saw above, Lupton argues that a hesitance by some patients to adopt a consumerist approach to healthcare (which for Lupton is congruent with Giddens' conceptual-ization of the reflexive project of the self) is a sign of the inadequacy of the concept; for Lupton, "late modernist notions of reflexivity as applied to issues of consumerism fail to recognize the complexity and changeable nature of the desires, emotions and needs that characterize the patient–doctor relationship" (1997a: 373). In its place, Lupton argues for a return to the psychoanalytic sociology that defines parts of Parsons' writings, not-ing that this would incorporate subjectivity into the analysis of the medical encounter and illness experience in a way that late modernist notions of reflexivity do not (Lupton, 1997c).

The psychoanalytic underpinnings of Parsons' sick role are not always emphasized in contemporary reviews of his work. This is almost certainly a reflection of the declining popularity of Freud and psychoanalytic theo-rizing among sociologists in the past few decades, as well as the difficulties associated with empirically testing psychoanalytic assertions. However, a close reading of Parsons indicates that Freud's concept of "transference" plays an important role in his understanding of the dynamics of the sick role and something that leads the medical encounter towards the activity–passivity model.

Transference, or the process by which a patient may project onto doctors attributes of the parental role, was critical for Parsons, who noted that "there is every reason to believe that it is always a factor in doctor–patient relationships, the more so the longer their duration and the greater the emotional importance of the health problem and hence relation to the physician" (Parsons, 1951: 453). Seen in this light, there is a strong force at play during the medical encounter, one that medical practitioners must deal with in a professional manner. At times, Parsons took this to an extreme in his writing, stating that illness may be thought of as a complete reversion to childhood (Lupton, 1997c). Such statements do little to account for the actions patients undertake to generate a more participatory mode of interaction with doctors, as seen in the studies by Werner and Malterud (2003) and Johannson et al. (1996), amongst others. However, the potential contribution of psychoanalytic theory for understanding the medical encounter is not diminished for Lupton, who argues that "if the assumptions of psychoanalytic theory are adopted, it may be argued that neither doctors nor patients adopt the social expectations of their roles without some degree of ambivalence and inner emotional conflict" (1997c: 577). Despite this potential, psychoanalytic theory remains largely divorced from medical sociological research, even though their synthesis was a hallmark of Parsons' work.

From the Micro-politics of the Medical Encounter to the Macro-politics of Inequities

Most of the studies discussed in this chapter have focused on the micro-politics of the medical encounter, perhaps at the neglect of underlying social, political, and economic forces. Indeed, a different picture emerges if we consider the medical encounter from the perspective of Marxist theory or political economy. Such a frame takes us away from an individualistic level of analysis and focuses on how medicine interacts with capitalism and patriarchy to "individualize patients' complaints rather than address the broader economic reasons for their ill-health" (Lupton, 1995: 158). In other words, such a perspective widens the nature of the "public issue" at hand.

This kind of approach is best exemplified in the writings of Howard Waitzkin, one of the leading researchers in this area. He has spent decades analysing medical discourse. His work has spanned the methodological spectrum, drawing from both quantitative and qualitative traditions. Like Lupton, Waitzkin has raised concern about the nature of discussion that occurs in doctors' offices. He writes

> Having been both a patient and a doctor, I hold a benign view of each party: I believe that patients seek assistance for concrete problems and that doctors genuinely want to help. Yet patient and doctor meet within a social context that is difficult and complicated. Medicine sometimes, but only rarely, involves a straightforward technical solution to a simple technical problem. One irony ... is that, by helping patients in little ways, doctors may reinforce the big problems that keep people distressed and unhappy.
>
> (1991: xiii)

His argument – one that is consistent with research on the social determinants of health – is that patients come to doctors with not only physical/mental ailments, but also with a social context. However, medical discourse is structured in such a way that, usually, contextual factors are ignored, at least at the primary care setting. For Waitzkin, doctor–patient encounters medicalize, "and thereby depoliticize, the social structural roots of personal suffering" (1983: 120). When contextual factors are given attention in a primary-care setting, this will usually involve a referral to specialist services, and the result there may often be a further medicalization of underlying social factors.

For Waitzkin, an important reason for why social context is ignored in the medical encounter is the

> doctor's own perception that their role is necessarily a limited one. From this viewpoint, a critical discussion of patients' social context goes beyond what doctors should reasonably be expected to do. Because many doctors recognize that delving into the social context of a patient can involve areas of life where they hold little special competence, they frequently feel more comfortable dealing with technical rather than contextual concerns.
>
> (1991: 5)

This implies a self-check on medicalization by doctors, which he would clearly support. However, Waitzkin's analyses of medical encounters suggest that whilst sometimes avoiding discussion of personal social context, doctor–patient interaction fundamentally serves as transmission of ideologic messages, with medicine *defining health as the ability to work* (recall that the sick role is only a temporary reprieve from social obligations). Consider the following comment from Waitzkin:

> [Doctors] regularly deal with patients' anger, anxiety, unhappiness, social isolation, loneliness, depression, and other emotional problems. Often these feelings derive in one way or another from patients' social circumstances, such as economic insecurity, racial or sexual discrimination, occupational stress, and

difficulties in family life. Such emotions, of course, are one basis of political outrage and organized resistance. How health professionals manage these sentiments is a question of great interest. One of medicine's most profound effects may be the defusing of socially caused distress.

(1983: 124)

His analysis of hundreds of medical encounters suggests that whilst most doctor–patient interactions conclude to the satisfaction of both parties, with the doctor truly caring for their patient and the patient appreciative of the doctor's concern, the social origins of the patient's troubles are almost always ignored. His analysis ultimately leads us to suggestions that do not readily fit expectations of medical care in Western societies; for instance,

When occupational toxins or stress produces physical symptoms...labor organizing is the preferred therapy, in addition to whatever physical treatment may be appropriate. For the tension headaches of tedious housework, sexual politics aim directly at social causes. Regarding alcoholism and other addictions that seek oblivion from the agonies of social life, social revolution may be the only remedy that even begins to correct the problem, as Engels and Allende noted long ago. These rather facile examples oversimplify the clinical issues; the point, however, is that a non-reformist doctor–patient relationship must foster long-term organized activism. Otherwise, the medical encounter dulls the pain of today, without hoping to extinguish it in the future.

(1983: 162)

Waitzkin's analysis, rooted as it is in political economy, emphasizes the material basis of health and illness; it steers us away from Fox's postmodern focus on discourse, from Parsons' focus on roles, and from Lupton's focus on psychoanalysis and brings us back to the social determinants of health.

Conclusion

As we have seen in previous chapters, work on contextual factors, or social determinants of health, has been the domain of research informed by political economy and conflict theory. Much of this work has focus on macro-level issues, primarily health inequities and health care reform. In many ways, analysis of the medical encounter pushes the boundaries of political economy theory, which has traditionally focused on issues of power and conflict at the macro, or structural, level of analysis (Lupton, 1995). A focus on an individual's experience in a clinical setting, and their interaction with medial professionals, has brought a more detailed understanding of health care to political economy. Qualitative studies, often including in-depth interviews with patients and sometimes with doctors, are contributing to the strengthening of the political economy perspective in health research. For Lupton, "in this perspective the medical encounter is not simply a self-contained microcosm, but the product of its encompassing political-economic framework in which struggle and inequality are central features" (1995: 158). This is an area of ongoing work in medical sociology, and much remains to be done to better integrate research on the micro-politics of the medical encounter with research on the macro-politics of health inequities.

8

Conclusion

Medical sociology is positioned at the cutting-edge of new developments in theory and method. At the same time, it has a remarkably interesting history, with ties to the pioneering work of Engels and Virchow in the nineteenth century and Parsons, Goffman, and Foucault in the twentieth century. And in the past 15 years, the writings of Wilkinson and Farmer – steeped in seemingly conflicting methodologies and epistemologies – have reminded us of the promise of this area of research: the ability to understand health in its context as a socially constructed and socially determined condition, at once a biomedical *and* a political issue. Medical sociologists using this frame are investigating some of the most important issues of our time: issues of inequality and discrimination, of gender and exploitation, of language, and of power.

In this book, I have tried to demonstrate that it is medical sociology's richness of theory and method that allows us to grasp how ill health – one of the most personal of all personal troubles – is inextricably intertwined with underlying public issues. This reflects the legacy of Mills' sociological imagination, a capacity of mind he believed central to understanding the complexity of the social world. This approach to social research acknowledges the often overwhelming power of large historical forces and social structure. At the same time, it upholds the argument that these must be understood with insight from lived experience. It is an open, contextual, question: how can and to what extent do situated actors and collectivities of actors have an impact upon these powerful forces?

Medical sociology achieves this by engaging in social research at the macro-, meso-, and micro-levels of investigation. For example, Chapter 4 tells of Wilkinson's income inequality hypothesis as primarily a story of social structure, of how the characteristics of the places where we live come to affect bodily processes – how unhealthy environments get "under the skin". In many ways, this is a direct continuation of the Durkheimian tradition of social research. It is primarily focused at the macro-level of investigation; the unit of analysis in many of the studies in this area is the nation-state or other geo-political entities such as provinces or counties. The primary epistemology at play here is positivism, albeit a sophisticated form of positivism that, whilst retaining a belief in elements of objectivity, measurement, and the testing of hypotheses, does not retain positivism's mandate of searching for laws of society. It also does not fall into the trap described by Mills as *abstracted empiricism* – because it does not focus on method at the expense of substance, nor gloss over history and politics. Whilst Wilkinson's work has not explicitly focused on class exploitation, ultimately, his model *is* about class differences; from Wilkinson's perspective, income inequality is a reflection of underlying (and unmeasured) class structures. In this respect, the work takes on elements of critical realism – that knowledge is not limited to that which can be directly measured, but also contains that which exists underneath the surface of observable phenomena and that can only be ascertained through theoretical reasoning. As this field of research continues to mature, more and more sociologists are paying attention not just to the health effects of income inequality, but also to the drivers of income inequality itself, which opens exciting areas of integration with political economy and a combination of positivist, interpretivist, and realist epistemologies.

Wilkinson's focus, and that of the neo-materialist theorists who have critiqued and refined his work in the past ten years, is clearly rooted at the macro-level of investigation. The primary concern is one of social structure and how it influences the health of individuals and populations. However, we also saw in Chapter 4 how Wilkinson's model incorporates insights from social psychology and health sciences regarding the pathways through which income inequality comes to affect the body. On this level, it actually has more to do with sociology's tradition of micro-level investigation, which is best exemplified in the work of Goffman – the interaction order in particular and symbolic interactionism in general. Theory, in this case, clearly guides the nature of empirical research, opening particular routes of questioning and directing our gaze to specific concepts and issues.

This book has been focused on three inter-related questions: To what extent has empirical research in medical sociology been informed or inspired by theoretical ideas? To what extent has empirical research been constrained by theoretical or epistemological assumptions? And has empirical research in medical sociology fed back to the larger discipline and led to the development or refinement of theoretical concepts? Merton's classic discussion of empirical research and social theory provides a frame for some concluding commentary on these questions, in relation to the substance of this book – health inequities, health care systems, medicalization, and the medical encounter.

The Bearing of Social Theory on Empirical Research in Medical Sociology

As we saw in Chapter 1, medical sociology's connection to social theory has been called into question, with Scambler (1987) and Johnson (1975) both decrying a certain theoretical impoverishment. For both, this was reflected in medical sociology's detachment from the larger discipline of sociology, and perhaps reflects a dominance of sociology *in* medicine over sociology *of* medicine in the early development of the field. In more recent years, researchers have begun to comment on medical sociology's increasing sophistication in terms of theoretical engagement, particularly in growing areas such as the sociology of the body and emotions, yet concern remains over the philosophical and theoretical foundation of contemporary research. Therefore, the following question becomes: has empirical work in this field been informed by theoretical developments in social science?

The works highlighted in this book, beginning with Engels' treatise on the condition of the working class in England and moving on to Parsons' classic conceptualization of the sick role and finally to contemporary research on the medical encounter, demonstrate that social theory has consistently and significantly guided empirical research in medical sociology. For example, it is conflict theory's overarching concern with social inequality that guides much of the contemporary empirical research on health inequities – from Wilkinson's income inequality hypothesis to the more qualitative, interpretivist research of Abraham, to the geographically broad and historically deep ethnography of Farmer.

As Chapter 5 discussed, theoretical constructs such as commodification and proletariatization have shaped empirical investigations of health care systems and health care reform. And Weberian ideal types have formed the basis of our understanding of health care systems around the world. In these ways, social theories originating in other areas of scholarship, including Esping-Andersen's work on welfare capitalism and Parsons' work on the sociology of the professions, have shaped strategies for empirical research.

Research on the medicalization of everyday life began as a theoretical endeavour in the writings of Zola and Illich. Over time, research on this concept has invoked both qualitative and quantitative research strategies whilst continuing to nurture important theoretical reflections, most recently in the writing of Ballard and Elston (2005). Interestingly, much of the research in this area eschews the structural functionalism that characterized Parsons' theorizing, yet continues to engage with his conceptualization of the sick role. The process of medicalization, from this perspective, is at least partly driven *by* patients' need to enter the sick role and receive its benefits.

Foucauldian notions of surveillance are also central to our thinking about medicalization; one can clearly see how rising rates of prescriptions for pharmaceutical products, including anti-depressants and anti-psychotics, may be seen as a product of an ever-expanding medical gaze and regime of control. It is this very concern over the expansion of the medical sphere guiding Lowenberg and Davis' (1994) qualitative study of holistic health practices featured in Chapter 6.

Chapter 7 examined the medical encounter – an area of medical sociology with a direct link to Goffman's groundbreaking work on the interaction order. It is Goffman's argument that it is the everyday interactions between people in socially defined contexts that should be the domain of sociology: that is where people define and negotiate roles, where power becomes manifest, and where people experience discrimination. From the perspective of health and illness, these interactions are critically important – for it is in this very interaction that society ("what is out there") influences our bodily systems, sometimes to pathological levels.

In all of these examples, social theory has influenced the design of empirical studies. Sometimes this has meant that particular variables are chosen for inclusion in the study, as has been the case with the concept of social capital in the income inequality–health literature. For Merton, "[t]he choice of concepts guiding the collection and analysis of data is, of course, crucial to empirical inquiry. [for] ... if concepts are selected such that no relationships between them obtain, the research will be sterile, no matter how meticulous the subsequent observations and inferences" (1967: 144). As we saw in Chapter 4, the choice of concepts/variables (and how to operationalize them) is rarely a straightforward affair – and in the case of the income inequality hypothesis, debate continues to unfold with respect to the operationalization of income inequality and health, social capital, and class.

The Bearing of Empirical Research on Social Theory in Medical Sociology

Merton argued that "empirical research goes far beyond the passive role of verifying and testing theory: it does more than confirm or refute hypotheses. Research plays an active role: it performs at least four major functions which shape the development of theory: It *initiates*, it *reformulates*, it *deflects* and it *clarifies* theory" (1957a: 103, emphasis in original). More specifically, he argued that empirical research initiated theory through serendipity – the process wherein observations reveal unexpected relationships, which can be used towards theory-building. He believed that empirical research also reformulates existing theory in the sense that repeated findings may exert pressure on theoretical frameworks, and that it deflects theory when new methods of empirical research open up new lines of theoretical elaboration. Finally, by debating operationalization strategies wherein complex, abstract concepts are defined in terms of measurable characteristics, empirical research may clarify the theoretical construct itself. Empirical research in medical sociology has fed back to social theory through all four of these mechanisms.

Indeed, it was empirical research, beginning with publications by Preston (1975) and Rodgers (1979) that enabled Wilkinson to develop his theory of the health effects of income inequality. Research on the income inequality hypothesis has subsequently contributed to the refinement of methodological tools, including advanced techniques of multi-level regression analysis (Goldstein, 2007; Merlo et al., 2006; Twisk, 2006). It has also contributed to the refinement of core sociological concepts like social capital. In doing so, it has extended debates regarding the definition of the construct, beginning with Durkheimian notions of social cohesion and moving on to Bourdieusian concepts of social capital as characteristics of individuals.

As we saw in Chapter 6, empirical studies on medicalization cast pressure on the early formulations of the concept with the result that it now is generally accepted as referring to a complex, multi-dimensional concept with contradictory tendencies. Empirical studies, including the qualitative work of Lowenberg and Davis, have played an important role in this development, which in Merton's terms is clearly a reformulation of theory. Many of the analyses and debates recorded here indicate that the lessons of empirical research regularly lead to a reformulation of theory, and also that these reformulations often involve the synthesis of concepts from different theoretical traditions. This indicates the wisdom of adopting an open, non-sectarian approach to theory and its application to empirical research.

Integrating Theory and Method

Although primarily focused on theory, methodology has also been a central concern of this book. Indeed, a key lesson from the material I have presented is that a nuanced understanding of the role of social theory in medical sociology can only be achieved if we also involve ourselves with methodological debates and bridge the deeply entrenched qualitative–quantitative divide. The subject matter of medical sociology is simply too complex and too varied for any one methodological or theoretical approach to hold a monopoly. Instead, a flexible approach, one that can, for example, integrate insights from Wilkinson *and* Farmer on health inequities, and one that can examine health care systems at an abstract level and through lived historical experience, is required. The medical encounter – perhaps the most "micro" of the issues examined in this book – similarly requires myriad methodological and theoretical approaches if we are to fully understand the nature of interaction that takes place between health care providers and patients and at the same time grasp the issues that shape their interaction. Clearly, the challenge of linking the micro-politics of the medical encounter with the macro-politics of health inequities and the social determinants of health requires multi-faceted research strategies. If medical sociology is to live up to the promise of social science, and if it is to be successful in presenting health in its context as a socially constructed and socially determined condition, further integration of theory and method, along with flexibility in terms of research design, is needed.

Notes

1 Introduction

1. Bryan Turner suggests that medical sociology has developed a much stronger connection to social theory since 1987, when in the first edition of *Medical Power and Social Knowledge* he noted that the field "did not have a sophisticated or systematic theoretical framework or tradition" (1995: 1).
2. Benton and Craib's (2001) excellent overview of the philosophy of the social sciences offers an insightful discussion of epistemological and ontological traditions.
3. The last few decades have seen increasing attention in methodological textbooks to mixed methods designs. However, the actual use of mixed methods – particularly a mixture of sophisticated statistical models and ethnographic research – remains rare indeed.

2 Foundations of Medical Sociology

1. Other notable writers working on the theme of the social production of disease include Edwin Chadwick, William Farr, and John Snow (Davey Smith et al., 2001; Hamlin, 1995; Whitehead, 2000).

3 Theoretical Contours

1. Freidson was careful to note that his typology was applicable to a "contemporary American middle class societal reaction" (1970a: 239); he was explicit about the limits to his analysis.

4 Health Inequities

1. Common mental disorders were assessed through a 12-item General Health Questionnaire (GHQ), which is included in the British Household Panel Survey. The GHQ is a screening instrument designed to identify psychopathology in primary care settings and in the community (Schmitz et al., 1999). It has been widely validated against structured clinical interviews. Importantly, the GHQ treats common mental disorders as a single dimension (Weich and Lewis, 1998; Weich et al., 2001) of "general dysphoria", which is understood to describe the two highly correlated conditions of anxiety and depression (Weich and Lewis, 1998).

2. This finding, however, was not robust to the choice of income inequality measure.
3. Recent research has also attempted to integrate international studies of Wilkinson's income inequality hypothesis with the framework of world-systems analysis (see Moore, 2006).

5   *Health Care Systems*

1. In particular, Poland et al. worry about a school of thought in population health research that emphasizes the health-producing properties of *overall* societal wealth; that perspective "emphasizes the generation of wealth without adequate attention to the social forces producing and reproducing poverty and inequality, and without adequate attention to either (re)distributive justice or environmental sustainability" (1998: 786).
2. Life expectancy at birth is the most commonly reported overall indicator of a country's population health. However, such aggregate indicators tell us nothing about how that life expectancy is shared within the population. In other words, aggregate indicators hide the inequities that exist within all societies (Braveman and Tarimo, 2002). One approach to overcoming this limitation is presented by De Maio, Linetzky, and Virgolini (2009) in our analysis of risk factors for non-communicable diseases in Argentina; in that paper, we use an "average/deprivation/inequality" framework to move away from relying on national averages and go on to identify the worst-off group as well as the difference between the worst-off and the best-off. Life expectancy at birth also does not tell us anything about the quality of life experienced by the population. To try to overcome this problem, some researchers have advocated the use of "Quality-Adjusted Life Years" (QALYs), which incorporate data on survival and quality of life. However, this notion has been criticized for being overly reductionist, and important methodological and conceptual problems associated with QALYs are yet to be solved (Busfield, 2000). The use of QALYs in social research, particularly medical sociology, is not as common as it is in economics.
3. Wiktorowicz (2006) notes that the systems of Germany and the Netherlands may also be considered privately financed (through sickness funds), although in both cases, government regulation and intervention ensures universal access to services.
4. For-profit delivery characterizes the US health care system, which delivers health care services via an assortment of bureaucratic arrangements, including Health Maintenance Organizations (HMOs), Preferred Provider Organizations (PPOs), and Independent Practice Organizations (IPAs) (Fry et al., 1997). For Caplan, whilst some of these organizations will be formally profit-seeking and others may not, they "all must seek to maximize their surplus income to survive .... the dictates of the market-place and the profit motive are important forces shaping American medicine" (1989: 1139).
5. Wiktorowicz's (2006) and Busfield's (2000) models share important features. They both outline varying mechanisms for financing and delivering health care services, and both highlight the important distinction between systems

based on public or private mechanisms. Both serve as ideal types with which we can compare the specifics of any given country's health care system.

6. Opposition by the medical profession to the CHA was intense. The Canadian Medical Association tried to block the legislation, and filed a lawsuit against the federal government, arguing that the act infringed upon doctors' rights to establish private contracts with patients (Clarke, 2004).

7. The one exception to this is Cuba, a country famous for its universal health care system and impressive levels of population health (Spiegel, 2006; Spiegel and Yassi, 2004; Waitzkin et al., 2001).

8. Muntaner et al. note that

> [i]n most Latin American countries, including Venezuela, health care became less a human right guaranteed by the state and more a commodity acquired in the marketplace.
>
> (2006a: 803)

9. Venezuelan *barrios* are akin to Brazilian *favelas* and Argentine *villas* (see Auyero, 2000) – shantytowns where housing construction is of particularly poor quality and where access to electricity is limited. In Venezuela, *barrios* encircle the capital city of Caracas.

10. Much of the government's new social programs are organized as "Social Missions". In the case of health, *Misión Barrio Adentro* (Inside the Barrio) is a program that has for the first time helped Venezuelans to implement the principle of universal access to health care.

11. Much has been written about the militaristic overtones of the Chávez government; he is, after all, a man raised in military service and much of his power derives from his popularity amongst the armed forces (indeed, if it was not for the support of low-ranking military personnel, the coup d'état of 2002 would likely have succeeded). But it should be noted that at first, "the Caracas Military Hospital was the only one that accepted referrals from *Barrio Adentro* for either diagnostic or hospital care" (PAHO, 2006: 28). In this case, it was the armed forces, and not the medical profession, that sought to ensure the public's access to needed health care services.

6 *Medicalization*

1. Interestingly, Lowenberg and Davis prefer to describe "medicalization" as a term, rather than a concept: "We speak of it as a term rather than a concept because there is as yet little scholarly consensus on exactly what attributes are to be subsumed under it or on the analytical weights to be accorded them" (1994: 582).

Further Reading

Bryan Turner's *Medical Power and Social Knowledge* (1995) and Uta Gerhardt's *Ideas About Illness* (1989) provide rigorous overviews of medical sociology and highlight with admirable clarity the theoretical foundations of the field. Turner's book is also a particularly engaging account of the philosophy of Michel Foucault. Eliot Freidson's *Profession of Medicine* (1970a) and Ivan Illich's *Limits to Medicine* (1976) are classics that warrant serious attention from readers. Freidson's book is perhaps the best way of approaching Talcott Parsons' work on the sick role, and Illich's compelling analysis of iatrogenic medicine offers an intellectually broadening account of the role of health care in industrialized societies. Lisa Berkman and Ichiro Kawachi's edited collection *Social Epidemiology* (2000) offers an important account of recent developments in epidemiology. Mel Bartley's excellent introductory text *Health Inequality* (2004) is also a very useful account of both theoretical concepts and empirical methodologies that shape the field. Richard Wilkinson's influential income inequality hypothesis was best developed in *Unhealthy Societies* (1996) and *Mind the Gap* (2000); Ichiro Kawachi and Bruce Kennedy's *The Health of Nations* (2002) provides an accessible treatment of that model. The psychosocial perspective is perhaps best described in Sir Michael Marmot's (2004) *Status Syndrome*. Vicente Navarro and Carles Muntaner provide an excellent collection of papers under the title of *Political and Economic Determinants of Population Health and Well-Being* (2004); the book is an indispensable source for readers interested in more examples from the neo-materialist perspective. Although I have found all of Paul Farmer's books inspiring, I would recommend *Infections and Inequalities* (1999) as perhaps his strongest statement on the nature of structural violence and health. Farmer's life and career are depicted in fascinating detail in Tracy Kidder's (2004) *Mountains Beyond Mountains*. Laurie Abraham's (1993) *Mama Might Be Better Off Dead* and Ronald Angel, Laura Lein, and Jane Henrici's (2006) *Poor Families in America's Health Care Crisis* provide rich and moving testimony of the hardship associated with a population's insecure access to healthcare. Joan Busfield's (2000) *Health and Health Care in Modern Britain* provides not only a useful framework comparing health care systems, but also insightful commentary on the causes of illness. Readers interested in medicalization would be well advised to consult Conrad's (2007) *The Medicalization of Society*, along with the recent analysis of the pharmaceutical industry by Ray Moynihan and Alan Cassels in *Selling Sickness* (2005). Howard Waitzkin's (1991) *The Politics of Medical Encounters* is the classic source on doctor–patient communication and provides thought-provoking passages on the quantitative–qualitative divide. Finally, a great deal of theoretical and empirical research in medical sociology is only published in journals, perhaps most notably in *Social Science & Medicine*, *Journal of Health and Social Behavior*, and *Sociology of Health & Illness*, along with the *British Medical Journal*, the *American Journal of Public Health*, and more recently, *Social Theory & Health*. It is in these publications that debates have been particularly constructive.

References

Abel, C., and Lloyd-Sherlock, P. (2000). Health policy in Latin America: themes, trends and challenges. In P. Lloyd-Sherlock (Ed.), *Healthcare Reform & Poverty in Latin America*. London: ILAS.

Abraham, J. (2005). Making regulation responsive to commercial interests: streamlining drug industry watchdogs. *British Medical Journal, 325*(7373), 1164–1169.

Abraham, L. K. (1993). *Mama Might Be Better Off Dead: The Failure of Health Care in Urban America*. Chicago: University of Chicago Press.

Abramson, J. (2004). *Overdo$ed America*. New York: HarperCollins.

Acheson, D. (1998). *Independent Inquiry into Inequalities in Health*. London: Stationery Office.

Adler, N. E., Boyce, T., Chesney, M. A., Cohen, S., Folkman, S., Kahn, R. L., and Syme, S. L. (1994). Socioeconomic status and health: the challenge of the gradient. *American Psychologist, 49*(1), 15–24.

Ainsworth-Vaughn, N. (1995). Claiming power in the medical encounter: the whirlpool discourse. *Qualitative Health Research, 5*(3), 270–291.

Ali, J., McDermott, S., and Gravel, R. G. (2004). Recent research on immigrant health from Statistics Canada's population surveys. *Canadian Journal of Public Health, 95*(3), 9–13.

Allende, S. (1939). *La Realidad Médio-Social Chilena [The Chilean Medico-Social Reality]*. Santiago: Ministro de Salubridad.

Angel, R. J., Lein, L., and Henrici, J. (2006). *Poor Families in America's Health Care Crisis*. New York: Cambridge University Press.

Arluke, A., Kennedy, L., and Kessler, R. C. (1979). Reexamining the sick-role concept: an empirical assessment. *Journal of Health and Social Behavior, 20*(March), 30–36.

Armstrong, D. (1995). The rise of surveillance medicine. *Sociology of Health & Illness, 17*(3), 393–404.

Aronson, J. (2002). When I use a word ... medicalization. *British Medical Journal, 324*(13 April), 904.

Atkinson, A. B. (1975). *The Economics of Inequality*. Oxford: Claredon Press.

Auyero, J. (2000). The hyper-shantytown: neo-liberal violence(s) in the Argentine slum. *Ethnography, 1*(1), 93–116.

Backlund, E., Sorlie, P. D., and Johnson, N. J. (1996). The shape of the relationship between income and mortality in the United States: evidence from the National Longitudinal Mortality Study. *Annals of Epidemiology, 6*(1), 12–20; discussion 21–12.

Badgley, R. F., and Wolfe, S. (1965). Medical care and conflict in Saskatchewan. *Milbank Memorial Fund Quarterly, 43*(4), 463–479.

Ballard, K., and Elston, M. (2005). Medicalisation: a multi-dimensional concept. *Social Theory & Health*, 3, 228–241.

Baltzan, M. (2002). The lockout of '62. *Canadian Medical Association Journal*, 167(9), 987–988; author reply 968–989.

Barker, K. K. (1998). A ship upon a stormy sea: the medicalization of pregnancy. *Social Science & Medicine*, 47(8), 1067–1076.

Bartley, M. (2003). Health inequality and societal institutions. *Social Theory & Health*, 1(2), 108–129.

Bartley, M. (2004). *Health Inequality: An Introduction to Theories, Concepts and Methods*. Cambridge: Polity.

Beck, C. A., Patten, S. B., Williams, J. V., Wang, J. L., Currie, S. R., Maxwell, C. J., and El-Guebaly, N. (2005). Antidepressant utilization in Canada. *Social Psychiatry and Psychiatric Epidemiology*, 40(10), 799–807.

Becker, H. S. (1963). *Outsiders: Studies in the Sociology of Deviance*. New York: Free Press.

Becker, H., Greer, B., Hughes, E., and Strauss, A. (1961). *Boys in White: Student Culture in Medical School*. Chicago: University of Chicago Press.

Becker, M. H., Drachman, R. H., and Kirscht, J. P. (1974). A new approach to explaining sick-role behavior in low-income populations. *American Journal of Public Health*, 64(3), 205–216.

Beckfield, J. (2004). Does income inequality harm health? New cross-national evidence. *Journal of Health and Social Behavior*, 45(3), 231–248.

Beiser, M. (2005). The health of immigrants and refugees in Canada. *Canadian Journal of Public Health*, 96 Suppl. 2, S30–44.

Benton, T., and Craib, I. (2001). *Philosophy of Social Science: The Philosophical Foundations of Social Thought*. New York: Palgrave Macmillan.

Berger, P. L. (1963). *Invitation to Sociology: A Humanistic Perspective*. New York: Doubleday.

Berkanovic, E. (1972). Lay conceptions of the sick role. *Social Forces*, 51(1), 53–64.

Berkman, L. (1995). The role of social relations in health promotion. *Psychosomatic Medicine*, 57, 245–254.

Berkman, L. F., and Kawachi, I. (Eds) (2000). *Social Epidemiology*. New York: Oxford University Press.

Berry, A. (Ed.) (1998). *Poverty, Economic Reform, and Income Distribution in Latin America*. Boulder: Lynne Rienner Publishers, Inc.

Bezruchka, S. (2006). Epidemiological approaches. In D. Raphael, T. Bryant, and M. Rioux (Eds), *Staying Alive: Critical Perspectives on Health, Illness, and Health Care*. Toronto: Canadian Scholars' Press.

Blakely, T., Atkinson, J., and O'Dea, D. (2003). No association of income inequality with adult mortality within New Zealand: a multi-level study of 1.4 million 25–64 year olds. *Journal of Epidemiology & Community Health*, 57(4), 279–284.

Blakely, T., Kennedy, B. P., and Kawachi, I. (2001). Socioeconomic inequality in voting participation and self rated health. *American Journal of Public Health*, 91(1), 99–104.

Blakely, T., Lochner, K., and Kawachi, I. (2002). Metropolitan area income inequality and self rated health – a multilevel study. *Social Science & Medicine*, 54, 65–77.

Blech, J. (2006). *Inventing Disease and Pushing Pills: Pharmaceutical Companies and the Medicalisation of Normal Life*. New York: Routledge.

Blendon, R. J., Schoen, C., DesRoches, C. M., Osborn, R., Scoles, K. L., and Zapert, K. (2002). Inequities in health care: A five-country survey. *Health Affairs, 21*(3), 182–191.

Bloom, S. W. (2002). *The Word as Scalpel: A History of Medical Sociology*. New York: Oxford University Press.

Bourdieu, P. (1984). *Distinction: A Social Critique of the Judgement of Taste*. London: Routledge.

Bourgeault, I. L. (2006). Sociological perspectives on health and health care. In D. Raphael, T. Bryant, and M. Rioux (Eds), *Staying Alive: Critical Perspectives on Health, Illness, and Health Care* (pp. 35–57). Toronto: Canadian Scholars' Press Inc.

Braveman, P., and Tarimo, E. (2002). Social inequalities in health within countries: not only an issue for affluent nations. *Social Science & Medicine, 54*, 1621–1635.

Broom, D. H., and Woodward, R. V. (1996). Medicalisation reconsidered: toward a collaborative approach to care. *Sociology of Health & Illness, 18*(3), 357–378.

Brown, P., Mayer, B., Zavestoski, S., Luebke, T., Mandelbaum, J., and McCormick, S. (2003). The health politics of asthma: environmental justice and collective illness experience in the United States. *Social Science & Medicine, 57*(3), 453–464.

Brown, T. M., and Fee, E. (2006). Rudolf Carl Virchow: medical scientist, social reformer, role model. *American Journal of Public Health, 96*(12), 2104–2105.

Brownlee, S. (2007). *Overtreated: Why Too Much Medicine is Making Us Sicker and Poorer*. New York: Bloomsbury.

Brunner, E. (1997). Stress and the biology of inequality. *British Medical Journal, 314*(7092), 1472–1476.

Bryman, A., and Teevan, J. L. (2005). *Social Research Methods: Canadian Edition*. Don Mills: Oxford University Press.

Busfield, J. (1996). *Men, Women and Madness: Understanding Gender and Mental Disorder*. London: Macmillan Press Ltd.

Busfield, J. (2000). *Health and Health Care in Modern Britain*. New York: Oxford University Press Inc.

Busfield, J. (2003). Globalization and the pharmaceutical industry revisited. *International Journal of Health Services, 33*(3), 581–605.

Busfield, J. (2004). Mental health problems, psychotropic drug technologies and risk. *Health, Risk & Society, 6*(4), 361–375.

Busfield, J. (2006a). Medicalisation. In J. Scott (Ed.), *Sociology: The Key Concepts* (pp. 99–103). London: Routledge.

Busfield, J. (2006b). Pills, power, people: sociogical understandings of the pharmaceutical industry. *Sociology, 40*(2), 297–314.

Buunk, B. P., Gibbons, F. X., and Reis-Bergan, M. (1997). Social comparison in health and illness: a historical overview. In B. P. Buunk and F. X. Gibbons (Eds), *Health, Coping, and Well-Being: Perspectives from Social Comparison Theory* (pp. 1–24). London: LEA.

Campano, F., and Salvatore, D. (2006). *Income Distribution*. Oxford: Oxford University Press.

Campion, P., and Langdon, M. (2004). Achieving multiple topic shifts in primary care medical consultations: a conversation analysis study in UK general practice. *Sociology of Health & Illness, 26*(1), 81–101.

Cantarero, D., Pascual, M., and Sarabia, J. M. (2005). Effects of income inequality on population health: new evidence from the European Community Household Panel. *Applied Economics, 37,* 87–91.

Caplan, R. L. (1989). The commodification of American health care. *Social Science & Medicine, 28*(11), 1139–1148.

Caplan, R. L., Light, D. W., and Daniels, N. (1999). Benchmarks of fairness: a moral framework for assessing equity. *International Journal of Health Services, 29*(4), 853–869.

Castro, A. (2005). Privatization and democracy in Venezuela. *Latin American Perspectives, 32*(3), 112–124.

Chafetz, M. E., and Demone, H. W. (1962). *Alcoholism and Society.* New York: Oxford University Press.

Champernowne, D. G., and Cowell, F. A. (1998). *Economic Inequality and Income Distribution.* Cambridge: Cambridge University Press.

Charmaz, K. (1983). The grounded theory method: an explication and interpretation. In R. M. Emerson (Ed.), *Contemporary Field Research* (pp. 335–354). Boston: Little, Brown and Company.

Choudhry, N. K., Stelfox, H. T., and Detsky, A. S. (2002). Relationships between authors of clinical practice guidelines and the pharmaceutical industry. *Journal of the American Medical Association, 287*(5), 612–617.

Clarke, J. N. (2004). *Health, Illness, and Medicine in Canada* (4th edn). Don Mills: Oxford.

Coambs, R. B., Jarry, J. L., and De Maio, F. G. (1999). Prescription medication noncompliance: the hidden nemesis. *Issues in Lipidology, 2*(3), 3, 15.

Coburn, D. (1988). Canadian medicine: dominance or proletarianization? *Milbank Memorial Fund Quarterly, 66 Suppl. 2,* 92–116.

Coburn, D. (2000). Income inequality, social cohesion and the health status of populations: the role of neo-liberalism. *Social Science & Medicine, 51*(1), 135–146.

Coburn, D. (2001a). Health, health care, and neo-liberalism. In P. Armstrong, H. Armstrong, and D. Coburn (Eds), *Unhealthy Times: Political Economy Perspectives on Health and Care in Canada* (pp. 45–65). Don Mills: Oxford University Press.

Coburn, D. (2001b). Reasons to be sceptical of Marmot and Wilkinson. *British Medical Journal,* Electronic letter published on 30 July 2001: http://bmj.bmjjournals.com/cgi/eletters/2322/7296/1233#15812

Coburn, D. (2004). Beyond the income inequality hypothesis: class, neo-liberalism, and health inequalities. *Social Science & Medicine, 58*(1), 41–56.

Coburn, D. (2006). Health and health care: a political economy perspective. In D. Raphael, T. Bryant and M. Rioux (Eds), *Staying Alive: Critical Perspectives on Health, Illness, and Health Care* (pp. 59–81). Toronto: Canadian Scholars' Press.

Coburn, D., Torrance, G. M., and Kaufert, J. M. (1983). Medical dominance in Canada in historical perspective: the rise and fall of medicine? *International Journal of Health Services, 13*(3), 407–432.

Cockerham, W. C. (1999). *Health and Social Change in Russia and Eastern Europe.* London: Routledge.

Cockerham, W. C. (2001). Medical sociology and sociological theory. In W. C. Cockerham (Ed.), *The Blackwell Companion to Medical Sociology* (pp. 3–22). Oxford: Blackwell.

Cockerham, W. C. (2004). *Medical Sociology* (9th edn). Upper Saddle River, NJ: Prentice Hall.

Cockerham, W. C. (2007). A note on the fate of postmodern theory and its failure to meet basic requirements for success in medical sociology. *Social Theory & Health*, 5(4), 285–296.

Coleman, J. S. (1990). *Foundations of Social Theory*. Cambridge, MA: Harvard University Press.

Colvin, P. (1994). Canadian health care financing. In K. Lee (Ed.), *Health Care Systems in Canada & the United Kingdom: Can They Deliver?* Keele: Ryburn Publishing.

Conrad, P. (1975). The discovery of hyperkinesis: notes on the medicalization of deviant behavior. *Social Problems*, 23(1), 12–21.

Conrad, P. (1985). The meaning of medications: another look at compliance. *Social Science & Medicine*, 20(1), 29–37.

Conrad, P. (1992). Medicalization and social control. *Annual Review of Sociology*, 18, 209–232.

Conrad, P. (2005). The shifting engines of medicalization. *Journal of Health and Social Behavior*, 46(1), 3–14.

Conrad, P. (2007). *The Medicalization of Society*. Baltimore: Johns Hopkins University Press.

Conrad, P., and Schneider, J. W. (1980). *Deviance and Medicalization: From Badness to Sickness*. St. Louis: C.V. Mosby Company.

Cooper, H., Arber, S., Fee, L., and Ginn, J. (1999). *The Influence of Social Support and Social Capital on Health*. London: Health Education Authority.

Corbin, J., and Strauss, A. (1990). Grounded theory research: procedures, canons, and evaluative criteria. *Qualitative Sociology*, 13(1), 3–21.

Cowell, F. A. (1995). *Measuring Inequality* (2nd edn). London: Prentice Hall.

Cowley, S., Mitcheson, J., and Houston, A. M. (2004). Structuring health needs assessments: the medicalisation of health visiting. *Sociology of Health & Illness*, 26(5), 503–526.

Craib, I. (1997). *Classical Social Theory*. Oxford: Oxford University Press.

Crossley, T. F., and Kennedy, S. (2002). The reliability of self-assessed health status. *Journal of Health Economics*, 21, 643–658.

Cwikel, J. (2006). *Social Epidemiology: Strategies for Public Health Activism*. New York: Columbia University Press.

Daly, M. C., Duncan, G. J., Kaplan, G. A., and Lynch, J. W. (1998). Macro-to-micro links in the relation between income inequality and mortality. *Milbank Memorial Fund Quarterly*, 76(3), 315–339.

Daniels, N., Kennedy, B., and Kawachi, I. (2000). *Is Inequality Bad for Our Health?* Boston: Beacon Press.

Davey Smith, G., Dorling, D., and Shaw, M. (Eds) (2001). *Poverty, Inequality and Health in Britain: 1800–2000*. Bristol: The Policy Press.

Davis, K., and Moore, W. E. (1945). Some principles of stratification. *American Sociological Review*, 10(2), 242–249.

De Maio, F. G. (2007a). Health inequalities in Argentina: patterns, contradictions and implications. *Health Sociology Review, 16*(3–4), 279–291.

De Maio, F. G. (2007b). Income inequality measures. *Journal of Epidemiology & Community Health, 61*(10), 849–852.

De Maio, F. G. (2008a). Ecological analysis of the health effects of income inequality in Argentina. *Public Health, 122*(5), 487–496.

De Maio, F. G. (2008b). Epidemiology. In Y. Zhang (Ed.), *Encyclopedia of Global Health*. Thousand Oaks, CA: Sage.

De Maio, F. G., and Kemp, E. (2009). The deterioration of health status among immigrants to Canada. *Global Public Health* (Global Public Health, forthcoming in 2009, DOI: 10.1080/17441690902942480.

De Maio, F. G., Corber, S. J., and Joffres, M. (2008). Towards a social analysis of risk factors for chronic diseases in Latin America. *LASA Forum, 39*(2), 10–13.

De Maio, F. G., Linetzky, B., and Virgolini, M. (2009). An average/deprivation/inequality (ADI) analysis of chronic disease outcomes and risk factors in Argentina. *Population Health Metrics, 7*(8).

De Vogli, R., Mistry, R., Gnesotto, R., and Cornia, G. A. (2005). Has the relation between income inequality and life expectancy disappeared? Evidence from Italy and top industrialised countries. *Journal of Epidemiology & Community Health, 59*(2), 158–162.

Dean, M. (2000). Implementing the 1998 Canadian asthma guidelines. *Canadian Family Physician, 46*(4), 761–762, 768–770.

Deaton, A. (2002). The convoluted story of international studies of inequality and health. *International Journal of Epidemiology, 31*(3), 546–549.

Diener, E., and Fujita, F. (1997). Social comparisons and subjective well-being. In B. P. Buunk, and F. X. Gibbons (Eds), *Health, Coping, and Well-Being* (pp. 329–358). London: LEA.

Diez-Roux, A. V. (2001). Investigating neighborhood and area effects on health. *American Journal of Public Health, 91*(11), 1783–1789.

Diez-Roux, A. V. (2002). A glossary for multilevel analysis. *Journal of Epidemiology & Community Health, 56*(8), 588–594.

Doyal, L. (1995). *What Makes Women Sick: Gender and the Political Economy of Health*. New Brunswick, NJ: Rutgers University Press.

Doyal, L. (2003). Sex and gender: the challenges for epidemiologists. *International Journal of Health Services, 33*(3), 569–579.

Durkheim, E. (1951 [1897]). *Suicide* (J. Spaulding and G. Simpson, Trans.). New York: The Free Press.

Durkheim, E. (1984 [1893]). *The Division of Labour in Society* (W. D. Halls, Trans.). London: Macmillan.

Ecob, R., and Davey Smith, G. (1999). Income and health: what is the nature of the relationship? *Social Science & Medicine, 48*(5), 693–705.

Eisenberg, L. (1986). Rudolf Virchow: the physician as politician. *Medicine and War, 2*(4), 243–250.

Ellison, G. T. H. (1999). Does income inequality influence the shape of the curvilinear relation between individual income and health? *Journal of Epidemiology & Community Health, 53*, 664.

Ellison, G. T. H. (2002). Letting the Gini out of the bottle? Challenges facing the relative income hypothesis. *Social Science & Medicine, 54*(4), 561–576.

Ellner, S. (2001). The radical potential of Chavismo in Venezuela: the first year and a half in power. *Latin American Perspectives, 28*(5), 5–32.

Elstad, J. I. (1998). The psycho-social perspective on social inequalities in health. *Sociology of Health & Illness, 20*(5), 598–618.

Engels, F. (1987 [1845]). *The Condition of the Working Class in England*. Harmondsworth: Penguin Books.

Esping-Andersen, G. (1990). *The Three Worlds of Welfare Capitalism*. Oxford: Polity Press.

Farmer, P. (1992). *AIDS and Accusation: Haiti and the Geography of Blame*. Berkeley: University of California Press.

Farmer, P. (1999). *Infections and Inequalities: The Modern Plagues*. Berkeley: University of California Press.

Farmer, P. (2003). *Pathologies of Power: Health, Human Rights, and the New War on the Poor*. Berkeley: University of California Press.

Feldberg, G., and Vipond, R. (2006). Cracks in the foundation: the origins and development of the Canadian and American health care systems. In D. Raphael, T. Bryant, and M. Rioux (Eds), *Staying Alive: Critical Perspectives on Health, Illness, and Health Care*. Toronto: University of Toronto Press.

Forbes, A., and Wainwright, S. P. (2001). On the methodological, theoretical and philosophical context of health inequalities research: a critique. *Social Science & Medicine, 53*(6), 801–816.

Foucault, M. (1965). *Madness and Civilization: A History of Insanity in the Age of Reason*. New York: Pantheon Books.

Foucault, M. (1977). *Discipline and Punish: The Birth of the Prison*. New York: Random House, Inc.

Foucault, M. (1984). Truth and power. In P. Rabinow (Ed.), *The Foucault Reader* (pp. 51–75). New York: Pantheon.

Foucault, M. (1994 [1973]). *The Birth of the Clinic: An Archaeology of Medical Perception* (A. Smith, Trans.). New York: Vintage.

Fox, N. J. (1993). Discourse, organisation and the surgical ward round. *Sociology of Health & Illness, 15*(1), 16–42.

Fox, N. J., Ward, K. J., and O'Rourke, A. J. (2005). The "expert patient": empowerment or medical dominance? the case of weight loss, pharmaceutical drugs and the Internet. *Social Science & Medicine, 60*(6), 1299–1309.

Freidson, E. (1970a). *Profession of Medicine: A Study of the Sociology of Applied Knowledge*. New York: Dodd, Mead.

Freidson, E. (1970b). *Professional Dominance*. Chicago: Aldine.

Freund, P. (2006). Socially constructed embodiment: neurohormonal connections as resources for theorizing about health inequalities. *Social Theory & Health, 4*, 85–108.

Frohlich, K. L., Corin, E., and Potvin, L. (2001). A theoretical proposal for the relationship between context and disease. *Sociology of Health & Illness, 23*(6), 776–797.

Fry, J., Light, D., Rodnick, J., and Orton, P. (1997). The US health care system. In P. Conrad (Ed.), *The Sociology of Health and Illness: Critical Perspectives* (5th ed., pp. 206–214). New York: St. Martin's Press.

Fukuyama, F. (1995). *Trust*. New York: Free Press.

Gafni, A., Charles, C., and Whelan, T. (1998). The physician-patient encounter: the physician as a perfect agent for the patient versus the informed treatment decision-making model. *Social Science & Medicine, 47*(3), 347–354.

Gallagher, E. B. (1976). Lines of reconstruction and extension in the Parsonian sociology of illness. *Social Science & Medicine, 10*(5), 207–218.

Gecas, V. (1989). The social psychology of self-efficacy. *Annual Review of Sociology, 15,* 291–316.

Gerhardt, U. (1979). The Parsonian paradigm and the identity of medical sociology. *Sociological Review, 27*(2), 235–251.

Gerhardt, U. (1989). *Ideas About Illness: An Intellectual and Political History of Medical Sociology.* New York: New York University Press.

Gillis, M., Perkins, D. H., Roemer, M., and Snodgrass, D. R. (1996). *Economics of Development.* New York: W.W. Norton & Company.

Glaser, B., and Strauss, B. (1967). *The Discovery of Grounded Theory.* Chicago: Aldine.

Glenton, C. (2003). Chronic back pain sufferers – striving for the sick role. *Social Science & Medicine, 57*(11), 2243–2252.

Goffman, E. (1961). *Asylums.* New York: Anchor.

Goffman, E. (1963). *Stigma.* Englewood Cliffs, NJ: Prentice-Hall.

Goffman, E. (1983). The interaction order. *American Sociological Review, 48*(1), 1–17.

Goldstein, H. (2007). Becoming familiar with multilevel modeling. *Significance, 4*(3), 133–135.

Gordis, L. (1970). "Medicalized" sex. *New England Journal of Medicine, 283*(13), 709–710.

Gordon, C. (2003). *Dead on Arrival: The Politics of Health Care in Twentieth-Century America.* Princeton: Princeton University Press.

Gott, R. (2005). *Hugo Chávez and the Bolivarian Revolution.* London: Verso.

Gravelle, H. (1998). How much of the relation between population mortality and unequal distribution of income is a statistical artefact? *British Medical Journal, 316*(7128), 382–385.

Guevara, A. (2005). *Chávez, Venezuela & the New Latin America.* New York: Ocean Press.

Gwatkin, D. R. (2000). Health inequalities and the health of the poor: what do we know? What can we do? *Bulletin of the World Health Organization, 78*(1), 3–18.

Hajdu, S. I. (2005). A note from history: Rudolph Virchow, pathologist, armed revolutionist, politician, and anthropologist. *Annals of Clinical & Laboratory Science, 35*(2), 203–205.

Hamilton, J. C., Deemer, H. N., and Janata, J. W. (2003). Feeling bad but looking good: sick role features that lead to favorable interpersonal judgments. *Journal of Social and Clinical Psychology, 22*(2), 253–274.

Hamlin, C. (1995). Could you starve to death in England in 1839? The Chadwick-Farr controversy and the loss of the "social" in public health. *American Journal of Public Health, 85*(6), 856–866.

Hankivsky, O. (2006). Beijing and beyond: women's health and gender-based analysis in Canada. *International Journal of Health Services, 36*(2), 377–400.

Harling, G., Ehrlich, R., and Myer, L. (2008). The social epidemiology of tuberculosis in South Africa: a multilevel analysis. *Social Science & Medicine, 66*(2), 492–505.

Harnecker, M. (2005). *Understanding the Venezuelan Revolution*. New York: Monthly Review Press.

Haug, M. R. (1988). A re-examination of the hypothesis of physician deprofessionalization. *Milbank Memorial Fund Quarterly, 66 Suppl. 2*, 48–56.

Health Canada. (2001). *Canada Health Act Overview*. Ottawa, Ontario, Canada: Health Canada.

Healy, D. (2003). *Let Them Eat Prozac*. Toronto: J. Lorimer & Company.

Hershberg, E., and Rosen, F. (Eds) (2006). *Latin America After Neoliberalism: Turning the Tide in the 21st Century*. New York: New Press.

Hey, J. D., and Lambert, P. J. (1980). Relative deprivation and the Gini coefficient: comment. *Quarterly Journal of Economics, 95*(3), 567–573.

Himmelstein, D. U. (2002). (Book Review) Navarro, V. (Ed.) The political economy of social inequalities: consequences for health and quality of life. *Social Science & Medicine, 55*(7), 1279–1280.

Hoffman, K., and Centeno, M. A. (2003). The lopsided continent: inequality in Latin America. *Annual Review of Sociology, 29*, 363–390.

Hollander, I. (2006). Viagra's rise above women's health issues: an analysis of the social and political influences on drug approvals in the United States and Japan. *Social Science & Medicine, 62*(3), 683–693.

Holton, R. (2008). Talcott Parsons. In R. Stones (Ed.), *Key Sociological Thinkers* (pp. 136–150). Basingstoke: Palgrave Macmillan.

Horowitz, A. (2002). *Creating Mental Illness*. Chicago: University of Chicago Press.

Hou, F., and Myles, J. (2005). Neighbourhood inequality, neighbourhood affluence and population health. *Social Science & Medicine, 60*, 1557–1569.

Hyman, I. (2004). Setting the stage: reviewing current knowledge on the health of Canadian immigrants. *Canadian Journal of Public Health, 95*(3), 1–8.

Idler, E. L., and Benyamini, Y. (1997). Self rated health and mortality: a review of twenty-seven community studies. *Journal of Health and Social Behavior, 38*(1), 21–37.

Illich, I. (1971). *Deschooling Society*. New York: Harper & Row.

Illich, I. (1976). *Limits to Medicine*. London: Marion Boyars Publishers.

Iriart, C., Merhy, E. E., and Waitzkin, H. (2001). Managed care in Latin America: The new common sense in health policy reform. *Social Science & Medicine, 52*, 1243–1253.

Jellinek, E. M. (1960). *The Disease Concept of Alcoholism*. Highland Park, NJ: Hillhouse.

Johansson, E. E., Hamberg, K., Lindgren, G., and Westman, G. (1996). "I've been crying my way" – qualitative analysis of a group of female patients' consultation experiences. *Family Practice, 13*(6), 498–503.

Johnson, M. L. (1975). Medical sociology and sociological theory. *Social Science & Medicine, 9*, 227–232.

Jones, R. W., and Herlich, A. R. (1972). Treatment of alcoholism by physicians in private practice: a national survey. *Quarterly Journal of Studies on Alcohol, 33*, 117–131.

Kahn, R. S., Wise, P. H., Kennedy, B. P., and Kawachi, I. (2000). State income inequality, household income, and maternal mental and physical health: cross sectional national survey. *British Medical Journal, 321*(7272), 1311–1315.

Kaplan, G., and Baron-Epel, O. (2003). What lies behind the subjective evaluation of health status? *Social Science & Medicine, 56*(8), 1669–1676.

Kassebaum, G. G., and Baumann, B. O. (1965). Dimensions of the sick role in chronic illness. *Journal of Health and Human Behavior, 6*(1), 16–27.

Kawachi, I. (2002). Social epidemiology. *Social Science & Medicine, 54*(12), 1739–1741.

Kawachi, I., and Kennedy, B. P. (1997). Health and social cohesion: why care about income inequality? *British Medical Journal, 314*(7086), 1037–1040.

Kawachi, I., and Kennedy, B. P. (2002). *The Health of Nations: Why Inequality is Harmful to Your Health*. New York: The Free Press.

Kawachi, I., Kennedy, B. P., and Glass, R. (1999a). Social capital and self rated health: a contextual analysis. *American Journal of Public Health, 89*(8), 1187–1193.

Kawachi, I., Kennedy, B. P., and Wilkinson, R. G. (1999c). *The Society and Population Health Reader: Income Inequality and Health* (Vol. 1). New York: The New Press.

Kawachi, I., Kennedy, B. P., Gupta, V., and Prothrow-Stith, D. (1999b). Women's status and the health of women and men: a view from the States. *Social Science & Medicine, 48*(1), 21–32.

Kawachi, I., Kennedy, B. P., Lochner, K., and Prothrow-Stith, D. (1997). Social capital, income inequality, and mortality. *American Journal of Public Health, 87*(9), 1491–1498.

Kennedy, B. P., Kawachi, I., Glass, R., and Prothrow-Stith, D. (1998). Income distribution, socioeconomic status, and self rated health in the United States: multilevel analysis. *British Medical Journal, 317*(7163), 917–921.

Kesey, K. (1962). *One Flew Over the Cuckoo's Nest*. New York City: Penguin Books.

Kidder, T. (2004). *Mountains Beyond Mountains*. New York: Random House.

Kim, J. Y., Millen, J. V., Irwin, A., and Gershman, J. (Eds) (2000). *Dying for Growth: Global Inequality and the Health of the Poor*. Monroe: Common Courage Press.

Kjaergard, L. L., and Als-Nielsen, B. (2002). Association between competing interests and authors' conclusions: epidemiological study of randomised clinical trials published in the BMJ. *British Medical Journal, 325*(7358), 249.

Kopec, J. A., Williams, J. I., To, T., and Austin, P. C. (2001). Cross-cultural comparisons of health status in Canada using the Health Utilities Index. *Ethn Health, 6*(1), 41–50.

Kovner, A. R., and Knickman, J. R. (Eds) (2005). *Health Care Delivery in the United States*. New York: Springer.

Krahn, M. D., Berka, C., Langlois, P., and Detsky, A. S. (1996). Direct and indirect costs of asthma in Canada, 1990. *Canadian Medical Association Journal, 154*(6), 821–831.

Krieger, N. (2005). Embodiment: a conceptual glossary for epidemiology. *Journal of Epidemiology & Community Health, 59*(5), 350–355.

Krieger, N., and Davey Smith, G. (2004). "Bodies count," and body counts: social epidemiology and embodying inequality. *Epidemiologic Reviews, 26*, 92–103.

Kuschner, W. G. (2000). Asthma guidelines: an assessment of physician understanding and practice. *American Journal of Respiratory Critical Care Medicine, 161*(1), 330.

Lagerløv, P., Leseth, A., and Matheson, I. (1998). The doctor-patient relationship and the management of asthma. *Social Science & Medicine, 47*(1), 85–91.

Laroche, M. (2000). Health status and health services utilization of Canada's immigrant and non-immigrant populations. *Canadian Public Policy, 26*(1), 51–75.

LeClere, F. B., and Soobader, M. J. (2000). The effect of income inequality on the health of selected US demographic groups. *American Journal of Public Health, 90*(12), 1892–1897.

Lesley, D. (1995). *What Makes Women Sick: Gender and the Political Economy of Health*. New Brunswick, NJ: Rutgers University Press.

Lexchin, J., Bero, L. A., Djulbegovic, B., and Clark, O. (2003). Pharmaceutical industry sponsorship and research outcome and quality: systematic review. *British Medical Journal, 326*(7400), 1167–1170.

Link, B. G., and Phelan, J. (1995). Social conditions as fundamental causes of disease. *Journal of Health and Social Behavior, 35*(Extra issue), 80–94.

Lochner, K., Kawachi, I., and Kennedy, B. P. (1999). Social capital: a guide to its measurement. *Health and Place, 5*(4), 259–270.

Lochner, K., Pamuk, E., Makuc, D., Kennedy, B. P., and Kawachi, I. (2001). State-level income inequality and individual mortality risk: a prospective, multilevel study. *American Journal of Public Health, 91*(3), 385–391.

Lofland, J., and Lofland, L. H. (1995). *Analyzing Social Settings: A Guide to Qualitative Observation and Analysis*. Belmont, CA: University of California.

Lopez, R. (2004). Income inequality and self rated health in US metropolitan areas: a multi-level analysis. *Social Science & Medicine, 59*(12), 2409–2419.

Lowenberg, J. S., and Davis, F. (1994). Beyond medicalisation – demedicalisation: the case of holistic health. *Sociology of Health & Illness, 16*(5), 579–599.

Lukes, S. (1985). *Emile Durkheim: His Life and Work*. Stanford: Stanford University Press.

Lupton, D. (1995). Perspectives on power, communication and the medical encounter: implications for nursing theory and practice. *Nursing Inquiry, 2*(3), 157–163.

Lupton, D. (1997a). Consumerism, reflexivity and the medical encounter. *Social Science & Medicine, 45*(3), 373–381.

Lupton, D. (1997b). Foucault and the medicalisation critique. In R. Bunton (Ed.), *Foucault, Health and Medicine* (pp. 94–110). Florence, KY: Routledge.

Lupton, D. (1997c). Psychoanalytic sociology and the medical encounter: Parsons and beyond. *Sociology of Health & Illness, 19*(5), 561–579.

Lupton, D. (2003). *Medicine as Culture: Illness, Disease, and the Body in Western Societies*. Thousand Oaks, CA: Sage.

Lynch, J., Davey Smith, G., Harper, S., Hillermeier, M., Ross, N., Kaplan, G. A., and Wolfson, M. (2004). Is income inequality a determinant of population health? Part 1: A systematic review. *Milbank Memorial Fund Quarterly, 82*(1), 5–99.

Lynch, J., Davey Smith, G., Kaplan, G. A., and House, J. S. (2000). Income inequality and mortality: importance to health of individual income, psychosocial environment, or material conditions. *British Medical Journal, 320*(7243), 1200–1204.

Macintyre, S., Ellaway, A., and Cummins, S. (2002). Place effects on health: how can we conceptualise, operationalise and measure them? *Social Science & Medicine, 55*, 125–139.

Mackenbach, J. P. (2009). Politics is nothing but medicine at a larger scale: reflections on public health's biggest idea. *Journal of Epidemiology & Community Health, 63*(3), 181–185.

Manners, S. (2006). *Super Pills: The Prescriptions Drugs We Love to Take.* Vancouver: Raincoast Books.

Marchildon, G. P. (2006). *Health Systems in Transition: Canada.* Toronto: University of Toronto Press.

Marmot, M. (2004). *Status Syndrome.* London: Bloomsbury.

Marmot, M., and Siegrist, J. (2004). Health inequities and the psychosocial environment. *Social Science & Medicine, 58*, 1461.

Marmot, M., and Wilkinson, R. G. (2001). Psychosocial and material pathways in the relation between income and health: a response to Lynch et al. *British Medical Journal, 322*(7296), 1233–1236.

Marmot, M., and Wilkinson, R. G. (Eds) (2006). *Social Determinants of Health* (2nd edn). Oxford: Oxford University Press.

Mathers, C. D., and Loncar, D. (2006). Projections of global mortality and burden of disease from 2002 to 2030. *PLoS Medicine, 3*(11), e442.

May, C., Allison, G., Chapple, A., Chew-Graham, C., Dixon, C., Gask, L., Graham, R., Rogers, A., and Roland, M. (2004). Framing the doctor-patient relationship in chronic illness: a comparative study of general practitioners' accounts. *Sociology of Health & Illness, 26*(2), 135–158.

Maya, M., and Lander, L. (2005). Popular protest in Venezuela: Novelties and continuities. *Latin American Perspectives, 32*(2), 92–108.

McCord, C., and Freeman, H. P. (1990). Excess mortality in Harlem. *New England Journal of Medicine, 322*(3), 173–177.

McCrea, F. B. (1983). The politics of menopause: the "discovery" of a deficiency disease. *Social Problems, 31*(1), 111–123.

McDonald, J. T., and Kennedy, S. (2005). Is migration to Canada associated with unhealthy weight gain? Overweight and obesity among Canada's immigrants. *Social Science & Medicine, 61*(12), 2469–2481.

McDonough, P., Duncan, G. J., Williams, D., and House, J. (1997). Income dynamics and adult mortality in the United States, 1972 through 1989. *American Journal of Public Health, 87*(9), 1476–1483.

McEwen, B. S. (1998). Protective and damaging effects of stress mediators. *New England Journal of Medicine, 338*(3), 171–179.

McKeown, T. (1976). *The Modern Rise of Population.* London: Edward Arnold.

McKinlay, J. B., and McKinlay, S. M. (1977). The questionable contribution of medical measures to the decline of mortality in the United States in the twentieth century. *Milbank Memorial Fund Quarterly – Health and Society, 55*(3), 405–428.

Mechanic, D. (1989). Medical sociology: some tensions among theory, method, and substance. *Journal of Health and Social Behavior, 30*, 147–160.

Merlo, J., Chaix, B., Ohlsson, H., Beckman, A., Johnell, K., Hjerpe, P., Rastam, L., and Larsen, K. (2006). A brief conceptual tutorial of multilevel analysis in social epidemiology: using measures of clustering in multilevel logistic regression to investigate contextual phenomena. *Journal of Epidemiology & Community Health, 60*(4), 290–297.

Merton, R. K. (1957a). *Social Theory and Social Structure* (Revised and enlarged edn). New York: The Free Press.

Merton, R. K. (1957b). *Student-Physician: Introductory Studies in the Sociology of Medical Education*. Harvard, MA: Harvard University Press.

Merton, R. K. (1967). *On Theoretical Sociology: Five Essays, Old and New*. New York: The Free Press.

Merton, R. K. (1968). *Social Theory and Social Structure*. New York: The Free Press.

Mhatre, S. L., and Deber, R. B. (1992). From equal access to health care to equitable access to health: a review of Canadian provincial health commissions and reports. *International Journal of Health Services, 22*(4), 645–668.

Mills, C. W. (1959). *The Sociological Imagination*. New York: Oxford University Press.

Mintzes, B., Barer, M. L., Kravitz, R. L., Kazanjian, A., Bassett, K., Lexchin, J., Evans, R. G., Pan, R., and Marion, S. A. (2002). Influence of direct to consumer pharmaceutical advertising and patients' requests on prescribing decisions: two site cross sectional survey. *British Medical Journal, 324*(7332), 278–279.

Mohan, J., Barnard, S., Jones, K., and Twigg, L. (2004). *Social capital, place and health: creating, validating and applying small-area indicators in the modelling of health outcomes*. London: Health Development Agency.

Moore, S. (2006). Peripherality, income inequality, and life expectancy: revisiting the income inequality hypothesis. *International Journal of Epidemiology, 35*(3), 623–632.

Moynihan, R. (2003a). The making of a disease: female sexual dysfunction. *British Medical Journal, 326*(7379), 45–47.

Moynihan, R. (2003b). Who pays for the pizza? Redefining the relationships between doctors and drug companies. 1: entanglement. *British Medical Journal, 326*(7400), 1189–1192.

Moynihan, R. (2003c). Who pays for the pizza? Redefining the relationships between doctors and drug companies. 2: Disentanglement. *British Medical Journal, 326*(7400), 1193–1196.

Moynihan, R., and Cassels, A. (2005). *Selling Sickness: How the World's Biggest Pharmaceutical Companies are Turning Us All Into Patients*. Vancouver: Greystone Books.

Mullings, L., and Schulz, A. J. (2006). Intersectionality and health: an introduction. In A. J. Schulz and L. Mullings (Eds), *Gender, Race, Class, & Health* (pp. 3–17). San Francisco: Jossey-Bass.

Muntaner, C. (2003). Social epidemiology and class: a critique of Richard Wilkinson's income inequality and social capital hypothesis. *Rethinking Marxism, 15*(4), 551–564.

Muntaner, C., and Lynch, J. (1999). Income inequality, social cohesion, and class relations: a critique of Wilkinson's neo-Durkheimian research program. *International Journal of Health Services, 29*(1), 59–81.

Muntaner, C., and Lynch, J. (2002). Social capital, class gender and race conflict, and population health: an essay review of Bowling Alone's implication for social epidemiology. *International Journal of Epidemiology, 31*, 261–267.

Muntaner, C., Lynch, J., and Davey Smith, G. (2000). Social capital and the third way in public health. *Critical Public Health, 60*(2), 107–124.

Muntaner, C., Lynch, J., and Davey Smith, G. (2001). Social capital, disorganized communities, and the third way: understanding the retreat from structural inequalities in epidemiology and public health. *International Journal of Health Services, 31*(2), 213–237.

Muntaner, C., Lynch, J., and Oates, G. L. (1999). The social class determinants of income inequality and social cohesion. *International Journal of Health Services, 29*(4), 699–732.

Muntaner, C., Salazar, R. M., Benach, J., and Armada, F. (2006a). Venezuela's Barrio Adentro: an alternative to neoliberalism in health care. *International Journal of Health Services, 36*(4), 803–811.

Muntaner, C., Salazar, R. M., Rueda, S., and Armada, F. (2006b). Challenging the neoliberal trend: the Venezuelan health care reform alternative. *Canadian Journal of Public Health, 97*(6), 119–24.

Navarro, V. (1975). The industrialization of fetishism or the fetishism of industrialization: a critique of Ivan Illich. *Social Science & Medicine, 9*(7), 351–363.

Navarro, V. (1976). *Medicine Under Capitalism*. New York: Prodist.

Navarro, V. (1986). *Crisis, Health and Medicine: A Social Critique*. New York: Tavistock Publications.

Navarro, V. (1988). Professional dominance or proletarianization?: neither. *Milbank Memorial Fund Quarterly, 66 Suppl. 2*, 57–75.

Navarro, V. (1999). Health and equity in the world in the era of "globalization". *International Journal of Health Services, 29*(2), 215–226.

Navarro, V. (2002a). A critique of social capital. *International Journal of Health Services, 32*(3), 423–432.

Navarro, V. (Ed.) (2002b). *The Political Economy of Social Inequalities: Consequences for Health and Quality of Life*. Amityville, NY: Baywood.

Navarro, V., and Muntaner, C. (Eds) (2004). Political and Economic Determinants of Population Health and Well-Being: Controversies and Developments. Amityville, NY: Baywood.

Navarro, V., and Shi, L. (2002). The political context of social inequalities and health. In V. Navarro (Ed.), *The Political Economy of Social Inequalities: Consequences for Health and Quality of Life* (pp. 403–418). Amityville, NY: Baywood.

Navarro, V., Borrell, C., Benach, J., Muntaner, C., Quiroga, A., Rodríguez-Sanz, M., Vergés, N., Gumá, J., and Pasarín, M. (2003). The importance of the political and the social in explaining mortality differentials among the countries of the OECD, 1950–1998. *International Journal of Health Services, 33*(3), 419–494.

Naylor, C. D. (1986). *Private Practice, Public Payment: Canadian Medicine and the Politics of Health Insurance, 1911–1966*. Kingston and Montreal: McGill-Queen's University Press.

Nettleton, S. (2006). "I just want permission to be ill": towards a sociology of medically unexplained symptoms. *Social Science & Medicine, 62*(5), 1167–1178.

Neufeld, V., MacLeod, S., Tugwell, P., Zakus, D., and Zarowsky, C. (2001). The rich-poor gap in global health research: challenges for Canada. *Canadian Medical Association Journal, 164*(8), 1158–1159.

Norris, J. L. (1976). Alcoholics anonymous and other self-help groups. In R. Tarter and A. Sugerman (Eds), *Alcoholism*. Reading, MA: Addison-Wesley.

Oakley, A. (1984). *The Captured Womb: A History of the Medical Care of Pregnant Women*. Oxford: Oxford University Press.

Olsen, W., and Morgan, J. (2005). A critical epistemology of analytical statistics: addressing the sceptical realist. *Journal of the Theory of Social Behaviour, 35*(3), 255–284.

Ostry, A. S. (2006). *Change and Continuity in Canada's Health Care System*. Ottawa: CHA Press.

Oxman-Martinez, J., Abdool, S. N., and Loiselle-Leonard, M. (2000). Immigration, women and health in Canada. *Canadian Journal of Public Health, 91*(5), 394–395.

PAHO. (2006). *Mission Barrio Adentro: The Right to Health and Social Inclusion in Venezuela*. Caracas: PAHO.

Parsons, T. (1951). *The Social System*. London: Routledge & Kegan Paul Ltd.

Payer, L. (1992). *Disease-Mongers: How Doctors, Drug Companies, and Insurers are Making You Feel Sick*. New York: Wiley & Sons.

Pearce, N. (2000). The ecological fallacy strikes back. *Journal of Epidemiology & Community Health, 54*(5), 326–327.

Pearlin, L. I., Menaghan, E. G., Lieberman, M. A., and Mullan, J. T. (1981). The stress process. *Journal of Health and Social Behavior, 22*, 337–356.

Pérez, C. E. (2002). Health status and health behaviour among immigrants. Supplement to *Health Reports*, volume 13. Ottawa: Statistics Canada.

Pevalin, D. (2003). More to social capital than Putnam. *British Journal of Psychiatry, 182*, 172–173.

Pevalin, D., and Rose, D. (2003). *Social Capital for Health: Investigating the Links Between Social Capital and Health Using the British Household Panel Survey*. Colchester: Institute for Social and Economic Research, University of Essex.

Pflanz, M., and Rohde, J. J. (1970). Illness: deviant behaviour or conformity. *Social Science & Medicine, 4*(6), 645–653.

Pickett, K. E., Kelly, S., Brunner, E., Lobstein, T., and Wilkinson, R. G. (2005). Wider income gaps, wider waistbands? An ecological study of obesity and income inequality. *Journal of Epidemiology & Community Health, 59*(8), 670–674.

Pidgeon, N. (1996). Grounded theory: theoretical background. In J. T. Richardson (Ed.), *Handbook of Qualitative Research Methods for Psychology and the Social Sciences* (pp. 75–85). Leicester: British Psychological Society.

Plummer, K. (Ed.) (1991). *Symbolic Interactionism*. Aldershot: Edward Elgar.

Poland, B., Coburn, D., Robertson, A., and Eakin, J. (1998). Wealth, equity and health care: a critique of a "population health" perspective on the determinants of health. Critical Social Science Group. *Social Science & Medicine, 46*(7), 785–798.

Pope, W. (1998). Emile Durkheim. In R. Stones (Ed.), *Key Sociological Thinkers* (pp. 46–58). New York: Palgrave Macmillan.

Porpora, D. V. (2001). Do realists run regressions? In J. López and G. Potter (Eds), *After Postmodernism: An Introduction to Critical Realism* (pp. 260–266). London: Athlone Press.

Porter, S. (1993). Critical realist ethnography: the case of racism and professionalism in a medical setting. *Sociology, 27*, 591–609.

Portes, A. (1998). Social capital: its origins and applications in modern sociology. *Annual Review of Sociology, 24*, 1–24.

Preston, S. H. (1975). The changing relation between mortality and level of economic development. *Population Studies, 29*, 213–248.

Putnam, R. D. (2000). *Bowling Alone: The Collapse and Revival of American Community*. New York: Touchstone.

Quick, A., and Wilkinson, R. G. (1991). *Income and Health*. London: Socialist Health Association.

Rafalovich, A. (2005). Exploring clinician uncertainty in the diagnosis and treatment of attention deficit hyperactivity disorder. *Sociology of Health & Illness, 27*(3), 305–323.

Ram, R. (2005). Income inequality, poverty, and population health: evidence from recent data for the United States. *Social Science & Medicine, 61*(12), 2568–2576.

Ramiréz, C. (2005). Venezuela's Bolivarian revolution: who are the Chavistas? *Latin American Perspectives, 32*(3), 79–97.

Ramiréz, C. (2006). Venezuela in the eye of the hurricane: landing an analysis of the Bolivarian revolution. *Journal of Latin American Anthropology, 11*(1), 173–186.

Raphael, D. (Ed.) (2004). *Social Determinants of Health: Canadian Perspectives*. Toronto: Canadian Scholars' Press.

Raphael, D., Bryant, T., and Rioux, M. (Eds) (2006). *Staying Alive: Critical Perspectives on Health, Illness, and Health Care*. Toronto: Canadian Scholars' Press.

Rather, L. J. (Ed.) (1985). *Collected Essays on Public Health and Epidemiology: Rudolf Virchow* (Vols 1 and 2). Canton, MA: Science History Publications.

Rawls, J. (1972). *A Theory of Justice*. Oxford: Oxford University Press.

Reese, D. M. (1988). Fundamentals – Rudolf Virchow and modern medicine. *Western Journal of Medicine, 169*, 105–108.

Reid, S., Whooley, D., Crayford, T., and Hotopf, M. (2001). Medically unexplained symptoms – GPs' attitudes towards their cause and management. *Family Practice, 18*(5), 519–523.

Robinson, W. S. (1950). Ecological correlations and the behavior of individuals. *American Sociological Review, 15*, 351–357.

Rodgers, G. B. (1979). Income and inequality as determinants of mortality: an international cross-section analysis. *Population Studies, 33*, 343–351.

Roghmann, M. C., and Sexton, M. (1999). Adherence to asthma guidelines in general practices. *Journal of Asthma, 36*(4), 381–387.

Romanow, R. J. (2002). *Building on Values: The Future of Health Care in Canada*. Ottawa: Commission on the Future of Health Care in Canada.

Ross, N. A., Wolfson, M. C., Dunn, J. R., Berthelot, J. M., Kaplan, G. A., and Lynch, J. W. (2000). Relation between income inequality and mortality in Canada and in the United States: cross sectional assessment using census data and vital statistics. *British Medical Journal, 320*(7239), 898–902.

Ruggie, M. (1999). The US, UK and Canada: Convergence or divergent reform practices? In D. Drache and T. Sullivan (Eds), *Health Reform: Public Success, Private Failure* (pp. 127–144). New York: Routledge.

Runciman, W. G. (1966). *Relative Deprivation and Social Justice: A Study of Attitudes to Social Inequality in Twentieth-Century England*. London: Routledge & Kegan Paul.

Samson, C. (Ed.) (1999). *Health Studies: A Critical and Cross-Cultural Reader*. Oxford: Blackwell Publishers, Ltd.

Saracci, R. (2009). Virchow, a model for epidemiologists. *Journal of Epidemiology & Community Health, 63*(3), 185.

Scambler, G. (2001). Critical realism, sociology and health inequalities: social class as a generative mechanism and its media of enactment. *Journal of Critical Realism, 4*, 35–42.

Scambler, G. (2004). Re-framing stigma: felt and enacted stigma and challenges to the sociology of chronic and disabling conditions. *Social Theory & Health, 2*(1), 29–46.

Scambler, G. (Ed.) (1987). *Sociological Theory and Medical Sociology*. London: Tavistock.

Scheff, T. J. (1966). *Being Mentally Ill: A Sociological Theory*. Chicago: Aldine Publishing Company.

Scheff, T. J. (Ed.) (1975). *Labeling Madness*. Englewood Cliffs, NJ: Prentice-Hall.

Schmitz, N., Kruse, J., Heckrath, C., Alberti, L., and Tress, W. (1999). Diagnosing mental disorders in primary care: the General Health Questionnaire (GHQ) and the Symptom Check List (SCL-90-R) as screening instruments. *Social Psychiatry and Psychiatric Epidemiology, 34*(7), 360–366.

Schneider, J. W., and Conrad, P. (1983). *Having Epilepsy: The Experience and Control of Illness*. Philadelphia: Temple University Press.

Schneider, J. W. (1978). Deviant drinking as disease: alcoholism as a social accomplishment. *Social Problems, 25*, 361–372.

Schulz, A. J., and Mullings, L. (Eds) (2006). *Gender, Race, Class, & Health: Intersectional Approaches*. San Francisco: Jossey-Bass.

Segall, A. (1976a). The sick role concept: understanding illness behavior. *Journal of Health and Social Behavior, 17*(June), 163–170.

Segall, A. (1976b). Sociocultural variation in sick role behavioral expectations. *Social Science & Medicine, 10*(1), 47–51.

Sen, A. (1999). *Development as Freedom*. Oxford: Oxford University Press.

Sen, A. (2002). Health: perception versus observation. *British Medical Journal, 324*(7342), 860–861.

Senn, S. (1998). Mortality and distribution of income: societies with narrower income distributions are healthier. *British Medical Journal, 316*(23), 1611.

Shaw, J., and Baker, M. (2004). "Expert patient" – dream or nightmare? *British Medical Journal, 328*(7442), 723–724.

Shi, L., and Starfield, B. (2000). Primary care, income inequality, and self rated health in the United States: a mixed-level analysis. *International Journal of Health Services, 30*(3), 541–555.

Shibuya, K., Hashimoto, H., and Yano, E. (2002). Individual income, income distribution, and self rated health in Japan: cross sectional analysis of nationally representative sample. *British Medical Journal, 324*(7328), 16.

Shilling, C. (2002). Culture, the "sick role" and the consumption of health. *British Journal of Sociology, 53*(4), 621–638.

Sica, A. (2008). Robert K. Merton. In R. Stones (Ed.), *Key Sociological Thinkers* (pp. 151–167). Basingstoke: Palgrave Macmillan.

Singh, G. K., and Siahpush, M. (2006). Widening socioeconomic inequalities in US life expectancy, 1980–2000. *International Journal of Epidemiology, 35*(4), 969–979.

Singh-Manoux, A., Clarke, P., and Marmot, M. (2002). Multiple measures of socio-economic position and psychosocial health: proximal and distal measures. *International Journal of Epidemiology, 31*(6), 1192–1199; discussion 1199–1200.

Smith, J. P. (1999). Healthy bodies and thick wallets: the dual relation between health and economic status. *Journal of Economic Perspectives, 12*(2), 145–166.

Soobader, M. J., and LeClere, F. B. (1999). Aggregation and the measurement of income inequality: effects on morbidity. *Social Science & Medicine, 48*(6), 733–744.

Spiegel, J. M. (2006). Commentary: daring to learn from a good example and break the "Cuba taboo". *International Journal of Epidemiology, 35*(4), 825–826.

Spiegel, J. M., and Yassi, A. (2004). Lessons from the margins of globalization: appreciating the Cuban health paradox. *Journal of Public Health Policy, 25*(1), 85–110.

Stocker, K., Waitzkin, H., and Iriart, C. (1999). The exportation of managed care to Latin America. *New England Journal of Medicine, 340*(14), 1131–1136.

Stones, R. (Ed.) (2008). *Key Sociological Thinkers* (2nd edn). Basingstoke: Palgrave Macmillan.

Straus, R. (1957). The nature and status of medical sociology. *American Sociological Review, 22*(2), 200–204.

Subramanian, S. V., and Kawachi, I. (2003). In defence of the income inequality hypothesis. *International Journal of Epidemiology, 32*, 1037–1040.

Subramanian, S. V., and Kawachi, I. (2004). Income inequality and health: what have we learned so far? *Epidemiologic Reviews, 26*, 78–91.

Subramanian, S. V., Blakely, T., and Kawachi, I. (2003a). Income inequality as a public health concern: where do we stand? Commentary on "Is exposure to income inequality a public health concern?" *Health Services Research, 38*(1 Pt 1), 153–167.

Subramanian, S. V., Delgado, I., Jadue, L., Vega, J., and Kawachi, I. (2003b). Income inequality and health: multilevel analysis of Chilean communities. *Journal of Epidemiology & Community Health, 57*(11), 844–848.

Subramanian, S. V., Kawachi, I., and Kennedy, B. P. (2001). Does the state you live in make a difference? Multilevel analysis of self rated health in the US. *Social Science & Medicine, 53*(1), 9–19.

Suissa, S., Ernst, P., Benayoun, S., Baltzan, M., and Cai, B. (2000). Low-dose inhaled corticosteroids and the prevention of death from asthma. *New England Journal of Medicine, 343*(5), 332–336.

Syliva, R., and Danopoulos, C. P. (2003). The Chávez phenomenon: political change in Venezuela. *Third World Quarterly, 24*(1), 63–76.

Szasz, J., and Hollender, M. (1956). The basic models of the doctor-patient relationship. *Archives of Internal Medicine, 97*, 585–592.

Szasz, T. (1961). *The Myth of Mental Illness: Foundations of a Theory of Personal Conduct*. New York: Harper & Row.

Tajer, D. (2003). Latin American social medicine: roots, development during the 1990s, and current challenges. *American Journal of Public Health, 93*(12), 2023–2027.

Takahashi, I., Matsuzaka, M., Umeda, T., Yamai, K., Nishimura, M., Danjo, K., Kogawa, T., Saito, K., Sato, M., and Nakaji, S. (2008). Differences in the influence of tobacco smoking on lung cancer between Japan and the USA: possible explanations for the "smoking paradox" in Japan. *Public Health, 122*(9), 891–896.

Taylor, R., and Rieger, A. (1984). Rudolf Virchow on the typhus epidemic in Upper Silesia: an introduction and translation. *Sociology of Health & Illness, 6*(2), 201–217.

Thompson, S. L., and Salmon, J. W. (2006). Strikes by physicians: a historical perspective toward an ethical evaluation. *International Journal of Health Services, 36*(2), 331–354.

Tomes, N. (2007). Patient empowerment and the dilemmas of late-modern medicalisation. *Lancet, 369*(9562), 698–700.

Townsend, P. (1979). *Poverty in the United Kingdom: A Survey of Household Resources and Standards of Living*. London: Allen Lane.

Townsend, P. (Ed.) (1970). *The Concept of Poverty*. London: Heinemann.

Townsend, P., and Davidson, N. (Eds) (1982). *Inequalities in Health: The Black Report*. Harmondsworth: Penguin Books.

Trigg, R. (1985). *Understanding Social Science: A Philosophical Introduction to the Social Sciences* Oxford: Blackwell.

Tumin, M. M. (1953). Some principles of stratification: a critical analysis. *American Sociological Review, 18*, 387–397.

Turner, B. (2003). Social capital, inequality and health: the Durkheimian revival. *Social Theory & Health, 1*(1), 4–20.

Turner, B. S. (1995). *Medical Power and Social Knowledge* (2nd edn). London: Sage.

Turner, J. H. (1991). *The Structure of Sociological Theory*. Belmont, CA: Wadsworth.

Twaddle, A. C. (1969). Health decisions and sick role variations: an exploration. *Journal of Health and Social Behavior, 10*(2), 105–115.

Twisk, J. W. (2006). *Applied Multilevel Analysis: A Practical Guide*. Cambridge: Cambridge University Press.

UNAIDS. (2007). *AIDS Epidemic Update: December 2007*. Geneva: UNAIDS/World Health Organization.

UNDP. (2007). *Human Development Report 2007/2008*. New York: United Nations Development Programme.

van Egmond, J. J. (2003). The multiple meanings of secondary gain. *American Journal of Psychoanalysis, 63*(2), 137–147.

Veblen, T. (1994 [1899]). *The Theory of the Leisure Class: An Economic Study of Institutions*. New York: Dover.

Veugelers, P. J., Yip, A. M., and Kephart, G. (2001). Proximate and contextual socioeconomic determinants of mortality: multilevel approaches in a setting with universal health care coverage. *American Journal of Epidemiology, 154*(8), 725–732.

Virchow, R. (1958). *Disease, Life, and Man: Selected Essays* (L. J. Rather, Trans.). Stanford, CA: Stanford University Press.

Virchow, R. (1985 [1848]). *Collected Essays on Public Health and Epidemiology*. Cambridge: Science History Publications.

Viruell-Fuentes, E. A. (2007). Beyond acculturation: immigration, discrimination, and health research among Mexicans in the United States. *Social Science & Medicine, 65*(7), 1524–1535.

Wainwright, S. P., and Forbes, A. (2000). Philosophical problems with social research on health inequalities. *Health Care Analysis, 8*(3), 259–277.

Waitzkin, H. (1983). *The Second Sickness: Contradictions of Capitalist Health Care*. New York: Free Press.

Waitzkin, H. (1991). *The Politics of Medical Encounters: How Patients and Doctors Deal with Social Problems*. New Haven, CT: Yale University Press.

Waitzkin, H. (2006). One and a half centuries of forgetting and rediscovering: Virchow's lasting contributions to social medicine. *Social Medicine, 1*(1), 5–10.

Waitzkin, H., and Iriart, C. (2001). How the United States exports managed care to developing countries. *International Journal of Health Services, 31*(3), 495–505.

Waitzkin, H., Iriart, C., Estrada, A., and Lamadrid, S. (2001). Social medicine then and now: lessons from Latin America. *American Journal of Public Health, 91*(10), 1592–1601.

Wallerstein, I. (1974). *The Modern World-System*. New York: Academic Press.

Ware, N. C. (1992). Suffering and the social construction of illness: the delegitimation of illness experience in chronic fatigue syndrome. *Medical Anthropology Quarterly, 6*(4), 347–361.

Waters, M. (1994). *Modern Sociological Theory*. London: Sage.

Weber, M. (1947 [1922]). *The Theory of Social and Economic Organization*. New York: Oxford University Press.

Weich, S., and Lewis, G. (1998). Material standard of living, social class, and the prevalence of the common mental disorders in Great Britain. *Journal of Epidemiology & Community Health, 52*(1), 8–14.

Weich, S., Lewis, G., and Jenkins, S. P. (2001). Income inequality and the prevalence of common mental disorders in Britain. *British Journal of Psychiatry, 178*, 222–227.

Weich, S., Lewis, G., and Jenkins, S. P. (2002). Income inequality and self rated health in Britain. *Journal of Epidemiology & Community Health, 56*(6), 436–441.

Weitz, R. (2007). *The Sociology of Health, Illness, and Health Care* (4th edn). Belmont, CA: Thompson Wadsworth.

Wen, M., Browning, C. R., and Cagney, K. A. (2003). Poverty, affluence, and income inequality: neighborhood economic structure and its implications for health. *Social Science & Medicine, 57*(5), 843–860.

Werner, A., and Malterud, K. (2003). It is hard work behaving as a credible patient: encounters between women with chronic pain and their doctors. *Social Science & Medicine, 57*(8), 1409–1419.

Whitehead, M. (1992). The concepts and principles of equity and health. *International Journal of Health Services, 22*(3), 429–445.

Whitehead, M. (2000). William Farr's legacy to the study of inequalities in health. *Bulletin of the World Health Organization, 78*(1), 86–87.

WHO. (2008a). *Closing the Gap in a Generation: Health Equity Through Action on the Social Determinants of Health.* Geneva: World Health Organization.

WHO. (2008b). *Towards Universal Access: Scaling Up Priority HIV / AIDS Interventions in the Health Sector.* Geneva: World Health Organization.

Wiktorowicz, M. E. (2006). Health care systems in evolution. In D. Raphael, T. Bryant, and M. Rioux (Eds), *Staying Alive: Critical Perspectives on Health, Illness, and Health Care* (pp. 241–262). Toronto: Canadian Scholars' Press Inc.

Wildman, J. (2001). The impact of income inequality on individual and societal health: absolute income, relative income and statistical artefacts. *Health Economics, 10*(4), 357–361.

Wileman, L., May, C., and Chew-Graham, C. A. (2002). Medically unexplained symptoms and the problem of power in the primary care consultation: a qualitative study. *Family Practice, 19*(2), 178–182.

Wilkinson, R. G. (1990). Income distribution and mortality: a "natural" experiment. *Sociology of Health & Illness, 12*(4), 391–412.

Wilkinson, R. G. (1992). Income distribution and life expectancy. *British Medical Journal, 304*(6820), 165–168.

Wilkinson, R. G. (1996). *Unhealthy Societies: The Afflictions of Inequality.* New York: Routledge.

Wilkinson, R. G. (1999a). The culture of inequality. In I. Kawachi, B. P. Kennedy, and R. G. Wilkinson (Eds), *The Society and Population Health Reader: Income Inequality and Health* (Vol. 1, pp. 492–498). New York: The New Press.

Wilkinson, R. G. (1999b). Income inequality, social cohesion, and health: clarifying the theory – a reply to Muntaner and Lynch. *International Journal of Health Services, 29*(3), 525–543.

Wilkinson, R. G. (2000). *Mind the Gap: Hierarchies, Health and Human Evolution.* London: Weidenfeld & Nicolson.

Wilkinson, R. G. (2002). Commentary: liberty, fraternity, equality. *International Journal of Epidemiology, 31*(3), 538–543.

Wilkinson, R. G. (2005). *The Impact of Inequality: How to Make Sick Societies Healthier.* New York: The New Press.

Wilkinson, R. G., and Pickett, K. (2006). Income inequality and population health: a review and explanation of the evidence. *Social Science & Medicine, 62*(7), 1768–1784.

Wilkinson, R. G., and Pickett, K. (2009). *The Spirit Level: Why More Equal Societies Almost Always Do Better.* London: Allen Lane.

Williams, A. P., Deber, R., Baranek, P., and Gildinder, A. (2001). From Medicare to home care: globalization, state retrenchment, and the profitization of Canada's health care system. In P. Armstrong, H. Armstrong, and D. Coburn (Eds), *Unhealthy Times: Political Economy Perspectives on Health and Care in Canada* (pp. 7–27). Don Mills: Oxford University Press.

Williams, G. H. (2003). The determinants of health: structure, context and agency. *Sociology of Health & Illness, 25*(3), 131–154.

Williams, S. J. (2003). Beyond meaning, discourse and the empirical world: critical realist reflections on health. *Social Theory and Health, 1*(1), 42–71.

Williams, S. J. (2005). Parsons revisited: from the sick role to...? *Health, 9*(2), 123–144.

Williams, S. J., and Calnan, M. (1996). The "limits" of medicalization?: modern medicine and the lay populace in "late" modernity. *Social Science & Medicine, 42*(12), 1609–1620.

Willis, E. (1983). *Medical Dominance: The Division of Labour in Australian Health Care*. Sydney: George Allen and Unwin.

Wilson, H. S., Hutchinson, S. A., and Holzemer, W. L. (2002). Reconciling incompatibilities: a grounded theory of HIV medication adherence and symptom management. *Qualitative Health Research, 12*(10), 1309–1322.

Wolfson, M., Kaplan, G., Lynch, J., Ross, N., and Backlund, E. (1999). Relation between income inequality and mortality: empirical demonstration. *British Medical Journal, 319*(7215), 953–955.

Zimmerman, F. J., and Bell, J. F. (2006). Income inequality and physical and mental health: testing associations consistent with proposed causal pathways. *Journal of Epidemiology & Community Health, 60*(6), 513–521.

Zola, I. (1972). Medicine as an institution of social control. *Sociological Review, 20*, 487–504.

Zola, I. (1983). *Socio-Medical Inquiries*. Philadelphia: Temple University Press.

Index